This book is dedicated to my loving mother Ekaty Spyropoulos

Colophon

AA Managing Editor: Thomas Weaver
AA Publications Editor: Pamela Johnston
Editorial Assistant: Clare Barrett
AA Art Director: Zak Kyes

Design: Stephen Spyropoulos

Production Team: Ryan Dillon, Sara Saleh, Faysal Tabbara,
Jorge Méndez-Cáceres, Mollie Claypool

Assisted by: Sebastian Andia, Rodrigo Roberto Chain Rodriguez,
Lisa Cumming, Apostolos Despotidis, Thomas Tørslev Jensen,
Justin Kelly, Ralph Andrew Merkle, Anais Mikaelian, Jared Ramsdell,
Gilles Felix Restin, Leila Ahmed Selim, Lukasz Szlachcic, Nada Ahmed,
Omran Taryam Alshamsi, Salih Topal

Special thanks to: Marie Ange Brayer, Frederic Migayrou, Collection
FRAC Centre Orléans, Computer History Museum, The Estate of R
Buckminster Fuller, Dominique Perrault Architecture, Glen Howard Small,
Japan Architect/Shinkenchiku, Karl Sims, Kevin Raskoff, MIT, Nicolas
Negroponte,
Rogers Stirk Harbour + Partners, Safdie Architects, Studio Fuksas,
Tange Associates, Toyo Ito Architects and Zvi Hecker Architects

Printed in Belgium by Cassochrome

ISBN: 978-190789613-2

For a catalogue of AA Publications visit
www.aaschool.ac.uk/publications
or email publications@aaschool.ac.uk

AA Publications, 36 Bedford Square, London WC1B 3ES
T + 44 (0)20 7887 4021
F + 44 (0)20 7414 0783

ADAPTIVE ECOLOGIES: CORRELATED SYSTEMS OF LIVING

BY THEODORE SPYROPOULOS

004   Architecture's Adaptation
Brett Steele

010   Constructing Adaptive Ecologies: Notes on a Computational Urbanism
Theodore Spyropoulos

024   In Conversation
John Henry Holland and Theodore Spyropoulos

035   A Case Study Approach: Organisational Frameworks (Unit/Cluster/Collective)
With Ryan Dillon

115   Urban Typologies: London, Shanghai, New York, Tokyo
With Mollie Claypool and Ryan Dillon

134   Continuing Experiment: Adaptive Ecologies
John Frazer

150   Parametric Order: Architectural Order via an Agent-Based Parametric Semiology
Patrik Schumacher

164   Morphogenetic Taxonomies
Mangal / Polyp Growth / Colonial Form / Phyllotaxis / Seeding

204   Induction Design versus the Human Brain: Computer Programs versus Freehand – What Can We Do Now, What Can't We Do Yet?
Makoto Sei Watanabe

218   Self-Organisational Taxonomies
Stigmergy / Hair-Optimised Detour Networks / Cellular Automata / Swarm Behaviour

268   Returning to (Strange) Objects
David Ruy

278   Behavioural Taxonomies
Surface Tension / Hele–Shaw Cell / Siphonophora / Cymatics / Soft Cast

316   Ideas and Computation in Contemporary Urban Design: Addressing the Disconnects
Mark Burry

4

ARCHITECTURE'S ADAPTATION

Brett Steele

'Diversity in itself does not necessarily yield complexity.'
Murray Bookchin, The Philosophy of Freedom

At the core of Theodore Spyropoulos' worldview lies a simple but potentially deadly assertion regarding what constitutes for many the core knowledge of architecture: the making of architectural form. For Theo architecture isn't so much a discipline dedicated to the making of form as it is a field of action, performance and knowledge that is itself always undergoing formation – and in exactly the same ways that buildings and cities are themselves constantly growing and evolving in line with new social and material realities. In the book that follows, we see this worldview in action; we see architecture shown for what it is – a world of constantly adapting behaviours, interdependencies.

In Adaptive Ecologies what is called architecture is barely distinguishable from the behaviours making up the natural world all around it – a world, that is, where bodies, organisms, systems and even disciplines share one thing above all else in common: their own malleability. Accordingly, even such ordinary things as buildings are reconceived in ways that emphasise less their physical features, and more the relationships that describe these entities to their surrounding worlds (whether artificial, like other buildings or infrastructures, or natural, in the sense of physical, environmental qualities). In such an account, architecture is alive: it changes, it aggregates, distributes, coheres and then undoes these and many other organisational processes as part of its ordinary (even everyday) existence.

Such a thesis is of course hardly new in architecture, and indeed the purpose of the first half of this volume is to lay bare a 'prehistory' of modern, adaptive, aggregative architectures, which are documented at three distinct scales of operation, from unit (house) to cluster (building) to collective (territory). This gives us a view of the ways in which Adaptive Ecologies is not only aligned with its time, with the early twenty-first century, but also has its own suppressed history within the field of architecture – a field whose best-known theories and histories have frequently treated a concept like architectural behaviour as a mere outlier to more established interests that privilege permanence and endurance as architecture's most 'legitimate' quality.

In what follows, the tables are turned. We see not only the dissolving of architectonic and natural worlds, but also the blurring of any meaningful difference between organic and non-organic life-forms, something most evident in the artificial, computational and digital design systems used as platforms for Theo's and his students' strange design proposals. What we see is a world of design intelligence where highly abstract, numeric modelling simulations are aimed at old-fashioned, heavy (and often quite messy) material systems. As Theo writes in his essay, 'The distinctions between information, matter and life display complexities that suggest the possibility of a much deeper synthesis'. Between these otherwise differentiated aspects of the universe he imagines a synthesis that operates to such a deep level that we are able to grasp that it is the unfolding of form, more than form per se, that is the key process in architecture (just as it is, he would be quick to add, in any other discipline, field of enquiry, art or form of culture).

Theo founded his studio Minimaforms in New York and London with his brother Stephen several years ago. As their previous book amply demonstrated, theirs is an architectural project as difficult to classify as it is to see or touch. As they have grown and matured Minimaforms the brothers have created everything from strange text-messaging late-night smoke signal installations to interactive installation spaces, animal masks, vehicles, buildings, pavilions and landscapes. A growing interest in recent years has been the making of behaviours themselves, as opposed to the imagined 'actions' of people and others engaging with the faces, spaces and interfaces of their work. Interestingly, Theo and Stephen have come to realise that they share this preoccupation with many other contemporary practitioners, scientists and artists who happen to operate across a broad spectrum of intellectual and cultural activity, often far from architectural convention. The Spyropoulos brothers have opened up a prominent and productive view on what lies at the core of architectural experimentation; undertaken by them deliberately, in ways that confound conventional definitions of the 'architectural object'.

Adaptive Ecologies also offers an overview of the design and research Theo has undertaken in recent years both in his own studio and in the AA's Design Research Lab, which he directs. The projects and speculations collected here update a survey of a body of work glimpsed way back in 2008, with the publication of *DRL Ten*, and 2010, with Theo's first monograph titled *Enabling*. Working with some of the most gifted graduate students in the world Theo has pushed, prodded and nudged their collaborative, team-based enquiries towards ever more vivid, life-like visions of architecture's unknown future, or better said, perhaps, its multiple possible futures.

The making of conflicting, complex and at times almost unimaginable futures is, I think, exactly the kind of architectural project that is noticeably absent amongst a younger generation of experimentalists today. In *Adaptive Ecologies* we are reminded that adaptation itself is only ever interesting as a cognitive model when it is able to coherently account for change, for life and death: when it promotes the primacy of time (and not, as architects tend to assume, space) as the determinant ordering force of all lives, whether those of an individual member of a species, a large, complex organisation, or a narrow, well-defined form of human knowledge such as architecture.

Much as self-recognition operates at a cognitive level of the individual to serve as a key stage of self-awareness and -organisation, Theo and his collaborators' deep embedding of today's most advanced electronic, digital and computational design platforms has created a catalogue of projects that themselves record a remarkable moment of architecture's own mirror-stage – a registration of its own rampant acceleration away from the bookish, literary circumstances that have long shaped its discourses, theories and practices towards a new era of disciplinary, collaborative and experimental convergence.

To enrich the cultural legacy and not only the strange, machinic appearance of today's synthetic, evolutionary architectures, Theo has compiled a genealogy of evolutionary tendencies – of sensibilities, design systems and conceptual tools that have percolated, intermingled and evolved within architecture for many decades, and which brought together here convincingly show how Minimaforms and the work of Theo's DRL students is hardly anything more than the latest iteration of a long-running, sustained larger project. Once seen together, these outlier projects appear far less weird than when they were first presented, far less the kind of 'non-architecture' so many architects have long considered them.

Adaptive Ecologies unfolds a century-long investment by experimental architects in the making of unexpected forms of inhabitation and dwelling. But to call this a book on modern housing would be to miss the mark wildly, for the multiple and at times openly schizophrenic assertions regarding what properly constitutes individual, solitary or domestic space is staggeringly open-ended and – like most productive ecologies – diverse. From David Greene's iconic Living Pod, to Moshe Safdie's structuralist near-megastructures, to UN Studio's Moebius House and Buckminster Fuller's irrepressible Dymaxion experiments, this is a veritable catalogue of architectural eccentricity. Clustering, aggregation, clumping and arraying are all telling verbs to describe the many projects (and nested design operations) made visible in both the new and older work included here. As Theo says elsewhere, picking up on a sensibility that lies at the core of contemporary 'deep' ecologies, complexity requires more than 'mere diversity'.

Structured, scripted and technically precise, controlled forms of differentiation are hallmarks of the many different examples of modern and contemporary architecture that follow. What becomes apparent, when viewing the recent work of Theo and his students against the background of projects like Kikutake's Tower-Shaped City or Chanéac's multi-purpose cell dwellings, is that iteration and repetition are key conceptual design operations. The design decision-making, in other words, is undertaken sometimes arbitrarily, sometimes rationally, even functionally or efficiently, but always with the same expectation: that decision-making will be the result of running interrelated design operations over and over. What we confront here in this collection are projects that are knowingly the outcome, not merely of repetitive or precisely describable design machines, but of deliberately multiple, repetitive models of design thinking. And it's the iterative multiplicity of these design behaviours that points to the inescapable presence of mathematics underlying architectural work of this kind today.

To be more precise, the kind of complex algorithmic description of relationships between entities – whereby components, units, frame members, individual buildings or spaces are 'wired' together in the scripting and programming languages of contemporary modelling systems – once invoked, can then be unleashed to self-arrange as visualisable behaviours forecasting projects. And these behaviours – the ones describing changes, evolutions, refinements and distortions, etc – reveal how fully a new concept of design is emerging today. It's that kind of revolution in form – the form of how a design process plays out in time over the life of a project, not the 'form' of a building in its appearance – that is the most important discovery on display here.

Far from being the operators and originators of 'cool form', architects are shown instead to be above all the makers of their own working realities, with decision-making procedures that emphasise neither utility nor the function of an architectural project, but rather its innate beauty.

In an infamous passage in his *Value of Science* first published in 1905, the great philosopher of science Henri Poincaré put it this way: 'A scientist worthy of the name is above all a mathematician, experiencing his work with the same improvisation as an artist … the most interesting facts are those which may serve us many times, in different ways; these are the facts which have a chance of coming up again.'[1] Later, Poincaré states a corollary question to this observation: 'Which then are the facts likely to reappear?' And he gives us the answer: 'They are first the simple facts.'

The search for 'simple' facts, accordingly, can be seen as a hugely important task. Whether facts are ever 'simple' or not is a matter of great interest not only for the overarching philosophy of a scientist like Poincaré but for any architect who sees his work as art, not science. 'All we can say is that we ought to pay attention to the facts which [at least] seem simple', Poincaré concludes. Indeed, the purpose of making life-like analogies between architecture and nature's evolving, behavioural tendencies is not to try to make architecture more 'scientific'. Quite the opposite. As Poincaré wrote more than a century ago now, 'A scientist does not study nature because it is useful'. He studies it, of course, because it is beautiful. The same applies, I would argue, to the reasons why architects study their world (a world where nature has become a far more complex concept than it was a century ago; at least, in regard to the life-like properties of everything from the performance of algorithms, to the movement of information across the electronically distributed design platforms that now occupy all studios). Enjoy the book that follows, at once a document of and a testament to architectural, and not only natural, form – a concept that owing to its own ecological bias is directed (now perhaps more than ever) to an even more enduring form of natural adaptation, the concept of beauty.

1   Henri Poincaré, *The Value of Science (*Modern Science Library, 2001 edition), 182.

CONSTRUCTING ADAPTIVE ECOLOGIES: NOTES ON A COMPUTATIONAL URBANISM

Theodore Spyropoulos

'Living systems are units of interaction; they exist in ambience.'
Humberto Maturana[1]

'I shall consider the physical environment as an evolving organism as opposed to a designed artefact. In particular, I shall consider an evolution aided by a specific class of machines. Warren McCulloch calls them ethical robots; in the context of architecture I shall call them architecture machines.'
Nicholas Negroponte[2]

György Kepes once proclaimed, 'In our new conceptual models of nature, the stable, solid world of substance, which in the past was considered permanent and preordained, is understood as widely dispersed fields of dynamic energies. Matter – the tangible, visible, stable substance in the old image of the physical world – is recast today as an invisible web of nuclear events with orbiting electrons jumping from orbit to orbit.[3] The fixed and finite tendencies that once served to categorise the natural and the man-made worlds have been rendered obsolete. Today the intersections of information, life and matter display complexities that suggest the possibility of a much deeper synthesis. Within this context, however, architecture is being forced to radically refactor its response to new social and cultural challenges and an accelerated process of urbanisation. All over the world, cities are emerging in the kind of timeframe that buildings are usually developed in, and outdated practices dictate that these cities are generic, unable to adapt to the ever-changing needs of the built environment. To counter this, architecture today must participate and engage with the information-rich environments that are shaping our lives by constructing computational frameworks that will allow for change, embracing a demand for adaptive models for living. Our approach to addressing these challenges explores a systemic form of interaction that engages behavioural features that are polyscalar, allowing biodiverse networks to operate between urban contexts, buildings and materials. An intimate correlation of material and computational interaction allows for the emergence of a generative time-based behavioural model of living, where the interplay of local agency and environmental stimulus constructs collective orders. Environmental stimulus gives rise to structures of elaborate complexity, as these systems are able to continuously adapt to local and global signalling. Unlike most man-made structures, the architectures of these structures are not embedded in a blueprint, but rather are correlated operations governed through emerging collective interaction.

'Technology is the answer – but what was the question?'
Cedric Price[4]

A Cybernetic Approach

In September 1969 a landmark issue of *Architectural Design*, guest-edited by Roy Landau, brought issues of interaction and digital computation into mainstream architectural media for the first time. Alongside articles by Nicholas Negroponte, Cedric Price and Warren Brodey, the issue featured an essay by the cybernetician Gordon Pask, who introduced the idea that 'architects are first and foremost system designers who have been forced to take an increasing interest in the organisational system properties of development, communication and control'.[5] Architecture, Pask argued, had no theory to cope with the pressing complexities of the time, and it was only through a cybernetic understanding of systemic processes that the discipline would evolve. Central to Pask's argument was an understanding of the world through the pursuit of 'communication and control' and the elucidation of what he termed 'aesthetically potent environments' – external spaces designed to foster pleasurable interactions. These interactions were to be framed through a commitment to novelty. 'Man', he wrote, 'is prone to seek novelty in his environment and, having found a novel situation, to learn how to control it'.[6]

Claude Shannon and experimental mouse maze
constructed to demonstrate machine learning, c 1952
Courtesy the Computer History Museum, Mountain
View, CA

In his foreword to John Frazer's seminal book *An Evolutionary Architecture* (1980), Pask presents a fundamental cybernetic thesis that 'architecture is a living, evolving thing. In a way this is evident. Our culture's striving towards civilisation is manifested in the places, houses and cities that it creates. As well as providing a protective carapace, these structures also carry symbolic value, and can be seen as being continuous with and emerging from the life of those who inhabit the built environment. It is appropriate to stress an important cybernetic feature of the work; namely that unity is not uniformity, but is coherence and diversity admixed in collusion.[7] In the work of Gordon Pask and other artists and scientists, the use of cybernetic methods resulted in new experiential forms of practice.[8] As telematic artist Roy Ascott notes, cybernetics has transformed our world by 'presenting us with qualities of experience and modes of perception which radically alter our conception of it'.[9] In addition, second order cybernetician Ranulph Glanville has argued that cybernetics constructs a new way of thinking about the material world: 'the knowledge we previously had from science was all about trying to remove the observer so we could talk about an artefactual world full of things, but it is very difficult to argue about a world that exists without our sensing it'.[10] Glanville emphasises the role of the active observer and the distinctions to be made between science and design. In design he sees a cybernetic process at work – a form of conversational interaction. For Glanville designers 'are not observers of the world, but observers in the world'.[11] Therefore, design as an activity should not limit itself solely to descriptive forms but rather use casual and circular relationships to identify generative qualities that will continuously redefine and evolve the design system itself. This is a process of continual formation rather than a state of fixed form.

Behavioural Machines: Singular vs Collective Agency

The dynamic and adaptive approach advocated by this publication is not one of form but of correlated formations – a model of collective living that addresses the spatial complexities of the city. A synthesis of material and computational interaction constructs a generative organisation of space and structure that explores a behaviour-based model of living through patterns found in nature.

'Many of the most striking (pattern) examples that we encounter around us are evidently the products of human hands and minds – they are patterns shaped with intelligence and purpose, constructed by design.'
Phillip Ball[12]

System-to-system interactions identified through simple rule-based protocols can collectively exhibit complex non-linear behaviour. The magnitude of these interactions is explored across varied scales to test the potential of self-structuring orders constructed through the interplay of local agency and environmental stimulus. Early analogue cybernetic experiments – such as Gordon Pask's Colloquy of Mobiles – address the significance of parameters dealing with the observer in order to understand our tendency to attribute life-like properties through simple, relational agent interaction.

As a result, embodied patterns emerge through goal-oriented systems that exhibit life-like characteristics. These social orders allow a synthetic interplay to construct a new breed of proto-animalistic architectures that evolve through negotiated interactions, creating a fusion of digital and analogue computation that draws on the pioneering work of the renowned neurophysiologist W Grey Walter. An interest in cognitive operations and biological systems led Walter to develop his machinae speculatrices (machines that watch) – autonomous robots that could demonstrate how simple organisms exhibit non-linear interactions. The first of these were named Elsie and Elmer, and they took the form of phototropic tortoises inspired by a character in Lewis Carroll's *Alice in Wonderland*. Designed with a primitive nervous system, the tortoises constructed social action and self-organisational patterns that were characteristic of animal behaviour and ritual. Walter's genius lay in his ability to recognise complex adaptive behaviours in simple interconnected systems that focused on goal orientation and adaptation through learning. This allowed the robots to be free-ranging autodidacts that built up intelligence through interaction.

After completing his experiments with the tortoises, Walter wrote in *The Living Brain* (1953) that there was a 'well-defined difference between the magical and the scientific imitation of life. The former copies external appearances; the latter is concerned with performance and behaviour. Until the scientific era, what seemed most alive to people was what most looked like a living being. The vitality accorded to an object was a function primarily of its form.' Through a fusion of synthetic and natural

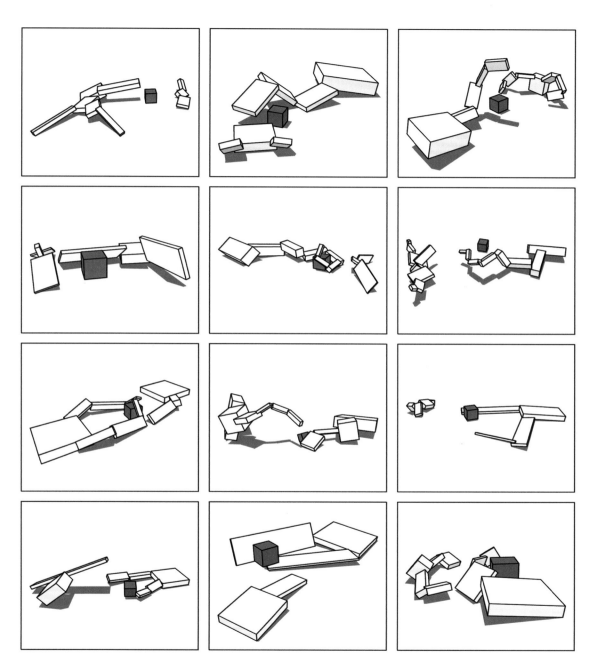

Evolved competing creatures. Courtesy of Karl Sims

systems, architecture can construct machines that are generative, evolving relationships that couple new forms of spatial organisation with fabrication. The ability to shift preoccupations from object to system allows our built environment to play an active and participatory role in the construction of adaptive forms through feedback.

From Object to System

György Kepes states in his introduction to *The Nature and Art of Motion* (1965) that 'to structure our chaotic physical and social environment as well as our knowledge and values, we have to accept the conditions of the new scale and learn to use the tools that have grown from it'.[13] New sensibilities have evolved in relation to communication through mediated and remote interaction, which are now critical to a research that explores the role of space and in particular the ways that the physical and public environment can communicate as an active agent. As Kepes's Bauhaus mentor and colleague László Moholy-Nagy once observed, 'design is not a profession but an attitude … thinking in complex relationships'.[14] Today, the role of science and technology offers architecture some of the most radical and thought-provoking scenarios if approached in a manner that enables participatory and collective emergence.

In a 1964 article titled 'The Construction of Change', Roy Ascott attempted to outline the terms for engaging art as a system based on the interrelations between artist, audience and environment.[15] His proposal stemmed from his belief that 'cybernetics was the science of behaviour and art was essentially behaviourist'. Through the interaction of these constituents, one could construct an environment in which new models of practice foreground participation, allowing aspects of play to evolve and thus creating new forms of knowledge. Ascott elaborated this idea further in his 1967 manifesto, *Behaviourables and Futuribles*, noting 'when art is a form of behaviour, software predominates over hardware in the creative sphere. Process replaces product in importance, just as system supersedes structure.' He went on to reinforce this sentiment by emphasising the importance of the societal and cultural: 'for a culture to survive it needs internal acrimony (irritation), reciprocity (feedbacks) and variety (change)'. In this way, the coupling of design and technology could bring about a discourse that was social and optimistic, buoyed by the shared belief that, through innovation, new channels of communication would emerge that would interconnect previously self-contained and isolated fields. Art and design was therefore seen as a tool enabling active collaboration with cultural and scientific disciplines.

The Architecture Machine Group led by Nicholas Negroponte produced Seek, a computer-controlled environment inhabited by gerbils as part of Jack Burnham's 1970 'Software' show in New York.
SEEK, © Nicholas Negroponte, Soft Architecture Machines

Detail of Minimaforms' Archigram revisit model of the living/high-rise pod exhibited at 'Mega-Structures Reloaded', Berlin (2008), alongside seminal works by Constant, Superstudio, Archizoom, Archigram and Yona Friedman.

*'We can communicate – that is, combine and reinforce our knowledge
with that of other men – by stimulating the circulation of ideas and
feelings, finding channels of communication that can interconnect
our disciplines and enable us to see our world as a connective whole.'*
György Kepes[16]

Architecture must Participate

György Kepes once wrote that 'The dynamic unity of constancy and
change has a fundamental role in our intellectual growth. Our clear-
est understanding of the nature of these complementary opposites has
been reached through a grasp of the principle of self-regulating systems.'
Similarly, our own systemic approach seeks to evolve research into new
forms of living and the structuring of human environments. Experimenting
through explicit models of interactions, observable patterns and proto-
animalistic agency, the work within this book explores the capacity for
design systems to evolve architectural elements with the capacity to self-
structure, respond and evolve. In the process, and beyond deterministic
methods of structuring space, issues of duration and populations evolve
into a new language of assemblies as collective structures.

Today, with greater opportunities and easier access to information, comes
the challenge to re-evaluate the conception and production of architecture.
These enabled communication networks have fostered the possibilities
for a shared and collective project – one that is not only available to all,
but affords a deeper understanding of the world and our participation in
it. In engaging with this shared project, it is important to recognise early
experiments within this domain, such as those explored by Nicholas
Negroponte and the Architecture Machine Group at MIT, which dealt with
the intimate association of man and machine within architecture, and of
Cedric Price, who in collaboration with Joan Littlewood and Gordon Pask
designed a Fun Palace that would operate as a time-based architectural
machine adapting and evolving through its everyday use. These projects
provided a model for the coupling of design and technology while
calling for a discourse that is both social and optimistic. Taken together,
architecture and design can be seen as a tool that enables an active
collaboration within cultural and scientific disciplines. Though not a new
pursuit in architecture, it should be recognised that we have greater
access to a collective understanding than ever before.

Design should be progressive and challenge people. We should be
enabling a diverse set of questions about how we live and the role that
architecture can play in our everyday lives. As John Frazer has reminded

us, 'perhaps computing without computers is the most important lesson to be learned by designing these tools. The real benefits are found in having to rethink explicitly and clearly the way in which we habitually do things.' Architecture today can serve as an emergent framework that displays a new nature, combining the biological, social and computational in an adaptive and evolving organism, reasserting Karl Friedrich Schinkel's belief that 'architecture is the continuation of nature in her constructive activity'.

1   Humberto R Maturana, *Biology of Cognition*, Biological Computer Laboratory Research Report BCL 9.0 (Urbana, IL: University of Illinois, 1970).

2   Nicholas Negroponte, *The Architecture Machine: Toward a More Human Environment* (Cambridge, MA: MIT Press, 1970).

3   György Kepes, *The Nature and Art of Motion* (New York: George Braziller, 1965), 2.

4   Quoted in Paul Brown et al, eds, *White Heat Cold Logic: British Computer Art 1960–1980* (Cambridge, MA: MIT Press, 2008), 37–51.

5   Gordon Pask, 'The Architectural Relevance of Cybernetics', *Architectural Design*, September 1969, 494.

6   Gordon Pask, 'A Comment, a Case History and a Plan' (1970) reprinted in J Reichardt, ed, *Cybernetic Art and Ideas* (London: Studio Vista, 1971), 77.

7   John Frazer, *An Evolutionary Architecture* (London: Architectural Association Publications, 1995).

8   Ascott and Pask worked together as part of the Cybernetics Sub-Committee, a consultancy of interdisciplinary minds organised by Pask to assist in the development of Cedric Price's Fun Palace.

9   Ascott, op cit note 1.

10   Stephanie Bunbury, 'It's time to learn to love your Dalek', 10 May 2005, retrieved 10 September 2007 from http://www.theage.com.au/articles/2005/05/09/1115584883777.html

11   Ranulph Glanville, 'Try again. Fail again. Fail better: The Cybernetics in Design and the Design in Cybernetics', *Kybernetes* 36: 9/10 (2007), 1199.

12   Philip Ball, *Shapes* (Oxford: Oxford University Press, 2009).

13   Kepes, *The Nature and Art of Motion*, 6.

14   László Moholy-Nagy, *Vision in Motion* (Chicago, P Theobald, 1947), 42.

15   Reprinted in Noah Wardrip-Fruin and Nick Montfort, eds, *The New Media Reader* (Cambridge, MA: MIT Press, 2003), 128–32.

16   Kepes, *The Nature and Art of Motion*, 6.

Osaka Expo 70, The Grand Roof and the
Festival Plaza Photo: Shinkenchiku-sha

JOHN HENRY HOLLAND AND THEODORE SPYROPOULOS IN CONVERSATION

Theodore Spyropoulos: One of the critical features of what we call 'Adaptive Ecologies' is the attempt to explore generative and behavioural forms of systemic interaction. Arising as a response to accelerated forms of urbanism, this agenda sought to ask if computation could help us to evolve a means to engage with the complex polyscalar relationships within architecture and urbanism today. Beyond issues of masterplanning, we wanted to use computation to examine principles that had the capacity to build relationships on three distinct scales: the masterplan (collective), the block/building (cluster), and the unit. Historically these scales have been treated with a degree of autonomy, but we set out to explore processes that considered them as part of an evolving system or ecology able to respond to uncertainty and latency. At the heart of this work were issues of adaptation and a search for systemic methodologies that would enable us to move toward a time-based and scenario-driven form of urbanism.

Your ideas on genetic algorithms and adaptation within these ecologies have been a great influence, so it would be interesting if you could discuss how these ideas have evolved since your seminal publication of 1975, *Adaptation in Natural and Artificial Systems*.

John Henry Holland: Well, let me start with adaptation and make a point of contrast. Even now, in almost all textbooks on biology, you'll find statements about mutation driving evolution. But in fact, if you start to look more closely, it's quite a different process. Each one of us is a combination of some characteristics – sets or clusters of values – of one parent and some characteristics of the other. This process occurs in every individual mammal in every generation: various things cross over, recombine, whatever you'd like to call it. And that is the main source of variation, whereas DNA mostly tries to protect from mutation, which is a one in a million to ten million occurrence.

This is the Lego block approach to adaptation, in the sense that you can make a tremendous variety of things with relatively few types of blocks. And these combinations of pre-established building blocks are what define or produce the interactions of agents – the signals they are supposed to be sending back and forth. Another way to frame this is in terms of grammars and so on and so on, where you can have a relatively small vocabulary and get a tremendous variation in your semantics.

TS: Yes, these simple rule-based grammars are very interesting as they evolve in a continual dialogue with their environment relative to their populations. And this interaction constructs fitness criteria.

JH: And it seems to me that if you trace the course of evolution you find a progressive building of hierarchy where a small set of building blocks at one level can serve, in selective combinations, to construct the building blocks at the next level up. Of course, in another sense, this is really the story of hierarchies in science, where you go from nucleons to atoms to chemistry and so on. Recognising this as a process of hierarchy seems to be a crucial step: even a biological cell contains a tremendous range of little bounded entities, organelles, each of which has functions, and then those functions become agents that trigger interaction within the cell.

So I would put a lot of emphasis on this co-evolution of boundaries and signals, some of which can go through the boundaries and some of which cannot. It seems to be a very important way of looking at how adaptation takes place.

TS: Yes, these are features that we've been trying to come to terms with. In designing these environments a series of questions became apparent. How could we articulate distinctions through interaction? How do we observe and evolve techniques and tools that could allow our systems to operate and co-evolve within this generative design environment? Could adaptation evolve through their ability to learn?

It brought to mind a lot of the early discourse that was coming out of second-order cybernetics, addressing the observer and the interpretation of what was being observed. As a design problem, coming from the perspective of an architect who is interested in this world of understanding, it became critical to identify distinction, variation and pattern – to see intelligence as a product of interaction that challenged the conventions of the generative vs parametric discourses that were symptomatic of the bottom-up vs top-down methods. Could you discuss the issue of control and the role of simulation in your thinking?

JH: I have a notion that may be helpful here. Let's think of an animal that is in an environment and is trying to learn about that environment, starting, in a certain sense, from a tabula rasa. This animal has a rule as an initial chance: if it sees anything moving out there, then it flees. Call that a default rule, and if it follows this rule all of the time, then it is never going to approach any moving object. The rule might be right, say, 60 to 70 per cent of the time, but it will lead it badly astray in other conditions – for example, if it preys on some moving objects, or wants to mate, or something like that. So then the next level is to have an exception rule, one that says: look it's moving, it's small, and on the wing. Now, if this rule is used with more detectors and more information it builds more exceptions, and there can be exceptions within exceptions and so on. We call this a default hierarchy.

The same principle works well in any learning system, because you learn the broadest correlations first – the default rules that are statistically better than random – and then you begin to build the exceptions which use more information, and the exceptions to those which use still more information. This system is also nicely scalable, and can be built much faster than if you were to try to discover all the rules at the level of greatest detail. So this notion of starting with very broad equivalent classes and then developing refinements of those classes is, again, a kind of building block approach based on the detectors or pattern-recognising devices that you're using. It seems to me it may also fit rather well with your notions of challenging the conventional bottom-up/top-down methods.

TS: It certainly does. I mean, one of the things we are reacting against is the conventional form of architectural thinking with respect to a 'masterplan', which makes the assumption of a fixed and finite condition, but on the contrary has to be flexible and open to evolve along with an ever-changing condition. Change over time is a certainty, and if the design of systems took this into account the city could evolve while the system maintained or mutated principal features of continuity.

In practice, when we look at computation, there have been two schools of thought. Both have emerged from a fundamental difference of control – parametric and generative – and they reinforce the top-down/bottom-up discussion in the most primitive form. With my students we've been speculating in the domain of the generative.

In a way we've been moving towards your work with second-order cybernetics and systems theory acknowledging the need to develop systems that allow for adaptability through their capacity to deal with latency and unknown parameters over time. This approach also features aspects which are more behavioural, in terms of defining environments – and engaging feedback to build up data sets that can start to influence these environments. On the other hand, we're really trying to respond to the fact that the masterplan isn't a blueprint and there are other more synergic models we could look at – like the termite mound and so forth – as a way of rethinking the construction and the making aspect.

JH: That sounds very good to me, but of course I am biased. This perhaps doesn't sound so relevant, but you may be interested in a software – a large simulation, I guess you'd call it – called Risk Assessment and Horizon Search (RAHS). It's used by businesses in Singapore, but it's open software, and the students in the university use it too. The idea is to try to anticipate things that may be a shock to the Singapore economy, such as rising fuel costs causing a reduction in tourism. As you know, it's a small island nation with no sort of defence against these things. So they're not aiming to predict in detail the effect of a shock: they're just trying to prepare ahead of time, so they can cope with the situation better than if they'd done nothing at all or done things randomly. And I find this to be very interesting. It's the only case that I know of where a kind of simulation of a nation has aimed in that direction.

In Singapore, partly because it's such a tightly controlled society, they can do things that would be much more difficult to achieve elsewhere. For instance, 60 per cent of the population own their own homes, essentially condominiums, and there's a law requiring that each of these relatively large units has roughly the same proportion of each ethnic group as in the city as a whole. This is remarkable! It means that all of the local markets have a wide variety of ethnic foods and ethnic entertainment and so on, and there are no ghettos with only Chinese or only Malay. It has a real effect on that city.

TS: Yes, I think this is definitely something for us to look into. Going back to this idea of learning – because I do think it's a critical part not only of the methods we are using but also of our approach to design research – one feature of our students' work is that it is team-based and collective. This doesn't sound radical in the scientific discourse, but in architecture students are taught generally as individuals.

JH: That is certainly largely true here as well.

TS: The role of a participatory and collective framework for design is an interest of mine. I've been looking at people like Gordon Pask and other second-order cyberneticians, particularly in the British camp. Pask in particular was influential at the AA, where I teach, as well with Nicholas Negroponte and his Architectural Machine Group at MIT.

When considering systemic practice one of the things that I find very important is allowing systems to interact and exhibit features or desires. For example, Pask talked about how man is very interested in novelty: as long as an environment constructs novelty and there is an active dialogue, adaptive features will exist. At the most straightforward level, he was trying to design systems that could get bored and start to intervene in the exchange if there was a certain repetition of patterns. I was wondering how you see this kind of aspect of the environment in relation to simulations or even to the projects you're working on, such as Echo models?

JH: You've started me thinking. Let's go to this notion, it's a little Echo-like. Let's assume that we're building a simulated agent which has some reservoirs that it must keep from running dry. So it has a reservoir for water, which is driven by thirst, and one for shelter, which is driven by fatigue, and so on. So we have one of these default hierarchies of rules, which for each environment's individual situation has something to do, and these rules are rewarded if eventually they link into something which fills one of the reservoirs. There are various reasons to do this in a reasonable, localised way, so you don't have to have referees outside the system telling you whether you did well or not – but I won't go into that here. Anyhow, it is possible to make a reservoir for novelty – a reservoir that is fed only in increments, when the agent encounters a situation that is not well handled by any of its rules. This is something that is actually quite easy to test and set up. Now, it turns out that these agent-based models yield some very interesting activity, where the agent certainly does try to keep the reservoirs reasonably full early on, but then starts seeking out novelty when it has met that basic requirement.

So, for me, the idea goes along the lines you were describing, where it is important not only that the organism is comfortable and feels that it knows what it needs to do, but also that it has complements that make it explore its world.

TS: Yes, I agree this is a very interesting area. But I'm curious to know whether you would consider an agent to be a designer? This necessity to explore resonates in a sense with the thinking of people like Victor Papanek, or the discourses of Heinz von Foerster, or the radical constructivists who took the approach that all aspects of cognition were constructed acts. Papanek was always saying that all humans were designers, that design was one of the most primal forms of human activity. He was talking about human behaviour and social change, but I think this idea perhaps extends to some of the more biological systemic aspects of reproduction and other features that agency and the life-like attributes exhibit over time.

As an architect, the role of design within an agent-based system is an open question. A move towards systems that exhibit tendencies towards self-awareness and varied decision-making as products of emergent hierarchies and complexities offers a form of knowledge and self-understanding within an environment. This embodied knowledge could allow a system to evolve or co-evolve. Do you see design as part of your discourse?

JH: Yes, though of course there are many interpretations of the concept of design. But from my perspective at least, once we allow for this kind of hierarchy of conditional interactions, we have co-evolution going on both within the agent and also between agents. If we look at the parts of a biological cell, the organelle, over evolutionary periods these have certainly co-evolved. So I am very much a constructivist in the sense that I do believe that these things are generated from well-defined basic building blocks. If you have to define the level at which you pick the things to be basic – whether we are talking about nucleotides or amino acids, or a range of organelles in a standard cell – that's a choice at the level of design, but from that point on, I don't see these things as emergent from the construction. It's a bit like me giving you a set of adjectives, then of course there will be a set of synonyms implied, but that doesn't mean that I know what they are.

TS: Establishing observable frameworks is very much part of the process that we've been engaging in the Adaptive Ecologies research. These observable features and the opportunities that are speculated in our work then have to come to terms with the generative capacity to drive issues of spatial organisation and implied materiality. What we've been trying to do is design architectural systems that are prototypical and scenario-based, with the idea that they will develop context-specific implementation through interaction. This seems to follow on from your Echo model, in which you strip away any situation-specific ideas. This is very important, as I am not interested in the generic, but in the hyper-specific. And from a research perspective this approach seems imperative, as it means we are not overly committed to the features of a particular site or a particular system and can actually build models that have a variety of applications. This is not very common in architecture. In fact, at times it is seen almost as blasphemous to have something not specific to a site as your starting point.

I am imagining that a lot of the discussions you have had must have changed over the decades since your first publication. I'm just wondering how? I recently read the preface to an edition of *Adaptation in Natural and Artificial Systems* where you mention that when the book first appeared it didn't seem to generate the same kind of involvement, but over time these things have obviously become much more applicable. The same has happened in architecture. Many of the people who were very forward-thinking, like Negroponte or John Frazer, were dealing with computation without having direct access to the much larger network society that we're living in now, so their work moved directly into communication and lost the physical properties of the architectural discourse.

JH: For almost two decades it was largely only my students, or their students in turn, who were interested in these particular ideas of adaptation. But then we began to get more of these problems that could not be solved in the classical way of optimisation, and people began to pay attention to heuristic methods like genetic algorithms, which were aimed more at improvement than optimisation. And these methods could be applied to real problems: I remember early on Canadian Air used them for scheduling pilots who had various priorities and various seniorities and they were surprised when they yielded much better results than the usual methods or guesswork. So this began to spread, and now you have two almost distinct groups: the large databases that we find in genomes and other areas, and those methods which are an adaptation, but not a big one, of the standard methods where you try to pick out the patterns using correlations. A large part of network theory has taken on these problems, with increased success, though it does not tackle the question of how these systems change and adapt over time. And so what is beginning – just beginning – is the penetration of some of these methods, including genetic algorithms, into this question of how networks evolve or co-evolve.

TS: One of the by-products of posing similar kinds of questions in relation to architecture was a turning towards models that suggested alternative approaches to ecological and material engagement: the stigmergic model that can be understood in the creation of termite ecologies was a very interesting one. It seems that issues of materiality or other features found in perhaps more primitive forms of architecture, like strategies of deposition, have somehow fallen out of the idea of making with the rise of industrial processes over the last hundred years or so. Against this, I think that computation has begun a process of unfolding a series of very interesting areas of research that look at onsite materiality through adaptive and subtractive CNC technologies as a viable way of thinking about a certain kind of architecture. Even though we didn't start out with the idea of the site-specific, what emerged from this approach – and moving beyond the abstraction about materiality and so forth – were these onsite features that started to become solutions or possible ways of addressing some of these concerns. I am a believer in these things, but to be honest, we're talking about a very new field of discourse. So your research has been important in helping us construct a conceptual framework for our work. We've also been looking at William Grey Walter's tortoises and at things like the homeostat. And working with the students I believe we have started to tease out some possibilities. This is by no means a new solution space but I think that it is suggesting alternatives and we've at least tried to take into account this issue of time, which I think is critical in architecture.

JH: This brings to mind of a couple of things. The 1930s Chicago World's Fair still has influences on the Near South Side, you know, with the

Museum of Science and Industry and even the campus of the University of Chicago. Also, when I was in Beijing recently, I saw the huge Olympic Forest Park, with its hills made from soil excavated from the construction of the Bird's Nest Stadium and other buildings. In a relatively short time-scale, it has become one of the city's most popular parks. Allowing for these kinds of unexpected outcomes seems to me terribly important.

TS: To be honest, this is the only way I can see for us to participate as architects in the conversation. We have to be able to develop systems that will not only show variations but will try to think beyond the building itself and see how these possible new uses or situations could evolve.

JH: Well, I am so much a fan of cross-disciplinary thinking as a way of generating metaphors which you can then take from one field to another and use to suggest new ways to move towards new possibilities.

TS: At the moment there is an opportunity for a conversation that is reminiscent of seminal meetings such as the Macy Conferences, with respect to the ever-pressing need to address problems in a creative, interdisciplinary manner. I am hopeful that social communication and computation will provide new means of communicating directly about the issues of today. There has been a recent process of demystification, too, that I believe will allow the collective interdisciplinary project to truly emerge. I am in complete agreement with you that we need more interdisciplinary approaches and your work on computation has been a very powerful suggestion to us of a model that needs to be actively engaged in. Thank you so much for this discussion.

R. Buckminster Fuller and heli-lifted dome, ca. 1954
Courtesy: The Estate of R. Buckminster Fuller

A CASE STUDY APPROACH

To communicate the continued and evolving relationship between each of the three distinct scales in our research we have adopted a case study approach highlighting seminal works. Departing from task-dependent models of spatial organisation, these case studies are presented in three sections that take the unit, the cluster and the collective as fundamental pattern-sensitive scales for consideration. Within each of these scales principles and ordering mechanisms are analysed in order to gain access to organisational frameworks that can evolve a time-based refactoring, as speculated in the *Adaptive Ecologies* thesis. This approach gives precedence to experimental architecture as a driver in fostering an operational form of research that learns through its attempts to realise alternative models of living.

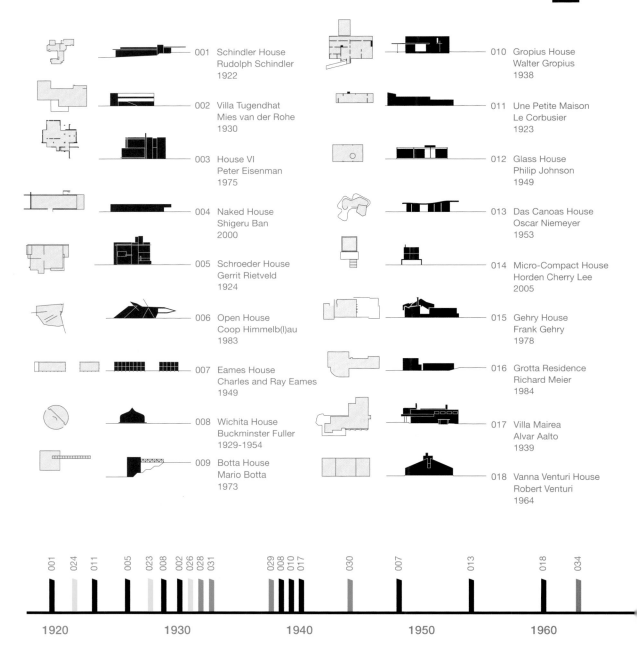

001 Schindler House
Rudolph Schindler
1922

002 Villa Tugendhat
Mies van der Rohe
1930

003 House VI
Peter Eisenman
1975

004 Naked House
Shigeru Ban
2000

005 Schroeder House
Gerrit Rietveld
1924

006 Open House
Coop Himmelb(l)au
1983

007 Eames House
Charles and Ray Eames
1949

008 Wichita House
Buckminster Fuller
1929-1954

009 Botta House
Mario Botta
1973

010 Gropius House
Walter Gropius
1938

011 Une Petite Maison
Le Corbusier
1923

012 Glass House
Philip Johnson
1949

013 Das Canoas House
Oscar Niemeyer
1953

014 Micro-Compact House
Horden Cherry Lee
2005

015 Gehry House
Frank Gehry
1978

016 Grotta Residence
Richard Meier
1984

017 Villa Mairea
Alvar Aalto
1939

018 Vanna Venturi House
Robert Venturi
1964

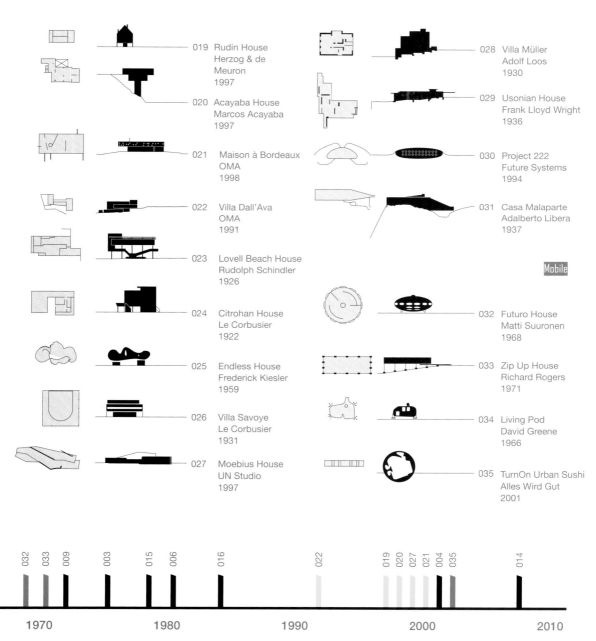

Elevated

019 Rudin House
Herzog & de
Meuron
1997

020 Acayaba House
Marcos Acayaba
1997

021 Maison à Bordeaux
OMA
1998

022 Villa Dall'Ava
OMA
1991

023 Lovell Beach House
Rudolph Schindler
1926

024 Citrohan House
Le Corbusier
1922

025 Endless House
Frederick Kiesler
1959

026 Villa Savoye
Le Corbusier
1931

027 Moebius House
UN Studio
1997

Embedded

028 Villa Müller
Adolf Loos
1930

029 Usonian House
Frank Lloyd Wright
1936

030 Project 222
Future Systems
1994

031 Casa Malaparte
Adalberto Libera
1937

Mobile

032 Futuro House
Matti Suuronen
1968

033 Zip Up House
Richard Rogers
1971

034 Living Pod
David Greene
1966

035 TurnOn Urban Sushi
Alles Wird Gut
2001

032 033 009   003   015 006   016   022   019 020 027 021 004 035   014

1970   1980   1990   2000   2010

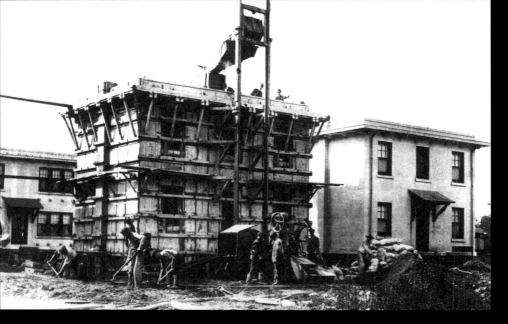

Thomas Edison, single-pour concrete system, 1906–19. In an attempt to address a chronic housing shortage in the US, Edison researched the untapped potentials of concrete as a building material and designed a rotary kiln that allowed a house to be completed in a single pour.

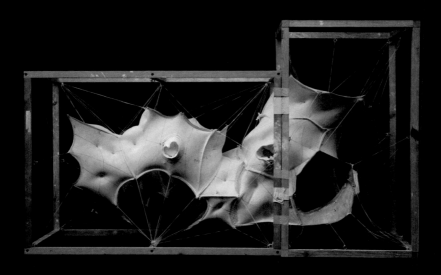

AADRL Team Anon: Mustafa El Sayed, Sara Saleh, Omrana Ahmed, Nick Williams, Project SoftCast

UNIT (HOUSE)

The unit has served as the most varied of all the scales examined, operating prototypically as the testing ground for new approaches to living. In its purest form, it synthesises a desire to experiment with new material processes, spatial conceptions and ways of engaging with the context. Here, the house stands as a materialised manifesto addressing a host of context-specific issues that challenge its fixity, relationship to the ground and material life-cycle: issues of fabrication, deployment and lightness are brought to the fore. This in turn prompts a consideration of the wider implications of these scenarios for the cluster and the collective. Buckminster Fuller's proposals illustrate this teasing out of pattern logic, showing how the design logic evolves as the singular engages with the collective, resulting in the coupling of production parameters (such as prefabrication, material efficiency and lightness) with issues of deployability and unit organisation.

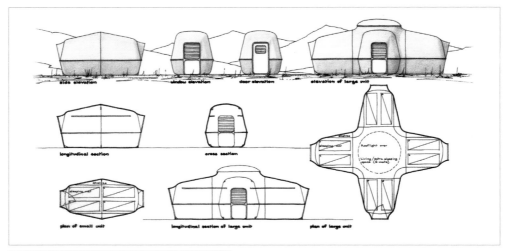

Arthur Quarmby, Emergency Mass Housing Units, Nº 1, 1962

Dimensions: 37m²
Material: Plastic, consisting of double-curved shells of three layers. The layers are made of polyester and fibreglass on the interior, and of polyester, fibreglass and an isolating phenol-based foam on the exterior
Fabrication: Designed to be assembled by four workers in seven and a half hours: the shapes of the building elements are defined by the constraints of stacking
Mobility: Just two trucks are needed to to transport enough building elements to provide housing for 114 people: the stock of elements is owned by the United Nations and stored all over the world
Flexibility: None

Matti Suuronen, Futuro House, 1978

Dimensions: Unit – diameter 8m; height 4m; cubic capacity 140m³; floor area 25m²; lot area 50m²; weight 2,500kg [without furnishings], 4,000kg total
Material: Unit – fibreglass-reinforced concrete and sandwiched polyester plastic; structure – four-leg steel foundation ring
Fabrication: The 16-part system could be dismantled and reassembled in two days
Mobility: Designed to be light enough for a helicopter to airlift the unit to difficult locations
Flexibility: Individual unit; plug-in system for hotel design

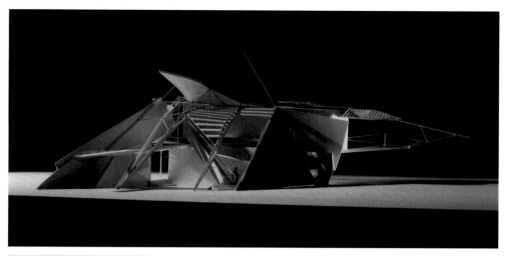

Coop Himmelb(l)au, Open House, 1983

Dimensions: Site area 9,000m²; floor area 190m²
Material: Double-glazed skin and double-shell structure
Fabrication: On-site bespoke fabrication of double-glazing, adjustable louvres, structural elements and staircase
Mobility: None
Flexibility: The flexibility resides in the 'open architecture', as there is no predetermined division of living spaces

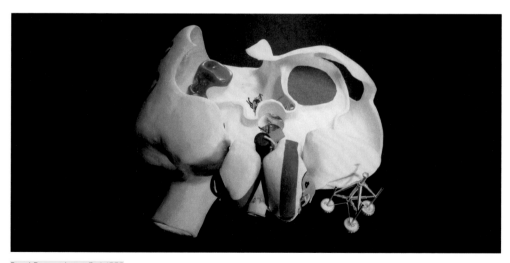

David Greene, Living Pod, 1965

Dimensions: Lot not specified as it is a mobile structure; floor area 85m²
Material: Unit – two-level fibreglass pod with an inner-bonded sandwich of insulation and/or finish; structure –
12 steel support nodes (6 tension, 6 compression)
Fabrication: Factory-fabricated, an 'appliance for carrying with you'
Mobility: Unit designed to move around to multiple locations and is adaptable for use as either a stand-alone
house or as part of an urban system
Flexibility: Single unit fully mobile

Wes Jones, Container House and Primitive Hut, 1998

Dimensions: Site 360 acres of inaccessible forest; multiple units ranging from 288 to 1,600ft² floor area; shipping container 20ft long x 8ft wide
Material: Unit – steel shipping container; structure – steel framing with levelling dunnage
Circulation: Telescoping armature, steel
Fabrication: Prefabrication with all interiors, plumbing and waste-disposal systems, power generator completed off site
Mobility: Unit transported to site via helicopter to avoid harming the landscape
Flexibility: Individual units can attach to each other, constructing diverse configurations

Future Systems, Une Petite Maison, 1982

Dimensions: N/A
Material: Semi-monocoque structure
Fabrication: Mass-produced and manufactured partly by robots
Mobility: On-site unit rests on inflatable cushions, two-person short-stay accommodation
Flexibility: Design has four different configurations

Richard & Su Rogers, Zip-Up Enclosures, 1971

Dimensions: Lot area not specified; floor area and weight vary; typical structural ring dimension 3ft wide x 30ft long
Material: DuPont materials including hybrid plastics, rubber and PVC; support structure, adjustable steel jack stilts
Fabrication: Floor, wall and roof components are fabricated off site and connected on site to form the structural ring: multiple structural rings are connected together to construct the house.
Mobility: Stand-alone individual unit can move and adapt to different sites, including multi-storey urban situations
Flexibility: Structural rings can be added to or removed from the overall house unit as the requirements of the owner change: rings have multiple options for colour, fenestration and texture

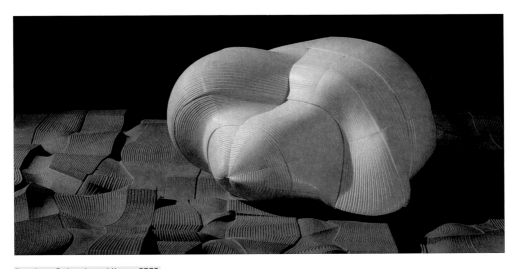

Greg Lynn, Embryological House, 2002

Dimensions: Variable
Material: Each unit is constructed entirely from wood
Fabrication: 14-month completion cycle for each house, including design, production, shipping and assembly
Mobility: Entire arrangement of units can be disbanded and reconstructed as required
Flexibility: The design of each unit allows for customisation and flexibility to adapt to a variety of situations: there is no original Embryological House – each unit is unique and individual

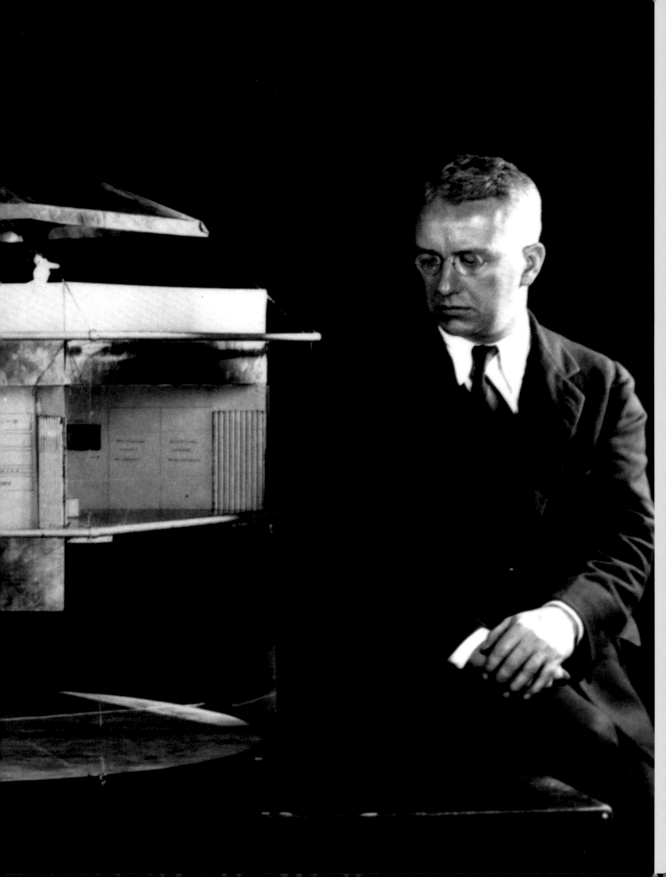

FULLER HOUSES

Through his early forays into mass-produced housing, Richard Buckminster Fuller (1895–1983) challenged how we design, fabricate and, most importantly, conceive of habitable space. These projects were guided by his 4D hypothesis, which posited that all designed objects located between the earth's crust and its atmosphere were time-based and moved dynamically around the earth, which was seen as fixed. Added to this was a belief that houses should be 'lightful' – a term evoking lightweight construction, an abundance of natural light and other 'delightful' qualities. A set of drawings for a single house offers a few radical glimpses of the approach that would come to define Fuller's most famous projects. While the plan is conventionally rectilinear, the structural core has a dual role: first, it contains all the mechanical systems required for the house to be self-sufficient; and second, it is the main structural support from which all the other components are hung, allowing the house to be raised above the ground.

In parallel with these individual house studies Fuller began to investigate the typology of the tower. Inspired by nature, and in particular botany, he produced a system that used the characteristics of the central trunk of a tree as the primary structure and the branches as secondary supports. This construction did not require a traditional foundation, but was suspended much like a tent, with the requisite compression strength being provided by a new, hexagon-shaped plan based on Fuller's investigations into the properties of crystals.

For Fuller, 4D was in essence a way of life, to be applied in its totality, from the scale of the house to transport infrastructures and the city as a whole. Over the next few decades, he attempted to revolutionise the human environment with a series of projects including the Dymaxion House, which challenged the heaviness of traditional house construction, the Wichita House, which redefined the concept of prefabrication, the Deployment Unit, which addressed reassembly and disassembly, and the 4D Tower, which offered a glimpse of how a single housing unit could be transformed into a collective housing structure.

The core of these studies was the Dymaxion House, where Fuller began to challenge the traditional focus of architecture on aesthetics and space (rather than the fourth dimension, time). To achieve the desired qualities of flexibility, mobility and efficiency, he freed the exterior walls from their structural role by transforming the core of the house into a central 'mast', much like a ship's mast, using a set of cables to support a hanging floor deck. These structural manoeuvres, besides freeing the house from the ground, provided certain functional advantages, increasing energy efficiency through natural ventilation. The house was also self-sufficient, with its own power and electrical systems and means of waste disposal, as well as its own cleaning system. All of its components, such as the bathroom unit, kitchen appliances, information systems and technological equipment, were designed to be easy to replace and recycle at the end of their useful life. This was a house conceived as a mobile unit – a challenge to the traditional permanence and stasis of architecture. As Fuller said, 'The modern automobile changes year by year, as we discover and develop new ways of improving it; so with the house.' The house was conceived according to the principles of industrial assembly and fabrication introduced by Ford Motors, known as Fordism. Fuller, always the inventor, began to speculate how this methodology could be implemented within architectural production, giving architects the possibility of 'doing more with less'. However he had to wait more than a decade, until 1944, before he could begin to fully explore this potential with the construction of a house in Wichita, Kansas.

The Wichita House was one of the few realised projects that embodied the radical vision of the Dymaxion House. As with the Dymaxion House, Fuller devoted his time to realising a living unit that was self-sufficient, cost-effective and based on industrial (rather than architectural) prefabrication. As Fuller was trained in multiple disciplines, including architecture and engineering, he was well aware of the advantages of a collaborative environment and he sought out a laboratory-type research and production space where a diverse team of engineers, designers, contractors and scientists could work side by side. After reviewing a handful of options the Beech Aircraft factory in Wichita was selected. The choice of location brought the team into direct contact with the highly technological, perfectionist approach to mass production in the aeroplane industry. It also allowed for a reimagining of the building trade definition of prefabrication, working towards Fuller's main goal of providing a house for everybody.

This ambitious aim resulted in a design that was a fully assembled industrial construction, in contrast to the standard prefabricated system, which could be defined as 'sub-assembled', with the panels and parts leaving the factory semi-finished and requiring additional fabrication on site. To achieve this, the earlier schemes underwent a series of modifications in terms of plan configurations, material selections and structural elements. Material studies on metals focused mostly on aluminium, chosen for its lightweight qualities. The use of aluminium required a stronger structure, so the hexagon-shaped floor plan was replaced by a round plan – which put the main structural loads back onto the walls and roof. While the core and mast of previous projects were retained, their roles changed: the mast became a key component during on-site assembly, as part of the mechanism for hanging the wheel-like floor frame, while the core housed mechanical systems and technological equipment such as the phone, television and information hub, as well as other programmatic spaces. Increasing the strength of the structure had the further added benefit of improving the house's resistance to tornados, hurricanes and earthquakes as well as fire. The aerodynamic qualities of the walls and the new curved roof, with its 'ventilator' cap, allowed for a natural flow of cool and hot air within the house, providing cost-effective air-conditioning and heating and minimising the need for bulky mechanical systems.

This evolution had begun to take shape with the Dymaxion Deployment Unit (DDU), which was originally conceived as a prefabricated house for a small family. It was here that material studies had revealed galvanised steel or aluminium to be self-supporting when erected vertically in a round plan – a configuration based on the grain silos constructed by the Butler Company of Kansas City. In 1940, when the British War Relief Organisation enlisted Fuller to develop an emergency shelter prototype that could be swiftly assembled and dismantled, he used the design of the prefabricated house as his template, but developed an aggregate system with two linked circular units of different sizes. The larger unit housed the main living and bedroom spaces, the smaller one the bathroom, kitchen and additional bedroom. The galvanised steel walls were cut and removed where the two circumferences intersected, providing fluid connections between the units and opening up the possibility for the prototype to continue attaching, in line with certain behavioural characteristics and needs, so as to form a cluster of modules.

However, this double clustering of modules did not originate in the Deployment Unit, but was a concept that Fuller had envisioned much earlier, at the start of the 4D proposals. This is seen most clearly in the 4D Tower, a vertical collection of Dymaxion House prototypes where Fuller deployed his favourite natural analogy of the tree, elongating the central core or trunk to accommodate more branches that supported up to 12 vertical towers. Each tower, itself a multi-storey apartment complex, functioned according to the same principles as the individual housing units, generating its own services for energy, light and heating as well as waste disposal. Never one to remain inside the box, Fuller speculated on a radical scale, visualising these aggregated towers being dropped all over the earth. This futuristic idea was buoyed by the lightweight qualities of the towers, which were designed, like the house prototypes, to be transportable from site to site. And if the tower had to be moved it could simply be lifted up by a Zeppelin airship and relocated to a new site on 'spaceship earth'.

Buckminster Fuller, Dymaxion House, 1920s

Dimensions: Floor area 1,600ft^2; weight 3,000lbs; lot area not specified
Material: Wire wheel-like steel frame hung from a central Duralumin 'mast' that suspends the floor and ceiling assemblies from pneumatic structures. All rigid supporting structures are thin aluminium tubes filled with air; walls are two-level fibreglass pod with an inner-bonded sandwich of insulation and/or finish; aluminium roof panels and Duralumin hood.
Fabrication: Mass-production process modelled after Ford car assembly line: all major systems and primary furniture are fabricated in the factory and sent to the site on a flatbed truck for assembly.
Mobility: The stand-alone individual unit is fixed to its site location.
Flexibility: Each unit designed independently of the masts so that it can be replaced whenever new and improved units become available; the material from the discarded unit can be recycled and used in the fabrication of new housing units.

R Buckminster Fuller, Dymaxion House, second model,
following the 1928 structural model, showing the
underground building elements (foundation and tanks)

Dymaxion House

The Dymaxion House was a commentary on and alternative to the orthogonal house plan constructed using traditional methods. By modelling the assembly, fabrication and life-cycle of the house on the automobile industry, the house would function like a car.

Hexagonal configuration of a unit system centred on a mast that allows for radial expansion at multiple levels

Factory-engineered prefabricated components are delivered to site in large preassembled 'packages'

The floor platform and mast are erected on site and the housing unit is fastened onto the mast

The tripod supporting mast is located in the centre of the unit from which cables stretch out to the floor decks

Modules are designed as independent entities from each other and are self-sufficient, but can be clustered vertically along the central mast

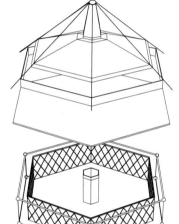

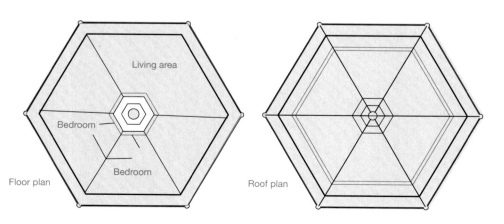

Floor plan

Living area

Bedroom

Bedroom

Roof plan

Buckminster Fuller, Wichita Dwelling Machine, 1944–46

Dimensions: Unit floor area 1,017ft²; weight 8,000lbs; diameter 36ft; interior volume 12,000ft³; interior height 16ft; exterior height 22ft; lot area not specified

Material: Steel wire-spoke horizontal wheel frame with sheet metal hung from a central 'mast' that is made from a bundle of steel tubes and network rings and struts. The exterior cladding is aluminium sheeting with thermal foil on the interior surface. Windows are of 'wrap-around' acrylic. The roof ventilator is made of aluminium sheeting. Interior walls and floors are plywood.

Fabrication: The house was produced on an assembly line and the finished products were packed in large metal tubes, which were shipped to the site. After assembling and erecting the 'mast', the floor, exterior sheeting, roof ventilator and interior assemblies followed in order. It took six workers approximately one day to erect the house.

Mobility: Stand-alone individual unit fixed to its site location

Flexibility: The house was designed independently of the mast so that it could be replaced as required when new units became available. Material from the discarded unit was recyclable and intended for use on future units.

R Buckminster Fuller, Wichita Dwelling Machine, exterior aluminium sheeting being installed during construction

Wichita Dwelling Machine

The project was a realised version and adaptation of the Dymaxion House prototype: standardised, lightweight, cost-effective homes with the components mass-produced on a factory assembly line and delivered to site for efficient construction.

Radial configuration for the most advantageous relationship between circumference and interior space

Factory-engineered and assembled prefabricated components are delivered to site in large 'packages'

Assembled on site in approximately one day

Structure is developed from the top of mast downward ensuring maximum rigidity within the house assembly

Modules are designed as independent entities and are self-sufficient, allowing for the free arrangment of clusters of units

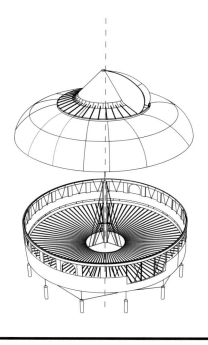

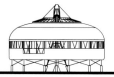

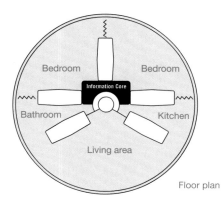

Floor plan

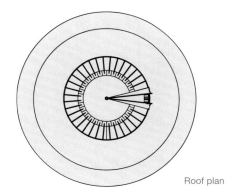

Roof plan

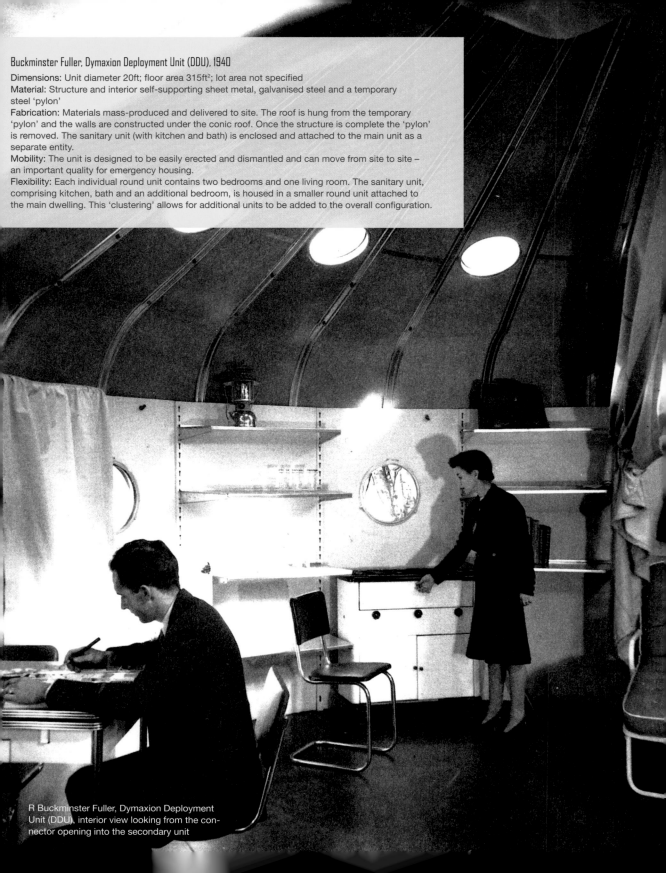

Buckminster Fuller, Dymaxion Deployment Unit (DDU), 1940

Dimensions: Unit diameter 20ft; floor area 315ft²; lot area not specified
Material: Structure and interior self-supporting sheet metal, galvanised steel and a temporary steel 'pylon'
Fabrication: Materials mass-produced and delivered to site. The roof is hung from the temporary 'pylon' and the walls are constructed under the conic roof. Once the structure is complete the 'pylon' is removed. The sanitary unit (with kitchen and bath) is enclosed and attached to the main unit as a separate entity.
Mobility: The unit is designed to be easily erected and dismantled and can move from site to site – an important quality for emergency housing.
Flexibility: Each individual round unit contains two bedrooms and one living room. The sanitary unit, comprising kitchen, bath and an additional bedroom, is housed in a smaller round unit attached to the main dwelling. This 'clustering' allows for additional units to be added to the overall configuration.

R Buckminster Fuller, Dymaxion Deployment Unit (DDU), interior view looking from the connector opening into the secondary unit

Deployment House

Initially conceived as a single-family house but used for wartime emergency shelters, the Dymaxion Deployment Unit (DDU) was made from off-the-shelf galvanised steel components and prefabricated furnishings and was designed to be easily assembled and disassembled in a speedy fashion, allowing the units to be transported from site to site.

 Radial configuration best suited for the galvanised steel materials of the unit

 Factory-engineered prefabricated steel materials are delivered to site for construction of the module

 Fast assembly and disassembly on site

 Self-supporting bent sheet metal that also provides beneficial interior space

 The two units (different sizes) are designed to connect and it is conceivable that more units can cluster

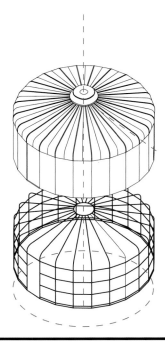

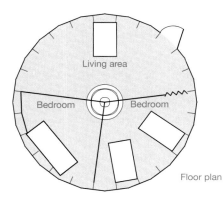

Living area

Bedroom   Bedroom

Floor plan

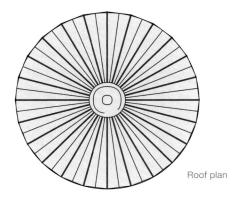

Roof plan

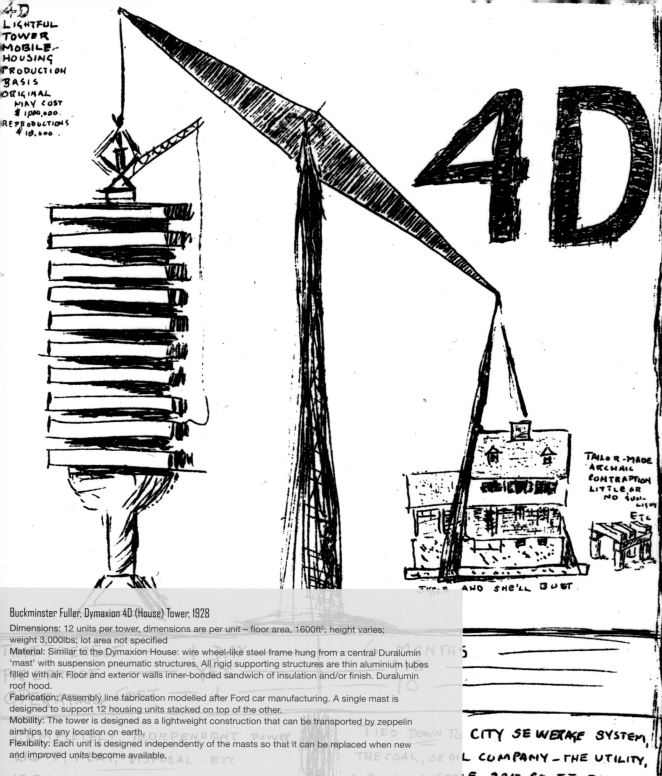

Buckminster Fuller, Dymaxion 4D (House) Tower, 1928

Dimensions: 12 units per tower, dimensions are per unit – floor area, 1600ft²; height varies; weight 3,000lbs; lot area not specified

Material: Similar to the Dymaxion House: wire wheel-like steel frame hung from a central Duralumin 'mast' with suspension pneumatic structures. All rigid supporting structures are thin aluminium tubes filled with air. Floor and exterior walls inner-bonded sandwich of insulation and/or finish. Duralumin roof hood.

Fabrication: Assembly line fabrication modelled after Ford car manufacturing. A single mast is designed to support 12 housing units stacked on top of the other.

Mobility: The tower is designed as a lightweight construction that can be transported by zeppelin airships to any location on earth.

Flexibility: Each unit is designed independently of the masts so that it can be replaced when new and improved units become available.

Dymaxion 4D Tower

The tower is a major component of Fuller's 4D vision and is a clustering of the single Dymaxion House module on an elongated central mast. Each tower is a self-sufficient entity and is highly efficient and mobile.

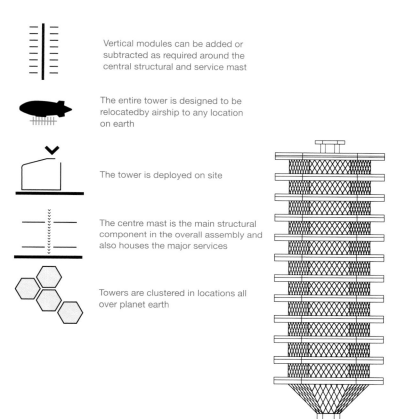

Vertical modules can be added or subtracted as required around the central structural and service mast

The entire tower is designed to be relocatedby airship to any location on earth

The tower is deployed on site

The centre mast is the main structural component in the overall assembly and also houses the major services

Towers are clustered in locations all over planet earth

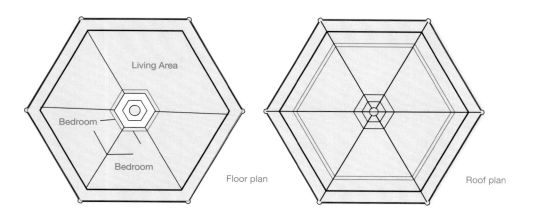

Living Area

Bedroom

Bedroom

Floor plan

Roof plan

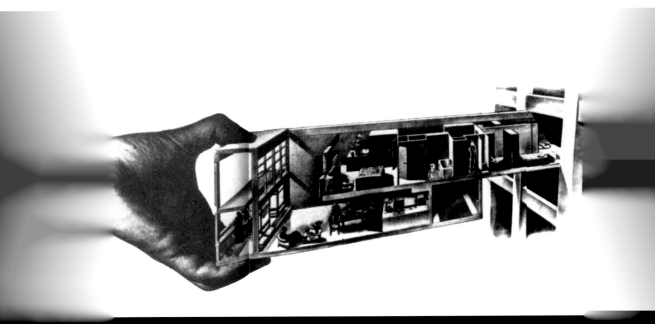

Corbusier, Unité d'Habitation, 1952

...ecursor to the plug-in system of the Unité d'Habitation was constructed from two components. First, a béton ...lattice-like frame that Corb referred to as a 'wine rack' formed the megastructure; next, the apartments, acting ...utonomous plug-in units, were slotted into the voids in the frame.

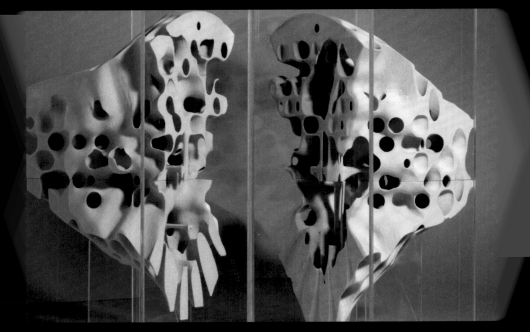

Team Farm: Marga Basquets, Sebastian Delagrange, Iain Maxwell, Project Agent Urbanism

CLUSTER (BUILDING)

The cluster affords the most detail-oriented models of spatial polyscalar organisation. The question of magnitude operates distinctly at this scale. Principles of vertical versus horizontal distribution identify urban typologies in which there is a correlation between circulation and unit distribution. From a systemic viewpoint, it is this coupling of circulatory dependence, unit distribution, structure and approaches to landscape that makes these models distinct. Density- and time-based distribution see unit-to-unit interaction evolve into collective relationships that challenge discrete building articulation. Examples such as the Japanese Metabolists' formal distribution of buildings in the sky or the Smithsons' interest in circulation corridors as public streets argue for new social frameworks that suggest an engaged form of collective dwelling that could be enabled through density.

Zvi Hecker's Ramot Housing of 1985 and Moshe Safdie's Habitat 67 offer two seminal examples of unit-based distribution models. In both, aggregation-based deployment – packing versus stacking organisations – show the varied range of unit-to-unit organisation that can be achieved within one housing cluster. Within Adaptive Ecologies computation is used to explore organisational principles that allow unit-to-unit interaction to emerge, engaging growth models that are based on both time and scenario, challenging the dominance of circulation-only distribution.

Jean Renaudie, Jeanne Hachette, Ivry-sur-Seine, 1970–75

Dimensions: 40 flats of varying size, from 38.9m² to 130.69m² (+27.50m² of garden space), 6,480m² of shops, 7,440m² of offices, 2,247m² of storage
Material: Precast concrete panels
Fabrication: Precast concrete panels assembled in situ
Mobility/flexibility: None
Number of units: 40 (27 different types)
Unit-to-unit organisation: Units are connected only through horizontal walkways
Typology: Horizontal
Circulation: Staircases provide vertical circulation and walkways provide horizontal circulation

Glen Small, Green Machine, 1977–80

Dimensions: Site 1 acre; modular box – length 19ft–30ft, width 8ft, height 9ft 7in
Material: Prefabricated Airstream trailers, steel space-frame megastructure, recycled materials, solar panels for energy use and consumption
Fabrication: Modular system and steel space-frame assembly on site; modules (Airstream trailers) are plugged into space-frame on site
Mobility/flexibility: None
Number of units: 24
Unit-to-unit organisation: Units are connected only through the horizontal walkways
Typology: Space-frame with pods plugged into superstructure
Circulation: Escalators for vertical circulation and interior walkways ('streets') for horizontal circulation

Archigram, Walking City, 1964

Dimensions: Undefined and ever-changing
Material: Unknown
Fabrication: Not realised
Mobility/flexibility: A nomadic city that plugs into its transient location to share and dissipate information technology
Number of units: Undetermined and ever-changing
Unit-to-unit organisation: Connected through plug-in system to the megastructure
Typology: Horizontal
Circulation: Unknown

Paul Rudolph, Oriental Masonic Gardens, 1971

Dimensions: Site 12.5 acres; unit 12ft wide and varying lengths (27ft, 39ft, 51ft)
Material: Each prefabricated unit made entirely from wood: a fire-wall is constructed on site prior
to the insertion of the units
Fabrication: Each unit, including plumbing, electrical and interior finishes, is fabricated and assembled
in a factory and delivered by truck to the site
Mobility/flexibility: The entire arrangement of units can be disbanded and reconfigured as required
Number of units: 148
Unit-to-unit organisation: Units grouped in fours around a utility core
Typology: Horizontal
Circulation: Exterior/interior pathways between the units

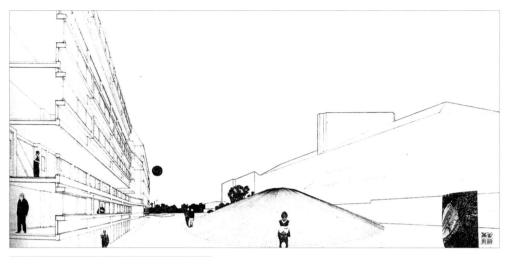

Alison and Peter Smithson, Robin Hood Gardens, 1972

Dimensions: Site zoning to 142 person/acre, 2 hectares; Block A: 10 storeys, Block B: 7 storeys
Material: Precast concrete slabs
Fabrication: On-site installation of precast concrete panels
Mobility/flexibility: None
Number of units: 213
Unit-to-unit organisation: Through a vertical concrete shaft
Typology: Horizontal
Circulation: Stairwells and outdoor aerial walkways ('streets in the sky')

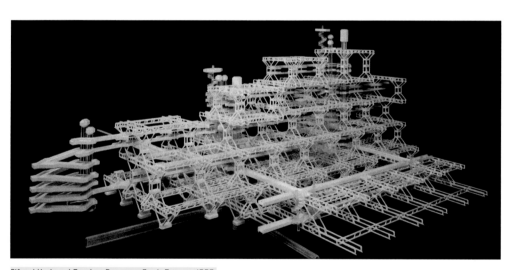

Elfried Huth and Günther Domenig, Stadt Ragnitz, 1969

Dimensions: Designed as a kit of parts that can expand infinitely
Material: Steel
Fabrication: Plug-in system into steel superstructure
Mobility/flexibility: As a unit none, however the system, as an entire kit of parts assembly, can expand and has multiple configurations providing a high level of flexibility
Number of units: Undefined
Unit-to-unit organisation: Connected through the superstructure
Typology: Horizontal and Vertical
Circulation: 'Multi-plex clusters' provide vertical circulation for inhabitants connected to horizontal walkways. Horizontal roads for vehicular traffic are woven through the mega-structure

Kisho Kurokawa, Nakagin Capsule Tower, 1972

Dimensions: Individual unit 8ft x 13ft; 14-storey superstructure
Material: Capsule – steel-trussed box clad with galvanised reinforced steel coated with rust-proof paint; vertical superstructure – steel frame partially encased in concrete
Fabrication: Capsules made off site and hoisted in by a crane
Mobility/flexibility: Multiple capsules can be modified to construct larger spaces and the system is designed for capsules to be replaced or removed as required
Number of units: 140
Unit-to-unit organisation: Through the vertical concrete shaft
Typology: Helicoidal and vertical
Circulation: Vertical circulation through elevator and lobby access

Kiyonori Kikutake, Osaka Tower Expo '70

Material: Solid truss with steel pipes and balls
Fabrication: A space frame consisting of group columns standing on the apexes of equilateral-triangular plans and connected by means of ball joints: the tower serves as a wireless reception base and communication system
Mobility/flexibility: None
Number of units: Six deck pods at different levels
Unit-to-unit organisation: Linked by staircases
Typology: Vertical
Circulation: Vertical circulation provided by staircases and elevators

Zvi Hecker, Ramot Housing I, 1972–85
Dimensions: Gross floor area 72,000m²
Material: Prefabricated precast concrete components, poured in-place concrete using traditional formwork and modular kitchen and bathroom units.
Fabrication: The housing complex was built in two stages using two different fabrication methods. Stage one units were connected through post-tensioning, high tensioning rods and welding. Specially designed prefabricated elements were brought to site, erected to form the living pods, and then lifted into place by crane. Stage two units were constructed using traditional masonry and mortar.
Mobility/flexibility: None
Number of units: 720 (varying in size and number of rooms)
Unit-to-unit organisation: Each housing block is organised around five interconnected external courts that are linked together by ground level walkways.
Typology: Horizontal plan-driven organisation
Circulation: Ground-level walkways lead to stairwells that provide vertical access

View of the pedestrian walkway that forms the central spine connecting the five star-shaped buildings of the complex

RAMOT HOUSING

Zvi Hecker's housing for the Ramot quarter in Jerusalem was influenced by his investigations into natural systems such as crystals, bee swarms and honeycombs, which took their cue from the research of the metabolist movement in postwar Japan. With Hecker, the enquiry into these organic structures inspired an interest in the structural and organisational properties of the dodecahedron – a 12-sided volume which became the singular aggregate that would ultimately generate the entire design.

The project was commissioned by the Israeli Ministry of Housing in 1972 – Hecker (1931–) was born and educated in Poland, but emigrated to Israel in 1950. It can be seen as an example of a new model of living based on the logic of organic spatial organisation where the individual constituent drives the collective. The 12-sided pods housing the living units are oriented around a skeletal frame that encloses the circulation of a series of arteries. The aggregation of the units creates a variety of spaces and conditions that allow for multiple configurations and sizes of rooms within the 720 individual apartments. A clustering both vertically and horizontally creates a terraced housing scheme consisting of five 'finger' complexes resembling the palm of a hand. Public spaces are formed through a central spine that weaves between the 'finger' complexes and connects five courts of green space. The units have the potential to continue aggregating within the internal logic of the system, making the cluster infinitely adaptable and expandable.

The prefabricated panels are prepared
for assembly on site

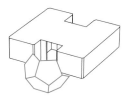

Unit aggregation

Each individual 12-sided aggregate clusters around the rectilinear apartment plans forming the building facade and interior spaces

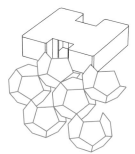

Apartment aggregation

The design and geometry of the 12-sided aggregate allows for a variety of apartment sizes and configurations

Third floor apartment

01. Bedroom
02. Bathroom
03. Living area
04. Dining/kitchen
05. Balcony
06. Storage
07. Communal stairway

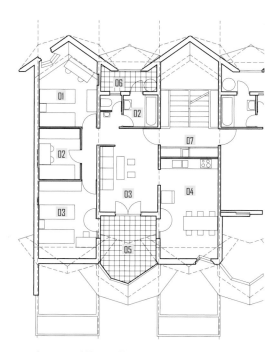

Apartment N5, type Z

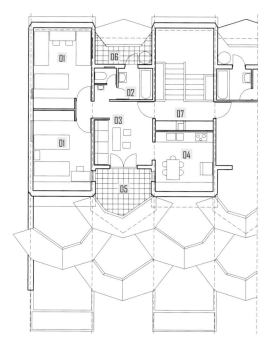

Apartment N9, type M

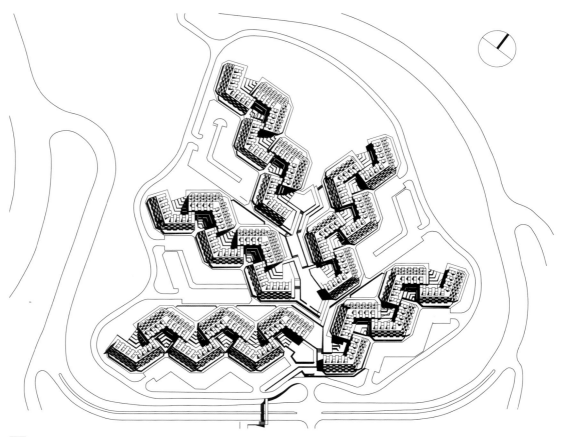

Plan

The overall layout consists of five 'fingers' of clustered housing blocks with each 'finger' representing a different phase of the construction process. Two stages were constructed using specially designed prefabricated concrete panels and elements. For three stages the housing blocks were built using traditional masonry in-situ methods of construction.

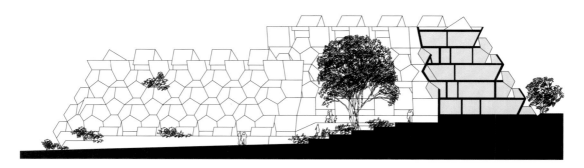

Section

Each of the five buildings has a dedicated 'court' and these exterior spaces provide a connector between the clusters of housing. The flexibility of the building section allows for apartments of varying sizes and numbers of rooms.

Prefabricated concrete panels are hoisted into place to form one of the housing pod components

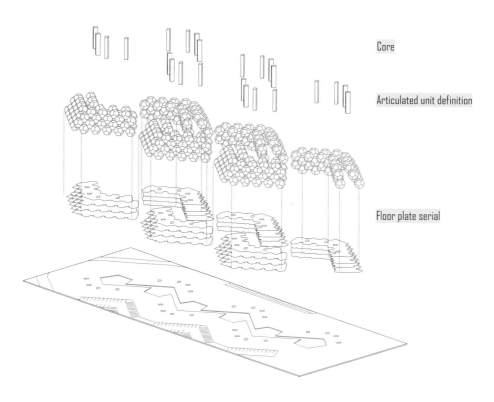

Core

Articulated unit definition

Floor plate serial

Housing complex under construction

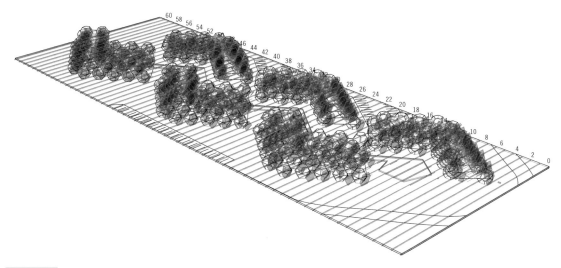

Section slices

This series of section cuts highlights the multiple configurations that the 12-sided aggregates form throughout the entire housing complex.

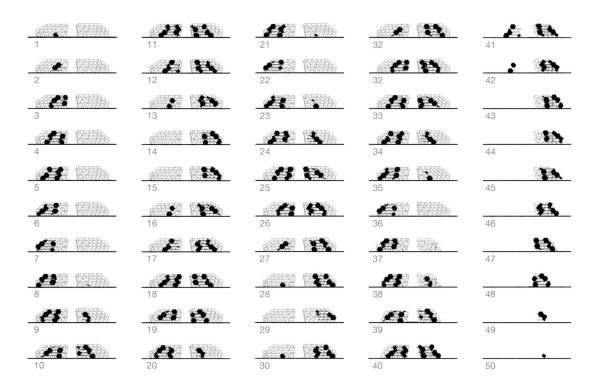

Moshe Safdie, Habitat '67, Montreal, 1964–67

Dimensions: Each modular box 5.3m x 117m; 354 modules form a total
of 15 different housing types ranging from 55.7m² (one-bedroom) to 157.9m²
(four-bedroom)
Material: Precast concrete modules; structural steel rods and cables; fibreglass
bathroom fixtures
Fabrication: Modular boxes and other concrete circulation components produced
on site in a purpose-built factory. Interior components, eg bathroom fixtures and
kitchen units, fabricated off site. Completed modules hoisted into place by crane
and connected by post-tensioning, high-tensioning rods, cables and welding.
Mobility/flexibility: None
Number of living units: 158 (made up of 354 modules)
Unit-to-unit organisation: Each unit conceived as a self-contained housing unit
for privacy and acoustics
Typology: Vertical non-load bearing pods plugged into superstructure
Circulation: Three elevator cores, outdoor pedestrian streets located every
four floors and vertical access stairwells

HABITAT '67

Habitat '67 by Israeli-born architect Moshe Safdie (1938–) exemplifies an attitude towards housing that focuses always on the idea of the singular generating the collective. From a conceptual point of view, the project emerged from a bottom-up design approach that used the development of an individual habitation prototype as the catalyst for the overall system of the housing complex.

Influenced by Buckminster Fuller's housing projects, this prototype was conceived as a factory-assembled container equipped with kitchen, bathroom and all service equipment. However, the Habitat unit departed from Fuller's preferred aluminium materials in utilising precast concrete for its speed of construction, prefabrication characteristics and load-bearing structural capabilities – here the inspiration was Thomas Edison's single-pour concrete house. The individual modules were then stacked and paired, creating a variety of living unit configurations (15 different housing types) that grew as a collective massing of housing.

Based on the assembly of prefabricated modules, Habitat on the surface resembles proposals developed by the Japanese metabolists, such as the Nakagin Capusle tower, which rely on a megastructure and 'plug-in' system. However, in contrast to those projects, the modules in the Habitat complex are linked by post-tensioning components not just to each other but to the vehicular circulation bridges, 'pedestrian streets' and mechanical cores – thus taking the structure out of the megastructure.

This structural and spatial organisation is a designed system that knows no boundaries: the modules and circulation and mechanical components have an infinite capacity to add to the overall collective of the network. In this way, the complex is not a static object but an ever-evolving dynamic of housing, enhanced by 'semipublic' spaces along the pedestrian streets that provide gardens for things to grow, areas where children can play, and where families and neighbours can interact together and with the built environment. Clearly, Habitat '67 was conceived not as a building but as a city – a synthesis of streets, shops, residences, people and infrastructure that grows organically as a collective organism. Habitat '67 provides an alternative to the rigidity of two-dimensional urban planning by introducing a 'three-dimensional community' that allows for alteration and growth. The only thing left for the architect to decide is when to stop the aggregation.

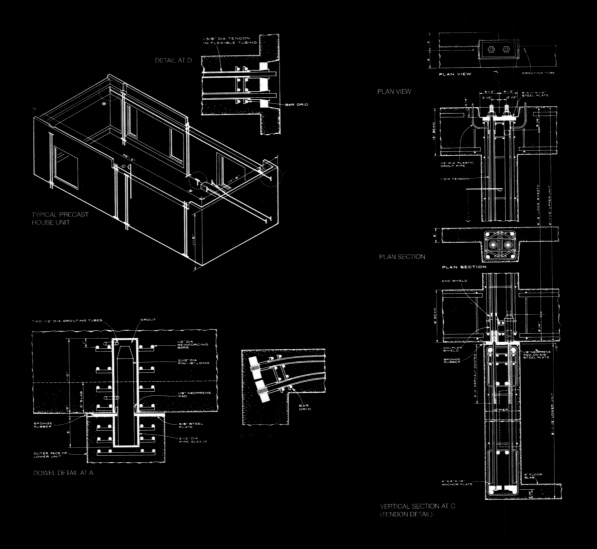

DETAIL AT D

TYPICAL PRECAST
HOUSE UNIT

DOWEL DETAIL AT A

PLAN VIEW

PLAN SECTION

VERTICAL SECTION AT C
(TENDON DETAIL)

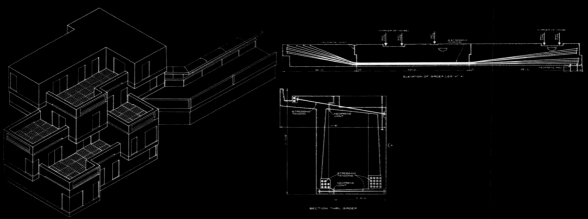

Construction drawings detailing how the individual modules are
connected to each other through post-tensioning, high-tensioning
rods, cables and welding

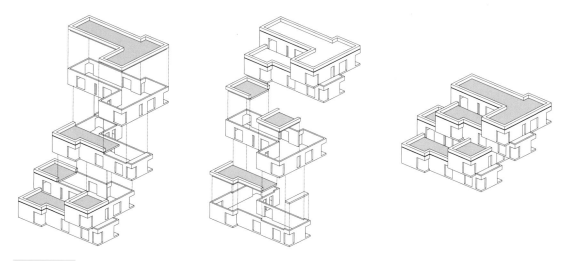

Unit aggregation

Through different orientations and stacking 354 modules construct the entire aggregated cluster housing complex of 158 living units. The modules are stacked in a staggered and cascading arrangement to give each apartment an outdoor terraced space and to maximise natural light.

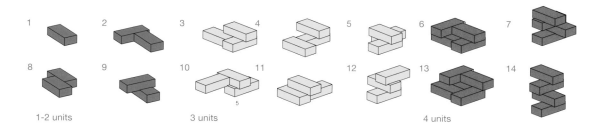

| 1 | 2 | 3 | 4 | 5 | 6 | 7 |
| 8 | 9 | 10 | 11 | 12 | 13 | 14 |

1-2 units   3 units   4 units

Apartment matrix

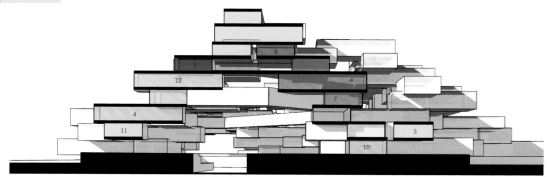

Sectional spatial relationships

A crane hoists one of the prefabricated modular
housing units into place

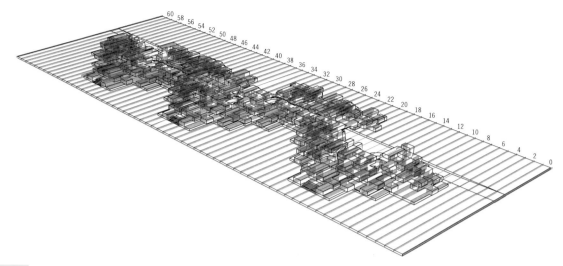

Section slices

The individual modular units cluster and aggregate to form multiple configurations throughout the housing complex.

001

Unit-to-apartment configurations

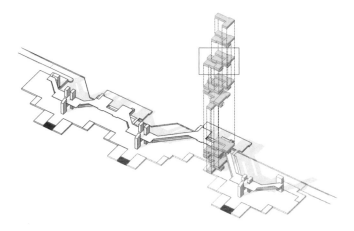

002

Groupings of apartments
aggregate to form the
building formation

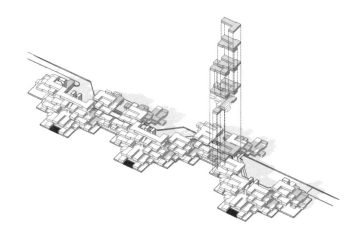

003

Aggregation of complex clusters

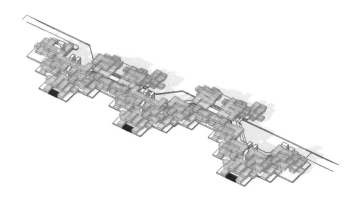

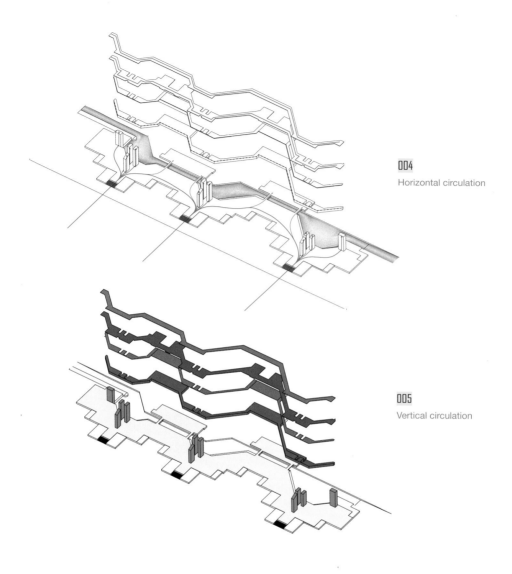

004

Horizontal circulation

005

Vertical circulation

The individual units are designed to attach to other units to form apartment groupings (001). There are 15 different apartment types that aggregate collectively in the formation of the building (002). This aggregation results in a large-scale cluster (003). The cluster is stitched together by two different circulation systems. Entry into each apartment is gained through continuous 'pedestrian streets' acting as the horizontal circulation artery (004). The pedestrian streets, located every fourth floor, are accessed and occupied by the elevator cores and stairwells, which provide the vertical circulation (005).

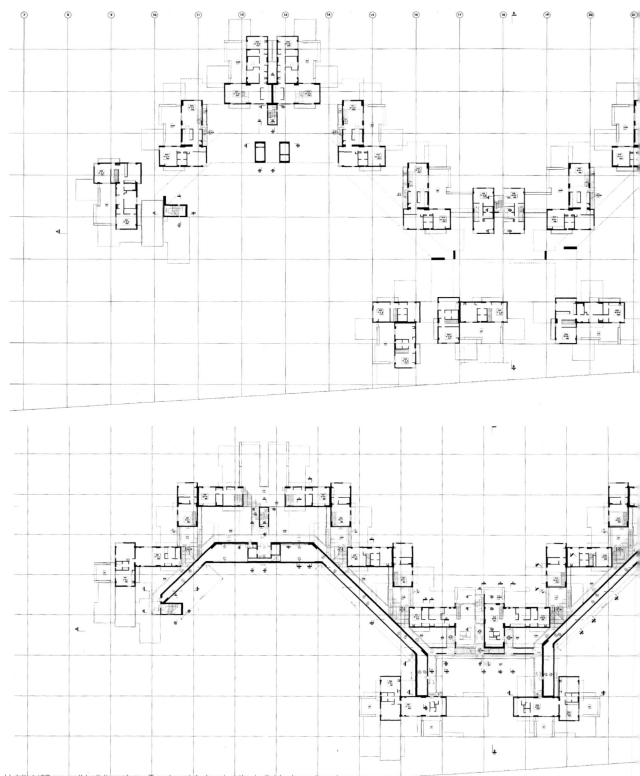

Habitat '67, overall building plans. Top: Level 4 showing the individual apartments connected by the pedestrian streets; Bottom: Level 5 shows the mechanical chase housing the systems for the housing complex.

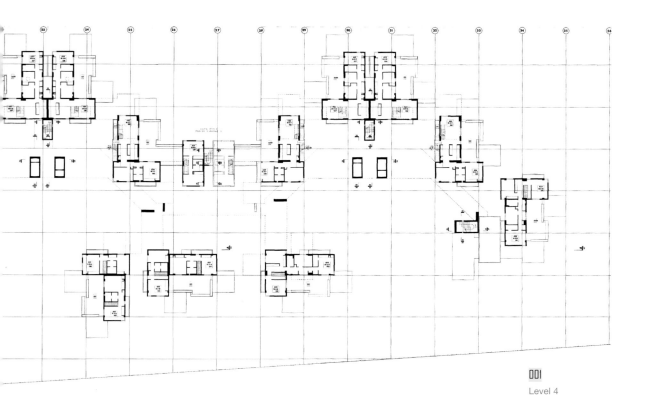

001

Level 4

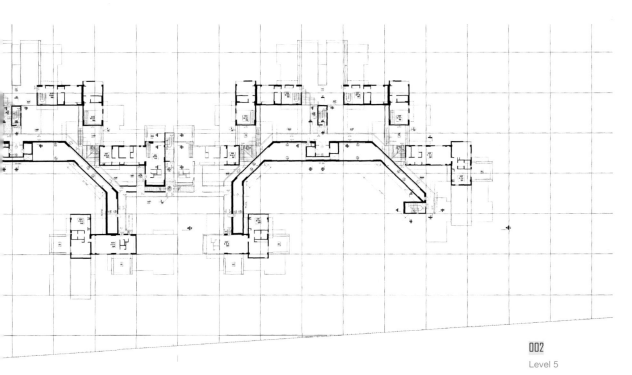

002

Level 5

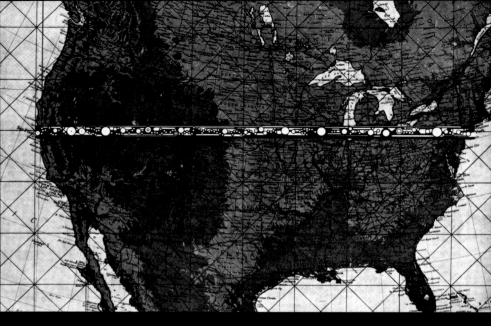

Alan Boutwell and Mike Mitchell, Continuous City for 1,000,000 Human Beings, 1969. The enormous city, erected on 100m-high pillars, spans across the entire United States, linked across the linear masterplan by transport systems of varying speeds and capacities.

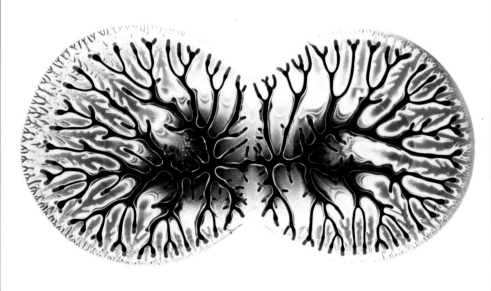

Team Egloo: Pankaj Chaudhary, Jwalant Mahadevwala, Mateo Riestra, Drago Vodanovic Egloo proposes a decentralised connective neighbourhood model developed through the interplay and transcoding of material and digital computation.

COLLECTIVE (MASTERPLAN)

The collective scale has historically informed the tradition of master planning the city. Within this discourse, evolved cluster-based organisations have incorporated pattern-based distribution and combinatorial typologies. Whether radical or reactionary in intent or the result of the technological advances in mobility, the sheer magnitude of these operational collectives tends to produce a fixed and finite vision of future living and societal function.

To counteract this inflexibility – and to allow the design of the city to accommodate the latent and the unknown – Adaptive Ecologies speculates on a form of computational urbanism that could enable the city to evolve with the times. Rather than resisting change, we could incorporate into the design of the contemporary city systems that are able to evolve and forecast future possibilities. The main obstacle to this is not a limit on the imagination, as demonstrated for example by Chanéac's continually evolving Crater City, or by the Ocean City projects of Kiyonori Kikutake, which embody a metabolic and generative ecological life-cycle. Rather, the challenge is to see computation as a means to further explore these implications through our capacity to simulate, communicate and forecast. Our argument is that time-based versioning is the most rigorous means of addressing the adaptive and knowledge-based development pursued within these models. For us, it is the means to allow cities to develop at a pace with the contemporary accelerated forms of urbanism in participatory and informed ways.

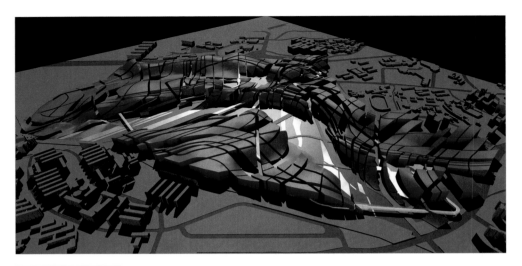

Zaha Hadid, One North, 2001
Location: Singapore
Population: 138,000 (estimated)
Density: 72,631 people per km^2
Total site area: 1.9 km^2
Classification: Urban masterplan
Typology: Technopole
Duration of project: 20 years

Richard Neutra, Rush City, 1928
Location: United States
Population: 22,040
Density: 5,485 people per km^2
Total site area: 4,018,591m^2
Classification: Urban utopian scheme based on hierarchical planning and modernist grid
Urban typology: A plan based on zoning separating industrial, green spaces, leisure, multi-family housing, single-family housing and different modes of transportation
Duration of project: Each section of the city was based on a 'sector' allowing additional sectors to be added to the overall city for infinite growth

Le Corbusier, Algiers Masterplan, 1931

Location: Algeria
Population: 250,000 (with a capacity for 180,000 more)
Density: N/A
Total site area: N/A
Classification: Urban and suburban scheme that acts as a link to connect fractured parts of the city
Urban typology: Linear city plan that provides development of rapid movement by means of an expressway, with living space integrated into the transport system
Duration of project: Undefined

Constant, New Babylon, 1960

Location: Global proposal
Population: 500,000
Density: 36,438 people per km^2
Total site area: 13,720,107m^2
Classification: Urban, suburban, rural and linkages between city centres, organic in its growth
Urban typology: An infinite megastructure consisting of space-frames that house nomadic and ever-changing structures
Duration of project: Limitless

Paolo Soleri, The City in the Image of Man, 1969

Location: Noahbabel coastal waters
Population: 90,000
Density: 233 people per acre
Total site area: 380 acres
Classification: Urban condition located on coastal waters
Urban typology: Centralised plan, part subterranean
Duration of project: N/A

Paul Rudolph, Lower Manhattan Expressway, 1971

Location: New York City, NY
Population: 100,000
Density: Undefined
Total site area: Undefined
Classification: Linear linkage urban plan
Urban typology: Multi-horizontal megastructure layered system providing designated areas for different modes
of transportation (local vehicular, highway vehicular, people-movers and pedestrian) that are integrated within
the existing city fabric of NYC
Duration of project: N/A

Frank Lloyd Wright, Broadacre City, 1934

Location: US countryside
Population: 7,000
Density: 615 people per km^2
Total site area: 11,390,923 m^2
Classification: Suburban and rural
Urban typology: Decentralised, anti-urban and self-sufficient, based on sprawl and the automobile
Duration of project: 25 years

Archizoom, No Stop City, 1969

Location: Global proposal
Population: 20,000
Density: 41,801 people per km^2
Total site area: 478,457m^2
Classification: An urban 'well-equipped residential parking lot'
Urban typology: A non-hierarchical uniform neutral field with an infinite pattern of potential extensions
Duration of project: Limitless

Jean-Louis Rey (Chanéac), drawing of the Crater Cities
(Villes Cratères) urban scheme with a human resting in their
crater space, 1963 Courtesy FRAC Centre, Orléans

CHANÉAC

The architecture of Chanéac (real name Jean-Louis Rey, 1931–1993) combines synthetic fabrication and material exploration with concepts of biological growth. Originally trained as an artist, Chanéac's work sought 'an organic architecture which can evolve and move' based on individual 'cell' implants that operate across multiple scales from the unit to the city. Invigorated by the possibilities of the new technologies and materials available to postwar architects, but frustrated by the static architecture produced by the ubiquitous modern movement, he set out to conceive of an architectural prototype that was highly adaptable through a rigorous and radical (for architecture) testing of materials.

The testing of materials had two main outcomes – unit adaptability and industrial-based fabrication concepts. Experimenting with plastics, polyester and polymers, especially thermosets reinforced with glass, Chanéac developed a rhomboid-shaped 'multipurpose cell' that created a spontaneous architecture based on the malleability of the various materials and the speed of assembly. It took just two hours to assemble the multipurpose cells out of plastic precast components produced using standard industrial processes. The flexibility of the materials gave the inhabitants the ability to transform the interior space of the cell in response to their individual needs.

Parallel to these cell studies Chanéac began to investigate the rapid growth of European cities and the suburban conditions that were appearing on the periphery of the urban edge. As a solution to this urban sprawl he proposed 'Crater Cities' (Villes Cratères), where benign parasitic entities were hosted by the existing city fabric, creating a mutually beneficial relationship that consisted of six parts: circulation canyons (vehicular and motorised traffic), artificial hills (sound barrier slopes that housed living quarters and office areas), crater-residences (private and intimate spaces created by the artificial hills), an artificial plateau (pedestrian circulation and public spaces), superstructures (high-density housing and commercial) and parasite cells (mass-produced living units). Within these cells, Chanéac began to implant the polyvalent habitation cells of earlier projects, aggregating the units through stacking and pairing. Further material studies allowed the design of the habitation crater-cells to achieve more complex geometries and double curvatures, giving them the potential to fill the available space in the urban super-block. With their rapid fabrication and assembly methods the units can reproduce indefinitely and begin to create their own network and collective in the growing metropolis. The project gives the city back to the inhabitants by allowing them to participate in the formation of urban space.

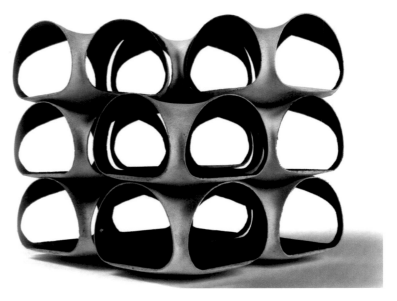

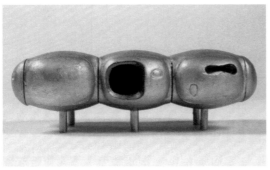

(Above)

Jean-Louis Rey (Chanéac), Multipurpose Cells – study models,
1958–60

Courtesy FRAC Centre, Orléans

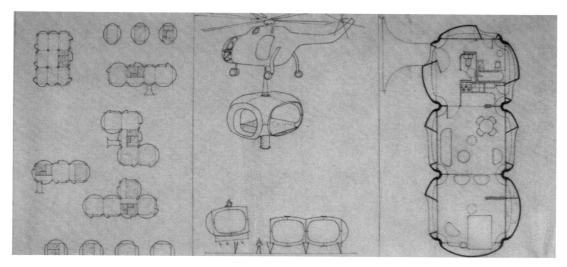

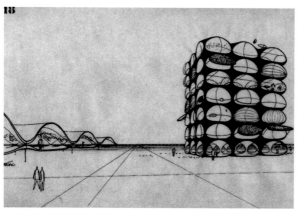

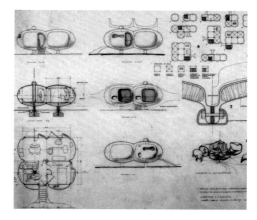

(Top)

Jean-Louis Rey (Chanéac), Multipurpose Cells – sketches of
several multipurpose cells grouping and being transported by
helicopter, 1958–60

(Bottom Left)

Jean-Louis Rey (Chanéac), proliferation cells (cellules proliférantes)
– perspective drawing showing multipurpose cells proliferating into
groupings within a superstructure, 1962

(Bottom Right)

Jean-Louis Rey (Chanéac), Multipurpose Cells – study models,
1958–60

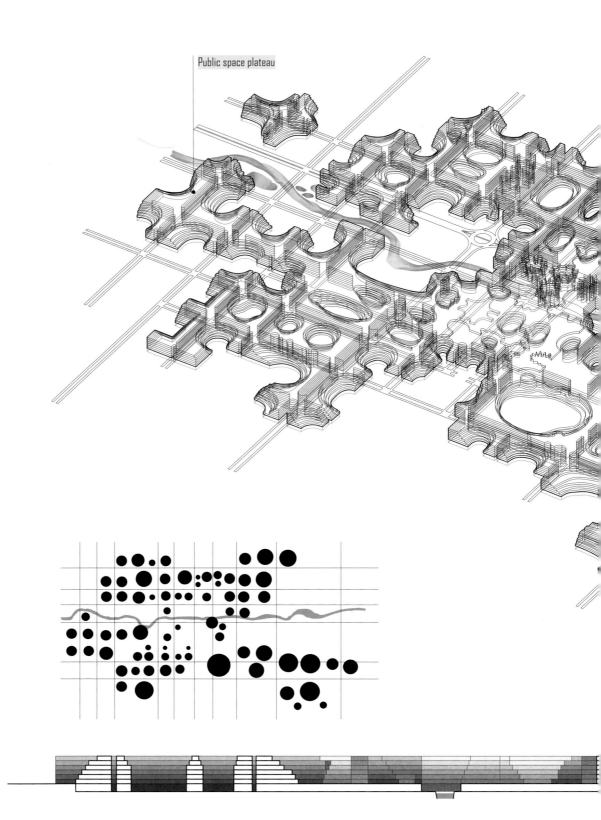

Public space plateau

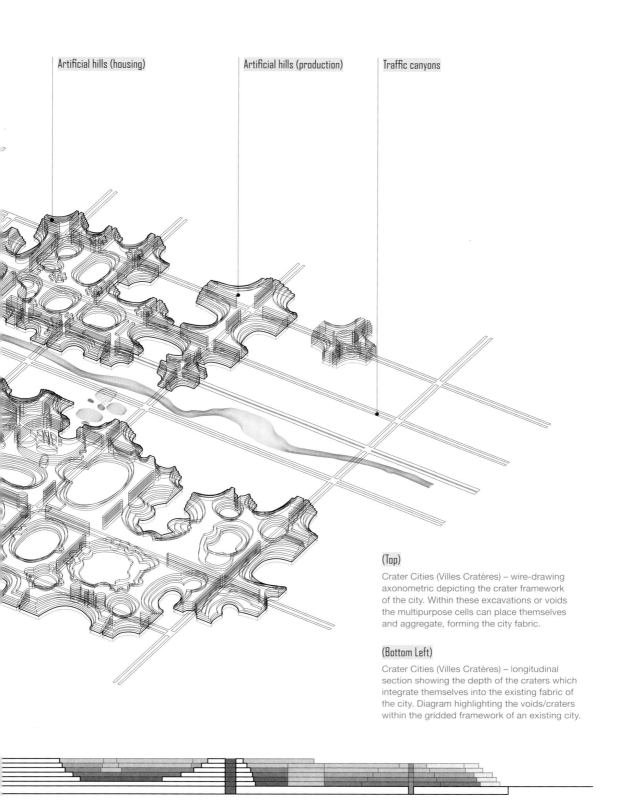

Artificial hills (housing)   Artificial hills (production)   Traffic canyons

(Top)

Crater Cities (Villes Cratères) – wire-drawing axonometric depicting the crater framework of the city. Within these excavations or voids the multipurpose cells can place themselves and aggregate, forming the city fabric.

(Bottom Left)

Crater Cities (Villes Cratères) – longitudinal section showing the depth of the craters which integrate themselves into the existing fabric of the city. Diagram highlighting the voids/craters within the gridded framework of an existing city.

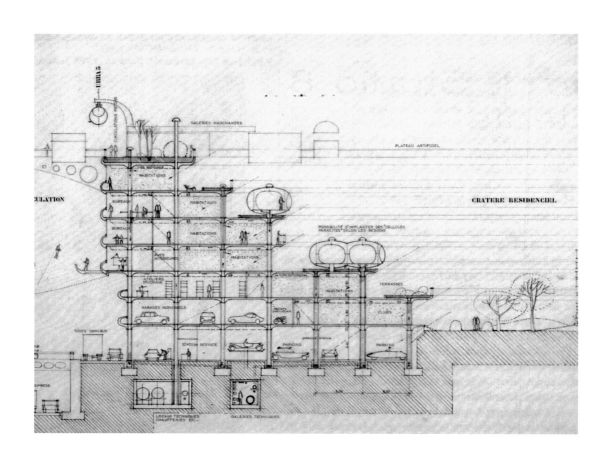

CRATERE RESIDENCIEL

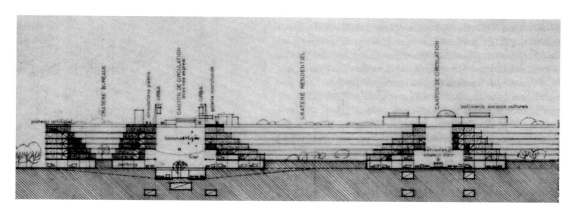

(Above)

Jean-Louis Rey (Chanéac), Crater Cities
(Villes Cratères) – cross section showing
the multipurpose cells aggregating within
the megastructure system, 1963

Courtesy FRAC Centre, Orléans

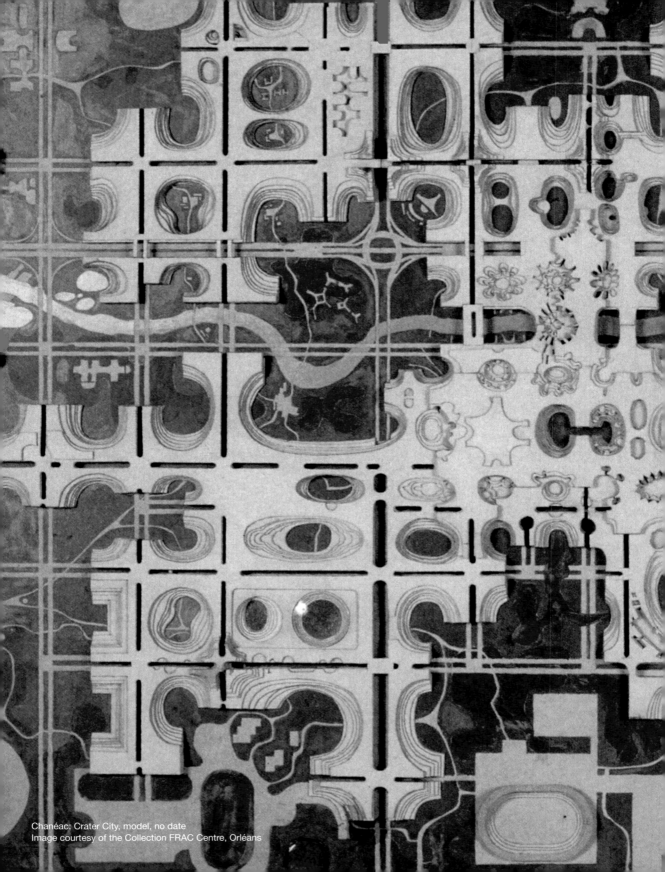

Chanéac: Crater City, model, no date
Image courtesy of the Collection FRAC Centre, Orléans

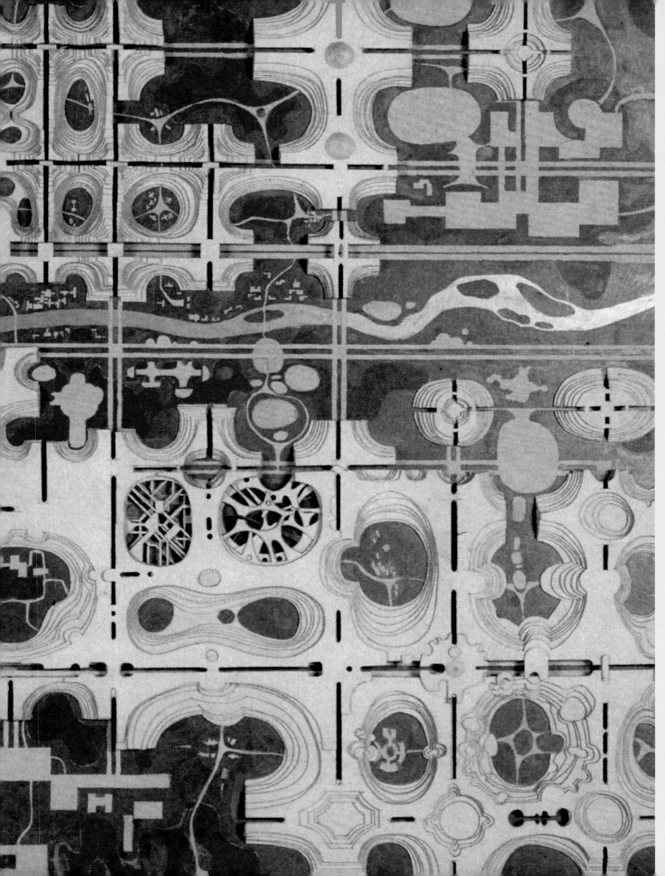

Kiyonori Kikutake, Marine City, 1963,
model view.

KIYONORI KIKUTAKE

Starting in 1958 Kiyonori Kikutake (1928–2011) proposed a series of urban schemes that became emblematic of the approach of the Japanese metabolists, and in particular their manifesto on city planning, *Metabolism: The Proposals for New Urbanism*. Like other idealised modern movement city plans Kikutake's early urban proposals were utopian, but they were distinguished by their understanding of the city as a generative process that works in a cyclical fashion and has the potential to further define and evolve the urban system itself. Emerging out of these concepts were three critical principles: the abandoning of the ground and investigation of alternative environments; the adaptability of the city and the housing unit, which had to be capable of being replaced as required; the conception of architecture and cities as ecological entities with lifecycles that could be renewed in response to their environment.

These principles were applied to his Tower-Shaped City, Marine City and Ocean City proposals, which are examples of new organisational attitudes towards natural systems embedded within synthetic urban schemes. In contrast to modernist schemes, which attempted either to erase existing parts of the city or to find a clear swath of land adjacent to existing metropolises, the metabolists' proposals were completely detached from typical urban environments – and thus freed from conventional modes of thinking about the city. Through the various forms they took – whether the artificial 'land' towers of Tower-Shaped City, or the floating cities of Ocean City or Marine City – Kikutake's proposals opened up a way of thinking about all of the earth's environments as viable settings for urban and architectural research and interventions.

With their removal from conventional urban conditions, the projects began to address the need of cities and their structures to keep pace with social and technological advances. As Kikutake states, 'Architecture that utilises a systemised modular and that allows for dismantling and reassembling … can become easily renewable and metabolic. In order to meet the needs of urban life which changes rapidly, it is necessary to make the environment renewable.' This was demonstrated by the replaceable plug-in housing units of Tower-Shaped City or the track system of Ocean City, which allowed the 'mova-block' residential buildings to slide on and off as required. These systems of living units could be replaced once their furnishings, appliances and mechanical services no longer fulfilled the needs of the inhabitants. Tower-Shaped City expanded on this by housing the fabrication facilities in the core of the tower, and by recycling and reusing the outdated units and materials in new assemblies. And on the urban scale Marine City, at the end of its lifecycle, was designed to locate a point out at sea where it would sink itself and regenerate into a mechanical fish bed on the ocean floor. As Kikutake states, the 'city is temporary, never can it be considered eternal'.

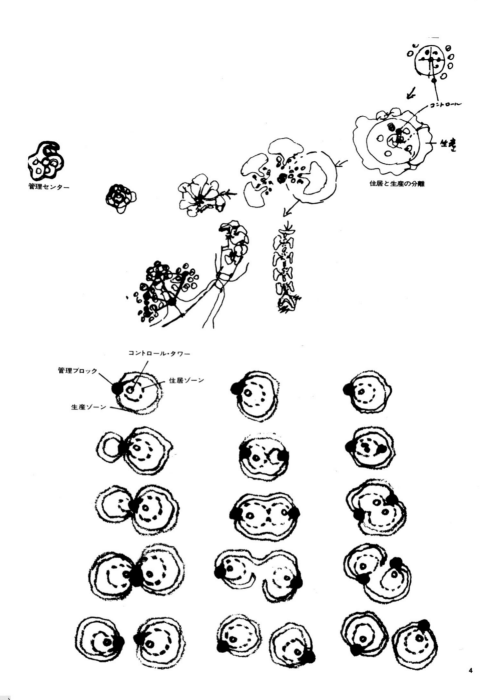

管理センター

住居と生産の分離

コントロール

生産

コントロール・タワー

管理ブロック

住居ゾーン

生産ゾーン

4

(Above)

Kiyonori Kikutake, sketches from the metabolist manifesto
depicting the city as a system through a concept of
organic growth, 1960

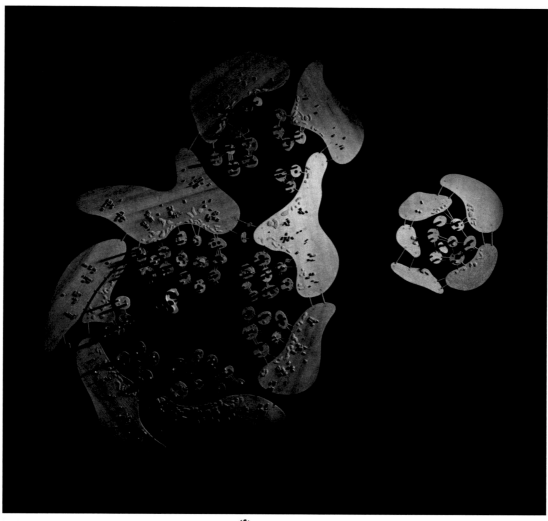

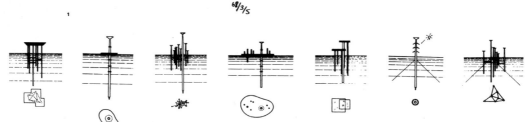

(Top)

Kiyonori Kikutake, bird's-eye view of the Marine City model,
a city relocated from land to sea, 1963

(Bottom)

Kiyonori Kikutake, sections of Marine City showing tower
habitation structures above and below sea, 1960

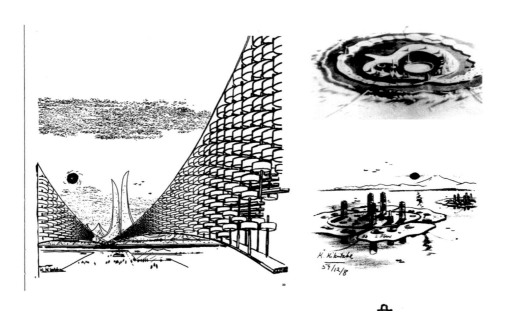

(Top Left)

Kiyonori Kikutake, sketch of Ocean City Mova-block housing complex with replaceable housing units, 1960

(Bottom Left)

Kiyonori Kikutake, Marine City sketch, 1958

(Top Right)

Kiyonori Kikutake, Ocean City model view and Marine City sketch, 1960

(Bottom Right)

Kiyonori Kikutake, sketch of Tower-Shaped City Habitation structures above and below sea, 1958

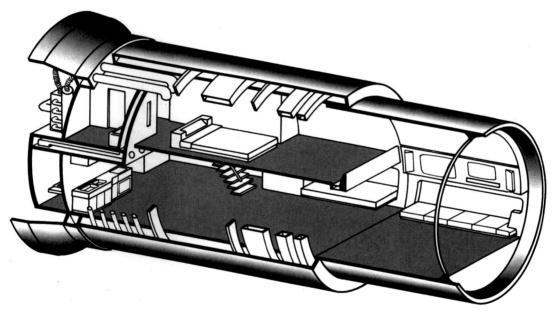

(Top)

Kiyonori Kikutake, Marine City model – a city relocated from
land to sea, 1963

(Bottom)

Kiyonori Kikutake, Tower-Shaped City – the replaceable plug-in
capsule is fabricated in the core of the housing towers, 1958

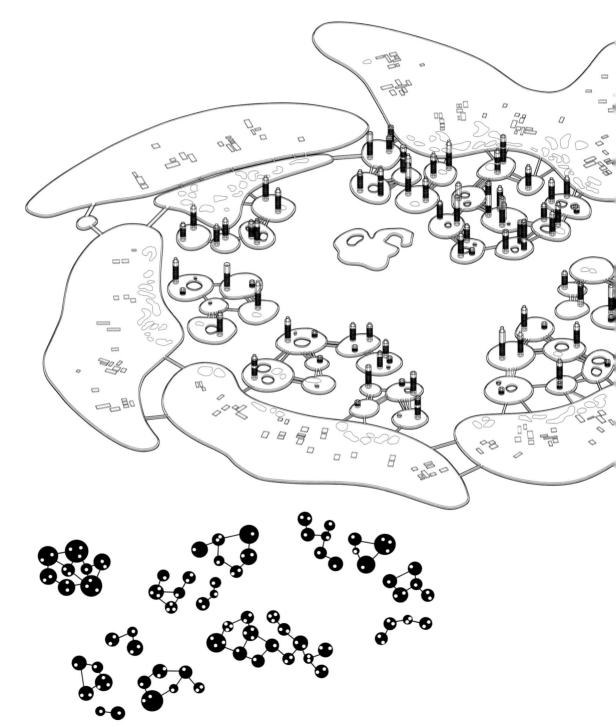

(Above)

Marine City axonometric showing the city floating on a series of pads located in the sea

(Opposite Left)

Marine City diagram highlighting the housing sector pads and housing towers

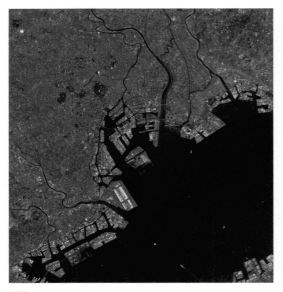

Tokyo
Data from the US Geological Survey

New York City
Data from the US Geological Survey

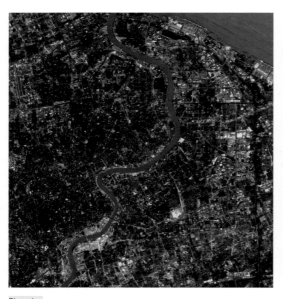

Shanghai
Data from the US Geological Survey

London
Data from the US Geological Survey

URBAN TYPOLOGIES

The research projects featured in this book have been developed through analytical case studies acting as design responses to contemporary prototypical scenarios of speculative urban development. The case studies are located in four cities: Tokyo, Shanghai, New York City and London. Each highlights architectural and urban interventions that address a variety of characteristics, ranging from visionary scenarios to tabula rasa conditions to the reuse of existing infrastructures and transitional planning.

The first of the four sites to be explored was the London Thames Gateway Development project in the Lower Lea Valley – site of the 2012 Olympics – which gave us a transitional model of planning encompassing both pre- and post-Olympic use. The agenda moved the research beyond the event nature of the Olympics to focus on the nodal landscape infrastructure that would be seeded within diverse ecological systems such as parks, canals and river estuaries – a vibrant platform for testing adaptive architectural and infrastructural models of living within a natural environment.

If the London project represented a staged and sequential time-based urban development, the megacity of Shanghai embodied the accelerated urban growth that has become symptomatic of rapidly developing economies. The reconfiguration of the Expo 2010 site provided our research with a tabula rasa condition for experimentation. Following Shanghai, we focused on the Hudson Yards area of New York City, where a series of competitions and proposals have attempted to envision possible models for the redevelopment of the site. Over the span of two decades this area has attracted proposals from radical architects as well as the most conventional of schemes, providing a laboratory of urban research strategies to be investigated.

To conclude our Adaptive Ecologies research we looked at Tokyo, focusing on Kenzo Tange's seminal Tokyo Bay proposal. The scheme was to be considered as if the project had been realised and augmented as part of an evolving urban generator towards speculative future development scenarios. Addressing the chronic housing shortage and uncontrolled urban growth of postwar Japan, the project turned its back on the existing city (its architecture and infrastructure) and relocated development just offshore – a radical ecological gesture that embodied Metabolist principles and set a precedent for organic, linear architectural and urban growth.

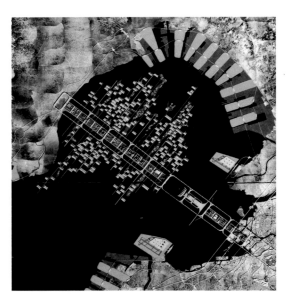

Plan for Tokyo
Photo: Akio Kawasumi

Tokyo Bay

The site of Kenzo Tange's 1960 Plan for Tokyo is Tokyo Bay itself, starting from the Outer Moat in Ichigaya and extending along a linear axis to the area of Tsukishima and beyond. A series of one-way streets reach out from the central spine of the new development into the neighbourhoods of Shinjuku, Shibuya and Ueno.

Population: 5,000,000
Site area/km^2: 204.40
Population density/km^2: 24,461

Hudson Yards Development
Photo Credit: © 2011 Google / Image © 2011 Digital Globe

Hudson Yards Development, New York City

The Hudson Yards development is located in West Midtown in Manhattan, extending south from West 42nd Street to West 30th Street and west from 8th Avenue to the Hudson River. This former manufacturing area was re-zoned in 2005 to a variety of uses, including commericial and residential.

Population: 63,382
Site area/km^2: 9.66
Population density/km^2: 6,561

Shanghai Expo

The 2010 Expo was located in downtown Shanghai, on both sides of the Huangpu River between the Nanpu and Lupu bridges. Prior to the 2010 Expo, the site hosted a large shipyard, over 250 factories and the homes of 18,000 people, which were relocated to make way for the new development. The site is just south of the Pudong district, the subject of a masterplan competition in the early 90s.

Population: 18,000 |
Site area/km²: 5.28 |
Population density/km²: 3,409   ▰

Shanghai Expo
Photo: © 2011 Google / Image © 2011 Digital Globe / Image © 2011 GeoEye

London Thames Gateway Development

Extending from London to the mouth of the River Thames, the Thames Gateway Development embraces a large swath of East London boroughs – Tower Hamlets, Havering, Bexley, Barking, Beckenham and Newham – including the area regenerated for the 2012 London Olympics.

Population: 861,800   ▬
Site area/km²: 139.43   ▬▬▬
Population density/km²: 6,181

London Thames Gateway Development
Photo: © 2011 Google / Image © 2011 Bluesky

LONDON

Thames Gateway Development

The London Thames Gateway project provided a model for transitional planning that allowed us to test the Adaptive Ecologies thesis within a European context. Over an eight-year period, beginning with London's selection as the host for the 2012 Olympics and the development of the cross-Channel rail link, the site underwent a continual transformation, from pre-Olympic planning to the Games themselves to post-Olympic 'legacy'. Encompassing 13 developments in eight different London boroughs – Hackney, Tower Hamlets, Barking and Dagenham, Bexley, Havering, Lewisham, Greenwich and Newham – this expansive terrain formed an ideal testing ground for time-based scenarios for hybrid conditions: housing, civic and ecological.

The development is situated within a rich urban ecology that includes rivers, parks and canal systems which will need to adapt to infrastructural and architectural interventions consisting of over two million square metres of cultural, residential, hotel, retail, commercial, event space and open space.

What actually resulted from the LTGD project was a collection of traditional urban development schemes. Our approach was to implement computational design processes within these proposals in an attempt to find adaptive systems and alternative models of living.

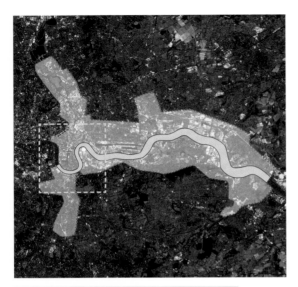

001 London Thames Gateway Development Corporation Site

⬚ Extent of development area
⬚ Focus of LTGDC site

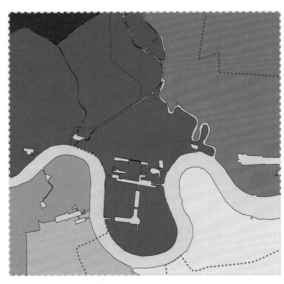

002 Boroughs in the development area

■ Hackney   ■ Southwark   ⬚ Extent of development area
■ Newham   ■ Lewisham   ■ Water
■ Tower Hamlets ■ Greenwich

003 Wood Wharf
454,000m²   ■
1,668 units   ■ ■

004 Hackney Wick
7,596m² |
1,820m² |
130 units |

005 District Centre Bromley-by-Bow
60,000m² |
2,400 units   ■ ■ |

006 Minoco Wharf
230,000m²   ■
3,500 units   ■ ■ ■ |

007 Leamouth Peninsula
170,000m² |
1,800 units   ■ ■

008 Greenwich Peninsula
350,000m²   ■
200,000m² |
10,000 units   ■ ■ ■ ■ ■ ■ ■ ■ ■ ■

009 Canning Town and Custom House
1,000,000m²   ■ ■
10,000 units   ■ ■ ■ ■ ■ ■ ■ ■ ■ ■

010 University Square Stratford
8,500m² |

011 Lea River Park
62,000m² |

012 Olympic Park & International Quarter
2.45 million m²   ■ ■ ■ ■ ■
112,000m²   ■ ■ |
17,600 units   ■ ■ ■ ■ ■ ■ ■ ■ ■ ■ ■ ■ ■ ■ ■ ■ ■

013 Westfield, Stratford City
2,000,000m²   ■ ■ ■ ■ ■

■ Commercial 1:500,000m²
■ Open space 1:500,000m²
■ Residential 1:1,000 units

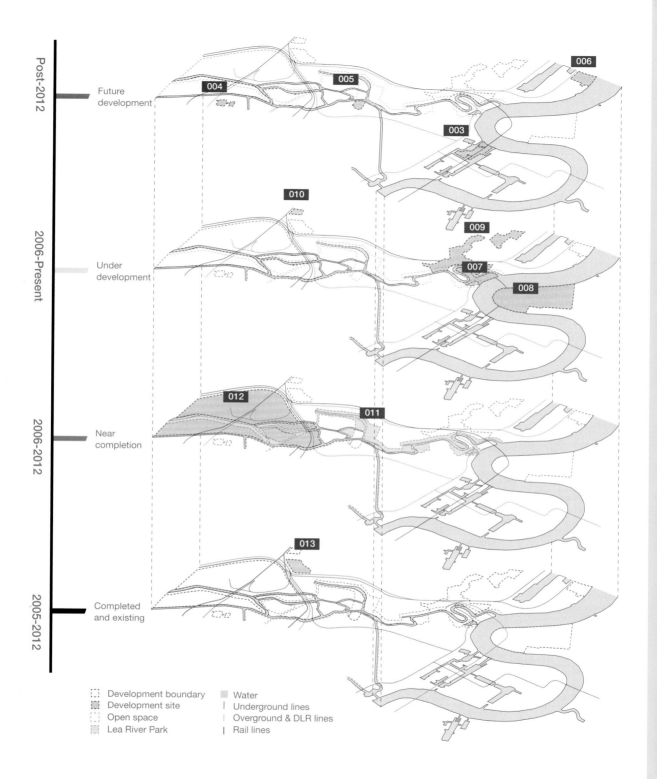

Post-2012

Future
development

004 005 006 003

2006-Present

010

Under
development

009 007 008

2006-2012

Near
completion

012 011

2005-2012

Completed
and existing

013

Development boundary   Water
Development site | Underground lines
Open space   Overground & DLR lines
Lea River Park | Rail lines

SHANGHAI

Shanghai Expo

The complexities of the Shanghai site lie not in its existing conditions and infrastructures but in the tabula rasa urban condition that was created for Expo 2010. After winning the bid for the international event, Shanghai officials began levelling the site in the Pudong industrial zone, demolishing some 200 factories and the Jiangnan shipyard while relocating 18,000 households. This created a wide open stage for urban and architectural exploration.

Adopting the Expo's theme of 'Better City – Better Life', which promoted the use of sustainable practices and technologies in everyday life, the Adaptive Ecologies projects in this location investigate how an environmental impetus can be achieved within time-based models of urban systems. The site itself was divided into five zones, each with a decentralised hub or 'square' for events, a network of open spaces and transport systems that link the complex as a whole. During the Expo a major influx of visitors (73 million) pushed the limits of the design for a period of six months. This was followed by a decompression in activity leading to the post-Expo reconfiguration, which envisioned the re-use of five buildings as a cultural and commercial hub for exhibitions and conferences, the development of the Expo village as an 'international community', the building of museums on the former shipyard site, and the creation of leisure areas along the river.

The speed of the timetable for the redevelopment – just six years from the razing of the site to its post-Expo incarnation – became a catalyst for intervention. Our Shanghai projects address the need for a multi-scalar system that can adapt to a variety of programmatic functions from the unit to the masterplan, from the architectural to the infrastructural, from the temporary to the permanent, and from the local to the global.

Massimiliano Fuksas
Image courtesy of Studio Fuksas

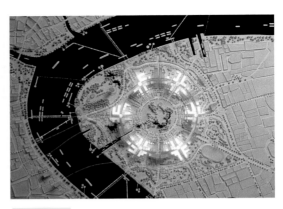

Richard Rogers
Image courtesy of Rogers Stirk Harbour & Partners

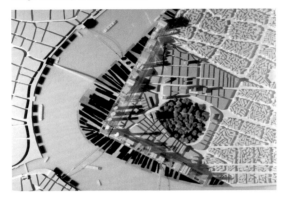

Dominique Perrault
Image courtesy of Michel Denancé / DPA / ADAGP

Toyo Ito
Image courtesy of Toyo Ito Architects

Skyline Map

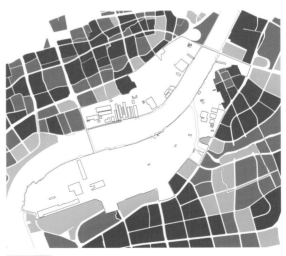

Density Map

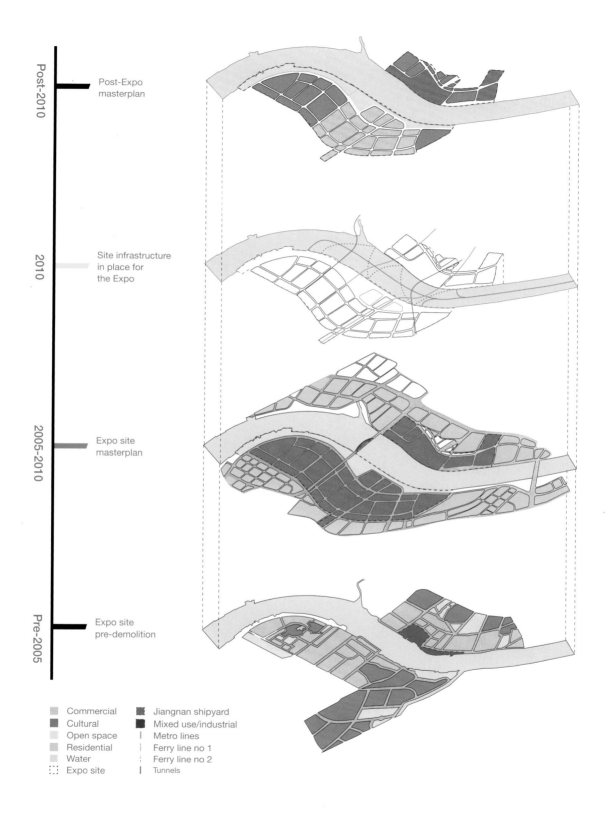

Post-Expo
masterplan

Post-2010

Site infrastructure
in place for
the Expo

2010

Expo site
masterplan

2005-2010

Expo site
pre-demolition

Pre-2005

Commercial
Cultural
Open space
Residential
Water
Expo site

Jiangnan shipyard
Mixed use/industrial
Metro lines
Ferry line no 1
Ferry line no 2
Tunnels

NEW YORK CITY

Hudson Yards Development

Since 1999 the Hudson Yards area of New York City has been a testing ground for architectural and urban redevelopment offering large-scale strategies both for the city of Manhattan and beyond. The site (encompassing 60 blocks running north to south from 42nd Street to 28th Street and east to west from 8th Avenue to the Hudson River) embodies a cross-section of urban infrastructures situated over an existing rail network that overlaps a series of park proposals, civic projects (convention centre expansions), hotel and residential schemes and extensions of existing subway networks, all framed within the rigid grid of Manhattan.

The first proposals of interest for the site were prompted by an architectural competition organised by the IFCCA (International Foundation of the Canadian Centre of Architecture) won by Eisenman Architects, with entries from Morphosis, Cedric Price, Reiser + Umemoto and UN Studio. After this, from 2001 to 2007, the area was the subject of a further series of proposals initiated by the Hudson Yards Development Corporation, including a 2005 scheme that was part of NYC's failed 2012 Olympics bid. This continual reworking of a prominent and under-utilised area of the city gave the DRL the means to experiment within the Adaptive Ecologies brief and add to this rich history of urban redevelopment.

Based on research into the area's infrastructures and the appropriation of previous schemes, our proposals for Hudson Yards develop iterative scenarios through the implementation of computational devices. This investigation attempts to exploit the diverse vertical section of the site. Through a series of generative urban organisational frameworks that address the section – its elevated train stations, subterranean subway systems, rezoned retail, commercial and residential space, and a raised park artery – the proposals interrogate a displacement of the ground plane.

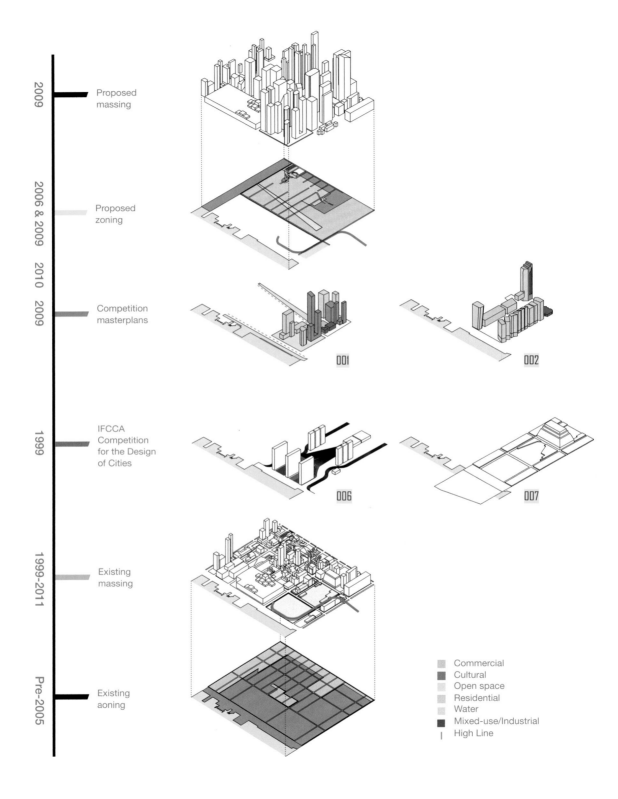

2009 — Proposed massing

2006 & 2009 — Proposed zoning

2010 2009 — Competition masterplans

001

002

1999 — IFCCA Competition for the Design of Cities

006

007

1999-2011 — Existing massing

Pre-2005 — Existing aoning

Commercial
Cultural
Open space
Residential
Water
Mixed-use/Industrial
High Line

001 Related Properties

with Kohn Pedersen Fox
Associates

002 Extell

with Steven Holl
Architects

003 Durst Organisation

and Vornado Realty Trust with
Pelli Clarke Pelli

004 Tishman Speyer Properties

and Morgan Stanley with
Helmut Jahn

005 Brookfield

with Skidmore, Owings & Merrill
LLP, Thomas Phifer & Partners,
ShoP Architects PC, Diller
Scofidio & Renfro, SANAA and
Handel Architects

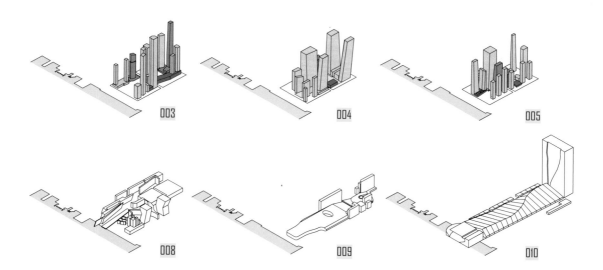

006 Reiser + Umemoto

Space-frame structure that
transforms over the site to
accommodate programme changes

007 Cedric Price

Proposed demolition of specific
areas of the site to allow for air flow
and direct sunlight

008 Morphosis

A multi-layered surface enhanced
by movement and changes in site
programme both horizontally and
vertically

009 UN Studio

Mapped the performance (user
flow, efficiency, etc) of the site as
a form-finding strategy

010 Peter Eisenman Architects

Digitally designed surface
topology mediating differently
programmed areas of the site

PLAN FOR TOKYO

Kenzo Tange, 1960

The Plan for Tokyo by Kenzo Tange (and various Metabolist collaborators) was presented as a realistic solution to the unprecedented expansion of the city, an entire urban scheme from micro to macro scale. Tange rejected the idea of a radial city focused around a centralised civic centre – the prevailing model in the first half of the twentieth century – in favour of a linear city along a 'civic axis' designed to marry urban, infrastructural and architectural systems.[1] Inspired by natural arrangements and organisms Tange took the body plan of a vertebrate and its linear axis as his model, which enabled the scheme to extend in a gradual development across the bay of Tokyo.

The task at hand for the Adaptive Ecologies investigation of the Tokyo Bay proposal was to interrogate how this visionary project could potentially be augmented through an in-depth synthesis of computational techniques and material studies. This combination of research could work on the vast poly-scalar system presented by Tange while challenging the repositioning of the man-made 'ground' plane that was supported by vertical columns (pilotis). These supports structured a three-level transport system and cyclical highways with the capacity to funnel approximately 2.5 million commuters a day into the city centre; open-air parks with parking space below; office buildings 200m long and 10 to 20 storeys high, clustered around a series of service cores; and, branching out perpendicularly from the civic axis, a parallel system of streets leading to residential units (triangular in section) with the capacity to house a projected population of five million inhabitants.

This combination of systems within an all-encompassing urban scheme provided us with a new model of city dwelling located in an extreme ecological environment – a city in the ocean. By looking at this proposal through a new computational lens we are able to challenge how visionary precedents can become a driving factor in architectural design.

---

1   'A Plan for Tokyo, 1960: Toward a Structural Reorganisation', in *Kenzo Tange: 1946–1969, Architecture and Urban Design*, ed Udo Kultermann (Pall Mall Press, London: 1970), 128.

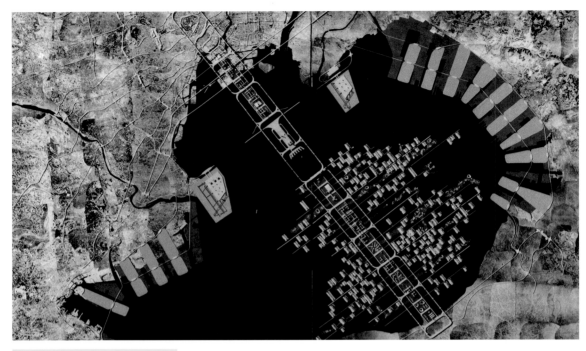

Tokyo Bay collage by Kenzo Tange, plan view

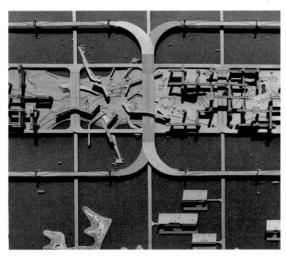

Tokyo Bay model

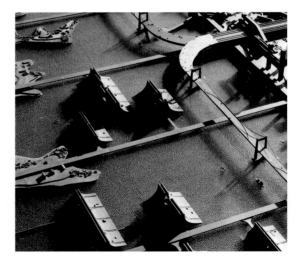

All photos on this page: Akio Kawasumi

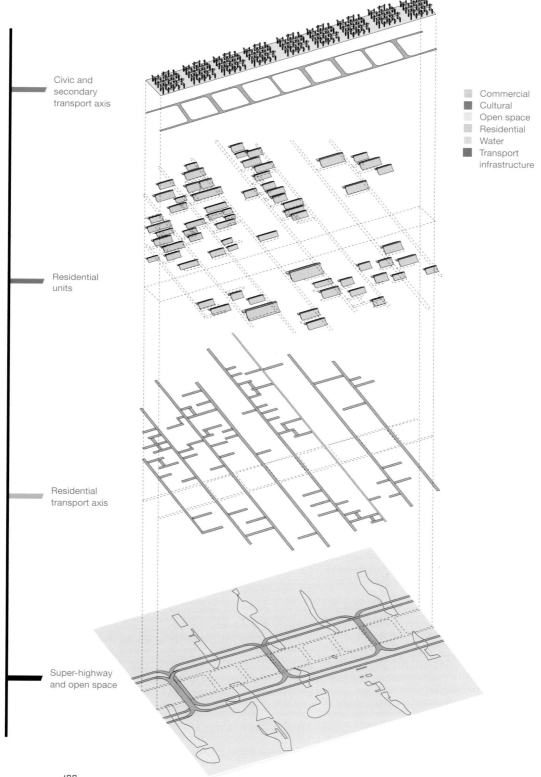

Civic and
secondary
transport axis

Residential
units

Residential
transport axis

Super-highway
and open space

Commercial
Cultural
Open space
Residential
Water
Transport
infrastructure

CONTINUING EXPERIMENT: ADAPTIVE ECOLOGIES

John Frazer

'Continuing Experiment' – the title I've chosen for my contribution sums up what this book on Adaptive Ecologies is all about. It also refers to the central role of experimentation at the Architectural Association and, more specifically, to the title of James Gowan's 1975 book on the AA.[1] But I will return to Gowan's role later.

My starting point for sketching a context for this work is Charles Jencks's *Architecture 2000*, which identifies six characteristics that have defined architecture over the last 100 years: Logical, Idealist, Selfconscious, Intuitive, Activist, Unselfconscious.[2] According to this schema Adaptive Ecologies bridges two categories – the Logical and the Intuitive – which both arise in the 1920s, the former exemplified by functionalism and constructivism, by Fuller and Wachsmann, and the latter by Gaudí and expressionism. By the 1960s and 1970s the streams are typified by Prouvé, Otto and parametrics on the one hand, and by pop, Archigram and inflatables on the other. By the 1980s and 1990s the two categories are represented by megastructures and by the biomorphic. All of these tendencies were explored at the AA at the time. *Adaptive Ecologies* seems to fit well into this model and to point to the next steps.

Tracing back the AA's contribution to these lines of development, and concentrating on those aspects I was personally involved with, the first and most obvious connection is with Diploma Unit 11 from 1989 to 1996.[3] The unit explored the use of the most advanced computer techniques to empower the idea of evolutionary architecture and take it beyond being a mere metaphor. Our intention was to create an evolutionary digital architecture that could be considered as a form of artificial life. We had access to advanced software because my wife Julia and I were running an award-winning company, Autographics, which developed the first microcomputer-based designing, drafting and modelling software before AutoCAD® came onto the scene. I was also head of a CAD research centre in Ireland where we were exploring the possible use of genetic algorithms for design applications. Julia and I combined these innovative techniques with generative techniques that we had already developed (mostly cellular automata) to create a very powerful software armoury. Our company, Autographics, also donated a significant amount of computing equipment to the AA, including flatbed plotters and a cabinet full of electronic equipment. The final ingredients were intelligent physical devices for which Julia and I held the patents.[4] As soon as the unit was set up we recruited Cedric Price as permanent visiting critic. We had worked with him on the Generator project ten years earlier (the working model that we built is in the Museum of Modern Art in New York), and were responsible for suggesting that microprocessors should be embedded into every building element so that the building could compute its own organisation. There was to be a crane permanently on site to move elements in response to instructions from the users, or the computer – or in this case the intelligent building itself.[5] We also borrowed the concept of boredom from Gordon Pask's musicolour machine:[6] if left unchanged, the building would get bored and start to suggest its own changes to provoke user interaction. So we recruited Gordon Pask too, as cybernetics tutor, and Guy Westbrook for programming, and we were off on another seven-year AA experiment.

Approaching architecture as an artificial life-form, we started by building three-dimensional reconfigurable array processors (the Universal Constructor 89/90) where there was an isomorphism between the processor configuration and the model structure. We worked our way through autopoiesis, exploring hierarchical cellular automata linked to genetic algorithms as our evolutionary engine (drawing heavily on the ideas of John Holland),[7] explored the genetic language of architecture and ended, in 1996, by applying all these techniques to the Groningen experiment – a small working prototype of a predictive urban computer model. The highpoint, however, was probably an exhibition at the AA in January 1995, and the accompanying book *An Evolutionary Architecture*.[8] The exhibition became renowned as it was the first one that could be

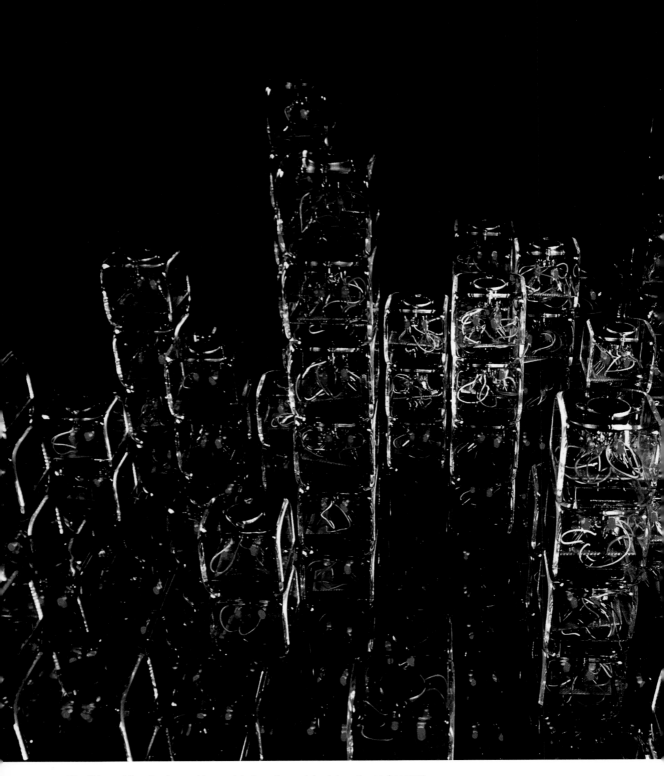

The Universal Constructor, working model of a self-organising interactive environment,
AA Diploma Unit 11 in collaboration with the University of Ulster, 1990.
Photo: Geoffrey Beeckman, courtesy of *Building Design*

visited online. Its central feature was an evolving interactive system that allowed interaction with exhibition visitors via an array of genetic switches, and virtual interaction via the web – another internet first.

So from 1989, Diploma Unit 11 had successfully experimented with genetic algorithms and their interaction with cellular automata, had successfully constructed working computers which represented what they were computing, had implemented architectural DNA in working form, and extended user interaction on the internet. All of these experiments are still continuing at the AA some 20 years later.

However, the story started much earlier. From 1973 to 1975 I ran an Intermediate Unit with Brit Andresen, and as the AA had no computer equipment at that time (apart from one exhausted teletype terminal!) we took the students to the Mathematics Laboratory at Cambridge University and introduced them to computation and computer graphics there. For a project we took James Gibbs's 'rules' for drawing a classical column and programmed them in Fortran and then plotted the column.[9] We then replaced all of Gibbs's carefully proportioned ratios with random number generators – the idea was to progressively weight the random number generators so that the system 'learned' to produce elegant proportions. What we actually produced, of course, were some very random columns. If I had known back then about genetic algorithms we might have got it to work. As it was, it took a further 20 years before we succeeded. Some experiments fail, or have to wait their time, but the spirit of experimentation was ever there.

The reason I could take the students to the Cambridge Mathematical Laboratory was that I was Director of Studies in Architecture for Trinity College at the time. Immediately before that, as a lecturer and First Year Master at Cambridge, I had gained access to my first graphics display screen and was at last able to finish my final year project, which was to generate a structure from a seed.

John Frazer, Reptile System, AA project: drawings produced on a flatbed plotter, 1967–69

And this is where James Gowan comes back into the story. Gowan was my final year tutor in 1968/69, when Peter Cook was year master (it was Cook, incidentally, who first introduced me to Cedric Price, Gordon Pask and Nicholas Negroponte). My final year thesis, titled 'Autotectonics', was about using technology – and specifically the computer and digital manufacturing – to change the choices available to the users of architecture.[10] And my task as a student was to show how this would be possible. To do that, I hypothesised as yet not-existing generative techniques and described a DNA-like language of architecture. In fact, I hypothesised the very techniques now used by Adaptive Ecologies and other groups at the AA and elsewhere.

The idea of a self-organising architecture was the central proposition in my thesis. As one of my demonstrations I developed a flexible enclosure system, Reptile, capable of many permutations of form – and of course I drew it by computer.[11] Thus my final year project is believed to be the first student project ever to be drawn by computer, and it won me a year prize, largely thanks to another remarkable tutor, John Starling, who

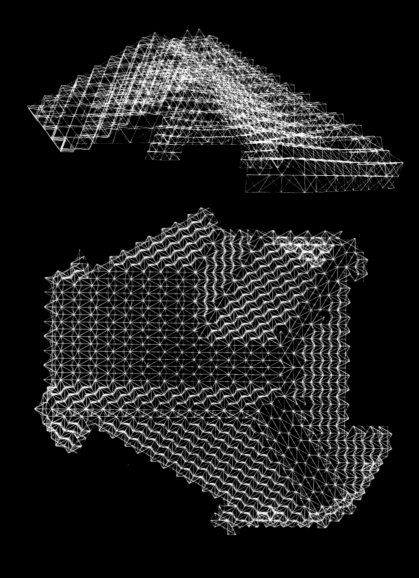

John Frazer, Reptile System, computer-generated plan, 1970

John Frazer, Reptile System, Cambridge University project: first generative algorithm
on a cathode-ray tube display, 1970

John Frazer, Reptile System, AA project: drawings produced on a flatbed plotter, 1967–69

John Frazer, Reptile System, AA project: drawings produced on a flatbed plotter, 1967–69

AA Diploma Unit 11 Interactor exhibition, 1992, seen here interacting with visitors Ken Yeang, Anna O'Gorman, Brit Andresen, Marcial Echenique, Samantha Hardingham and Sophie Hicks. Tutors John and Julia Frazer

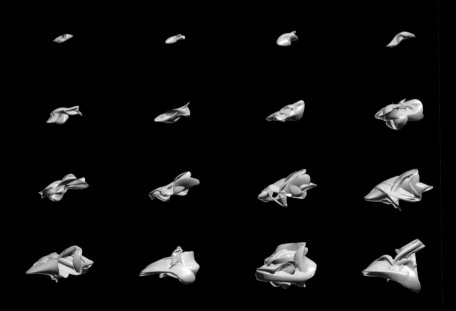

John Frazer, Reptile System, AA project: drawings produced on a flatbed plotter, 1967–69

the year before had given me fantastic encouragement to experiment with computing at a time when the AA's entire computing resource consisted of one teletype terminal (the very same one I found again in 1974!) connected to a remote timesharing mainframe. There was no software, there was no AutoCAD®, there was nothing – every line had to be programmed. And as the AA did not teach programming, John Starling found a programming course for me at the LSE. He also tracked down a commercial flatbed plotter that I could hire and wrote the perspective transformation routines for me. So for the Reptile System, we did the first ever student computer plots.

I believe there is an unbroken chain of development and experimentation that connects the thinking of some of the cohort that graduated with me – and indeed of those who came before – to the work seen in this book. And this connecting chain is the AA ethos as explained in James Gowan's book – a continuing experiment indeed.

1   James Gowan, *A Continuing Experiment: Learning and Teaching at the Architectural Association* (London: Architectural Press, 1975).

2   Charles Jencks, *Architecture 2000: Predictions and Methods* (London: Studio Vista, 1971), 46–47.

3   For its first year of operation, 1989/90, the unit was known as Diploma Unit 14.

4   John Frazer, Julia Frazer, 'Intelligent Physical Three-Dimensional Modelling System', *Computer Graphics* 80, online publications 1980, 359–70.

5   See 'Cedric Price Generator Project 1976' in Neil Spiller (ed), *Cyber_Reader* (London: Phaidon Press, 2002), 84–85.

6   Gordon Pask, 'A Comment, a Case History and a Plan', in Jasia Reichardt (ed), *Cybernetics, Art and Ideas* (London: Studio Vista 1971), 76–99.

7   John Holland, *Adaptation in Natural and Artificial Systems* (Ann Arbor: University of Michigan Press, 1975).

8   John Frazer, *An Evolutionary Architecture* (London: AA Publications, 1995). Long out of print, but still sought after, the book is available as a free download: www.aaschool.ac.uk/PUBLIC/AAPUBLICATIONS/outofprint.php?item=441

9   James Gibbs, *Rules for Drawing the Several Parts of Architecture*, 1732.

10   John Frazer, 'Autotectonics: The Choice of Choice', final year thesis, Architectural Association, 1969.

11   See John Frazer, 'Reptiles', *Architectural Design*, April 1974, 231–39.

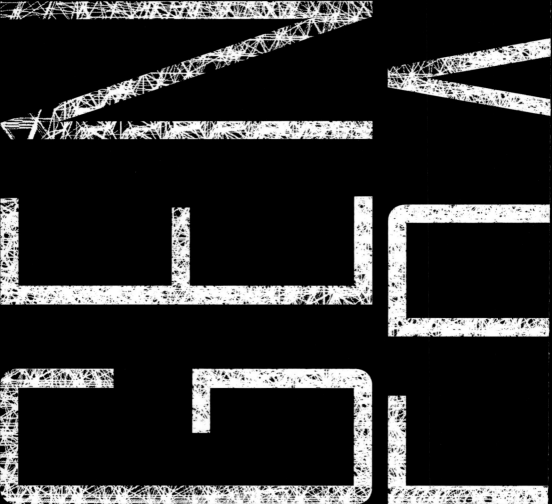

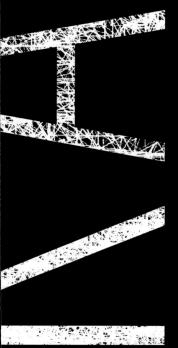
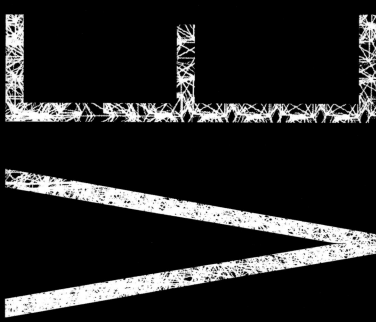

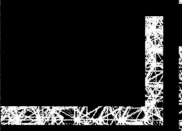

GENERATIVE

Morphogenetic / Self-Organising / Behavioural

'WHAT WAS MERE NOISE AND DISORDER OR DISTRACTION BEFORE, BECOMES PATTERN AND SENSE; INFORMATION HAS BEEN METABOLISED OUT OF NOISE.'

WM BRODEY AND N LINDGREN, 'SOFT ARCHITECTURE: THE DESIGN OF INTELLIGENT ENVIRONMENTS' 1967

COMPUTATIONAL TAXONOMIES

Within this thesis computational design thinking resides within three distinct frameworks that can be synthesised and understood as behavioural, self-organisational and morphogenetic approaches. Throughout, the underlying interest is in the critical response to the polyscalar challenges involved in attempting to integrate and correlate between unit, cluster and collective organisational models. Computational taxonomies are an attempt to communicate the project-based research undertaken through their core computational drivers. Each project aims at constructing a framework in which natural and synthetic ordering parameters can be identified, deployed and synthesised through the scale-dependent articulation that shifts principles from generic strategies to hyper-specific ordering mediums.
In this context the move towards a computation-driven urbanism seeks to go beyond the simplistic and at times generic notions of organisational development that are commonly classified as top-down or bottom-up. The work of Adaptive Ecologies situates itself in-between these two opposing positions as it attempts to address the complexities of scale-dependence through behaviours that afford organisational parameters to evolve through systemic forms of interaction.

001

Mangrove / Mangal

The mangrove biome (mangal) operates as a collective of saline woodland or shrub land characterised by aerated and migratory root networks found in depositional coastal environments. Mangal foster diverse ecology and operate as model of emergent singular / collective environments.

002

Polyp Growth / Colonial Form

Corals are marine animals that live in colonial environments constructed by populations of genetically identical polyps. Environmental stimuli influence the iterative development of their diverse exoskeletons.

003

Phyllotaxis

Defined through the organisational properties that arrange leaf distribution in botany, phyllo-taxis serves as a model that seeks sunlight and moisture. Phyllotactic patterns emerge as self-organising processes in dynamic, self-propagating systems.

004

Seeding

As in an agricultural context, the process of seeding is designed to foster growth and production within the natural cycles of the given ecology.

005

Stigmergy

Stigmergic behaviour is demonstrated in eusocial creatures that construct their complex habitations through simple decentralised rule sets. A network of complex relations built up through the use of pheromones creates an adaptive model of agent-based communication.

006

Hair / Optimised Detour Networks

One of the seminal analogue computational experiments developed by Frei Otto and his researchers at the Stuttgart Institute for Lightweight Structures used a radial apparatus of slack wet wool strands to demonstrate that the fusion of threads would result in the overall length of the path system being reduced.

007 / 009

Cellular Automata

Simplified rule-based cellular automata offer a discrete model that consists of a matrix of interacting cells with one of a finite number of states. Examples such as John Conway's Game of Life illustrate this model of computability which is studied in complexity science and mathematics.

008

Swarm

Emergent collective behaviour exhibited by self- propelled agents found in natural and synthetic systems. Population dependent, swarm organisations exhibit migratory behaviours that include social animals flocking and herding.

010

Surface Tension / Hele-Shaw Cell

Examining properties of the cohesive forces of surface tension, viscous fluids are placed between two pressurised parallel plates demonstrating properties of connective microflows.

011

Siphonophora

Operating as a model of colonial and complex multi-cellular organisms, siphonophora consist of specialised populations of singular zoids that evolve symbiotic relationships and hyper-specific functions as part of the emergent ecology.

012

Cymatics

Modal Phenomena, otherwise known by Hans Jenny's naming of cymatics, derives from the Greek as a description of the periodic effects that sound and vibration have on matter.

013

Soft-Cast

Flexible formwork approaches material computation through soft cast form-finding. Utilising phase change through pattern management, elastic textile properties allow a process of formation that coupled with contemporary digital techniques constructs a digital materialism.

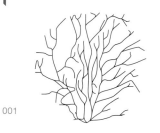

001

005

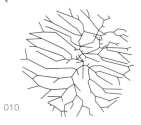

010

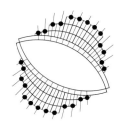

002

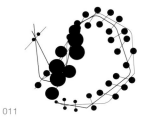

006

011

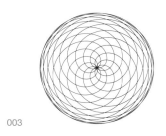

003

007

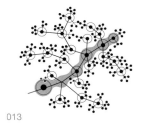

012

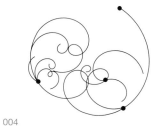

004

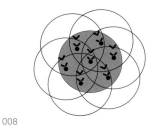

008

013

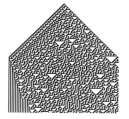

009

149

PARAMETRIC ORDER
ARCHITECTURAL ORDER VIA AN AGENT-BASED PARAMETRIC SEMIOLOGY

Patrik Schumacher

As Theodore Spyropoulos points out in his introduction, architecture is challenged to respond to new social and cultural complexities that demand networked systems that are dynamic, flexible and participatory. According to him this implies a new model of the city, an adaptive ecology; he also talks about correlated formations. In this context, the first task is to define the relevant 'systems' or urban 'formations' that are to be networked, correlated and adapted to each other. The question thus arises: what is the most pertinent way to analyse the contemporary city, to decompose it into its subsystems or components?

Guided by architecture's lead distinction of form vs function we may distinguish the formal-spatial decomposition/analysis of the city from the functional-social decomposition of the city. Each of these yields a set of components/subsystems. The former may deliver different fabric typologies, the latter different function types understood as typical patterns of communicative interaction (social institutions).

The pendant of decomposition/analysis is composition/synthesis, the concept of synthesis understood as composition. Parametricism has transmuted this into the concept of synthesis understood as (scripted) *correlation*, making correlation the new fundamental basis of architectural design. However, we must take care to distinguish not only the functional and the formal-spatial correlations (the primary focus of the discourse on parametricism to date).[1] It is important to expand the concept to include a third type: form-function correlations, ie the correlations of the patterns of the built environment with the patterns of the social communication that unfold within it. Here, the functions of spaces are not conceived in terms of static schedules of accommodation, but are seen as parametrically variable, dynamic event scenarios.

Significantly, these form-function correlations can now be defined using the same computational techniques that are applied to formal correlations. For the first time in the history of architecture, it is possible to model the functional layer of the city and incorporate it into a dynamic design process. Agent-based models can be used to reproduce/predict collective patterns of movement, including the emergence of formations such as stop-and-go waves and the spontaneous separation of opposing flows of pedestrians in two-way traffic. Tools such as 'MiArmy' or 'AI.implant' (available as plug-ins for Maya) now make behavioural modelling within designed environments accessible to architects.

Crowd modelling is also starting to program agents with rudimentary 'perceptual' capacities. While most crowd simulation softwares are based on analogies with physical systems, such as Newtonian repulsive forces between agents, a new approach to crowd modelling is being developed by cognitive science researchers Mehdi Moussaïd, Guy Theraulaz and Dirk Helbing. This 'cognitive' approach assumes that pedestrians try to minimise any obstruction of their field of vision, moving through gaps between some people while keeping a safe distance from others, and adjusting their walking speed accordingly.[2]

Agent modelling should not be limited to crowd circulation flows, but should encompass all patterns of occupation and social interaction in space. Research into these areas is already taking place at the University of Pennsylvania (at the Center for Human Modelling and Simulation) and George Mason University, for example. Jan M Allbeck of George Mason University emphasises this new departure, away from mere crowd flow engineering to the programming of *functional crowds*:

'Most crowd simulation research either focuses on navigating characters through an environment while avoiding collisions or on simulating very large crowds. Our work focuses on creating populations that inhabit a space as opposed to passing through it. Characters exhibit behaviours that are typical for their setting. We term these populations functional crowds ... We use roles and groups to help specify behaviours, we use a parameterised

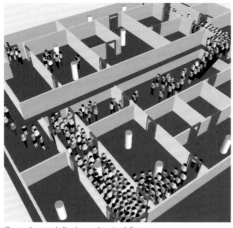

Crowds modelled as physical flows

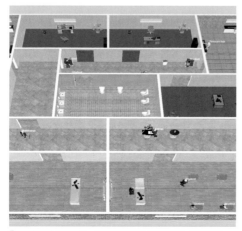

Differentiated crowds

Cognitive crowds with perception based behavioural heuristics

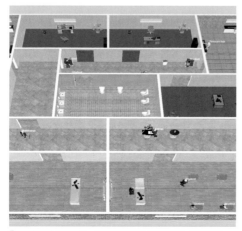

Functional crowds – crowds with aleatoric, reactive, opportunistic and scheduled actions

representation to add the semantics of actions and objects, and we implemented four types of actions (scheduled, reactive, opportunistic and aleatoric) to ensure rich, emergent behaviours. [13]

While this research seems primarily directed towards applications in the game industry, architects should be ready to appropriate both the tools and the analytic intelligence it provides.

The idea of functional crowds can be taken further: the agents' behaviour might be scripted so that it correlates with – responds to – elements of the designed environment such as colours, textures, stylistic features, configurations of furniture and other artefacts, and lighting conditions. The idea is to build up dynamic actor-artefact networks. Since an architectural space derives its meaning from the (nuanced) type of event/ social interaction enacted within its territory, these new tools allow for the re-foundation of architectural semiology as parametric semiology. The semiological project implies that the design medium (digital model) orders all form-function correlations into a coherent system of signification, mapping distinctions/manifolds defined within the domain of the signified (here, the domain of patterns of social interaction) onto distinctions/ manifolds defined within the domain of the signifier (here, the domain of spatial positions and morphological features) and vice versa. The system of signification works if the programmed social agents consistently respond to the coded positional and morphological clues so that expected behaviours can be read off the articulated environmental configuration. The meaning of architecture – the life-processes it potentially frames and sustains – is modelled within the design process, thus becoming a direct object of creative speculation and cumulative design elaboration.

The Semantic Dimension as a Crucial Aspect of Architectural Order

That architecture and urbanism inevitably have a semantic dimension is generally accepted. As yet, however, nobody seems to have succeeded in making this semantic dimension an arena of explicit, strategic design effort. Earlier attempts to develop an architectural semiology (under the auspices of postmodernism and deconstructivism) failed to convince, and were rejected in the early 1990s when 'operativity' was counterposed to 'representation'. This opposition – the expression of a necessary retreat from an unproductive engagement with architectural symbolism – was ultimately a false opposition. Architecture operates/functions through semantic associations as much as it does through physical separations/

connections. The built environment functions through its visual appearance, its legibility and its related capacity to frame and prime communication. The built environment does not just channel bodies: it orients sentient, socialised beings who must actively comprehend and navigate ever more complex urban scenes. A designed space is itself a communication, a framing device for all communications that take place within its territory.

The theory of architectural autopoiesis[4] posits the spatio-morphological *framing* of communicative interaction as the unique societal function of the design disciplines. In the second volume of my book, *The Autopoiesis of Architecture*,[5] I propose a definition of architectural order that poses organisation, phenomenological articulation and semiological articulation (signification) as three equally vital moments of a full-blown architectural/urban design project that can meet the challenges facing contemporary society. I distinguish three agendas – the *organisational*, the *phenomenological* and the *semiological* – for the re-tooling of architecture's expertise. These three dimensions, which together procure *architectural* order, are conceptually derived via two binary distinctions, as follows:

Organisation is based on the constitution/distribution of positions for spatial elements and their pattern of linkages. Articulation is based on the constitution/distribution of *morphological identities, similitudes and differences* across the architectural elements to be organised. Organisation is instituted via the physical means of distancing and barring, or alternatively connecting via vistas and/or circulatory channelling. These physical mechanisms can operate independently of all nuanced perception and comprehension and can thus, in principle, succeed without the efforts of articulation. However, deploying organisation without articulation – without facilitating the active navigation of the participants – severely limits the level of complexity possible in the patterns of social communication thus framed. Articulation presupposes cognition. It enlists the participants' perception and comprehension and thus facilitates their active orientation. The distinction of organisation vs articulation is thus based on the difference between handling *passive bodies* and enlisting active, *cognitive agents*. The two registers relate as follows: articulation builds upon and reveals organisation. It makes the organisation of functions apparent. In doing so it elevates organisation into order.

The dimension of articulation includes two distinct sub-tasks: *phenomeno-logical* articulation and *semiological* articulation. The phenomenological project enlists the users as cognitive agents, perceiving their environment along the lines of the cognitive principles of pattern-recognition or Gestalt-perception. It involves making organisational arrangements perceptually legible by ensuring that important points are conspicuous, avoiding visual overcrowding of the scene, etc. While phenomenological articulation enlists behavioural responses from cognitive agents, the semiological project, on the other hand, requires the communicative engagement of *socialised actors*. Comprehending a social situation involves more than the distinguishing of conspicuous features: it is an act of interpretation – more specifically, an act of reading the communication that the space itself constitutes, as a framing device for all communicative interactions within its ambit. Communication presupposes language, ie a *system of signification*. The built environment will spontaneously evolve into such a (more or less vague and unreliable) system of signification, but it is the task of architectural semiology to go beyond this spontaneous semiosis and build up a more complex and precise system of signification. To summarise, we can thus distinguish the contributions that the three fundamental dimensions of architecture make (via their respective design projects) to architecture's essential societal function:

Task Dimension	Framing Contribution	Engagement of Users	Soicicited Response
organisational project	as physical frame	as physical bodies	passive movement
phenomenological project	as perceptual frame	as cognitive beings	active behaviour
semiological project	as communicative frame	as socialised actors	communicative action

Why is this important now? The ability to navigate dense and complex urban environments is an important aspect of our overall productivity. In our post-Fordist network society, we need to keep continuously connected and informed, to coordinate our efforts with what everybody else is doing. Everything must communicate with everything. In terms of urban environments this implies that we should be able to see and participate in as many events as possible, always remaining exposed to many further choices from which to select our next move. This is best achieved if the visual field presents a rich, ordered scene of manifold offerings and also provides clues about what lies behind the currently visible layers. The speed and confidence with which one can make new experiences and meaningful connections is decisive. The design of environments that facilitate such hyper-connectivity must be very dense and complex and yet highly ordered and legible.

As urban complexity and density increase, effective articulation becomes more important.

A talented designer will intuitively adapt to and intervene within the spontaneous and historically evolving semiological system of the built environment. The aim of parametric semiology is to move from an intuitive participation within an evolving semiosis to an explicit agenda that understands the design of a large-scale architectural complex as an opportunity to create a new, coherent system of signification, a new artificial architectural language (without relying on the familiar codes found in existing built environments). The maturing style of parametricism is geared up – in terms of its computational techniques and attendant formal-spatial repertoire – to order and compose unprecedented levels of spatio-morphological complexity. *Parametric urbanism* – the application of parametricism to urban design – provides an accomplished point of departure for the *parametric semiology* yet to be accomplished.

Parametric Urbanism

At the beginning of this text we asked: how should contemporary urbanism analyse/decompose the city into subsystems? The most general, abstract decomposition of the city is evoked by Frei Otto's distinction of occupation vs movement, which entails differentiating and correlating the fabric system and the circulation/street system of the built environment. This conceptualisation already encapsulates architecture's lead distinction of form (internal reference, self-reference) vs function (external reference, world-reference): the distinction of fabric vs streets is a distinction in the domain of form, while the distinction of occupation vs movement is a distinction in the domain of function (social action). Although it lacks richness or variety in terms of its response to the challenges facing contemporary society, this basic conceptualisation is perhaps adequate with respect to early/primitive societies – those based on segmented differentiation, with simple settlement structures built up from the agglomeration of undifferentiated units. The medieval city and the built environment of the era of feudalism were characterised by a stratified order: the built environment was segregated according to the order of the estates – the nobility's castle/palace, the clerisy's monasteries, the burgher's walled city and the farmer's village. Starting with the Renaissance, this stratified order evolved into what Niklas Luhmann calls modern, functionally differentiated society,[6] which found its ultimate expression in the modernist city, differentiated according to the following basic function types: production, administration, consumption, recreation, habitation. For each of these function types (types of social interaction) the modernist architect/urbanist developed functionally specialised urban typologies, instantiated as distinct, separate, specialised, internally repetitive zones. Le Corbusier's Ville Radieuse, a generic design for the ideal modernist/functionalist city, makes explicit this approach. The modernist principles of separation, specialisation and repetition are clearly demonstrated; zones are distinct and sharply set apart.

Deconstructivism initiated a surprising, radical expansion of the compositional repertoire. The synthesis of subsystems moved from the layout of separated, adjacent zones to the superposition of layers, as demonstrated, for example, by Bernard Tschumi's competition-winning entry for the Parc de la Villette in 1983. The basic modernist function types were the starting-point for a studio that Zaha Hadid and I taught at Columbia University in 1993.[7] Rather than seeing these functional subsystems as separate zones, the premise of the studio was to interpret them as interpenetrating layers. The intention was to go beyond deconstructivist superposition/collage and allow the layers to adapt to each other via mutual, dynamic distortion. However, the results remained rather chaotic.

About ten years later, I started to revisit the problem of urbanism, first with masterplanning projects at Zaha Hadid Architects, and then more systematically with the AADRL research project 'Parametric Urbanism'.[8] New tools and techniques allowed us to develop our earlier intentions in a much more convincing way. By this time, we had the capacity to produce smooth, continuous differentiations. The task of complex multi-system urbanism was now posed once more in terms of layered subsystems, each of which displays its own ontology and internal logic of differentiation as the basis for scripted subsystem-to-subsystem correlations (as opposed to zoning or collage).

The project presented here used Maya fluid as tool for the initial generation of a basic urban geometry. The tool simulates the dynamic of a fluid and makes its typical characteristics subject to parametric control. The particle flow is sensitive to contextual features such as boundaries and obstacles. Two fluids flowing into each other form complex patterns of nesting and intermixing. The field of particles or vectors might be analysed in terms of particle directions, densities and velocities, thus producing a data-set delivering input parameters for the scripted definition of geometry (urban morphology). The most diverse transcoding scripts are imaginable

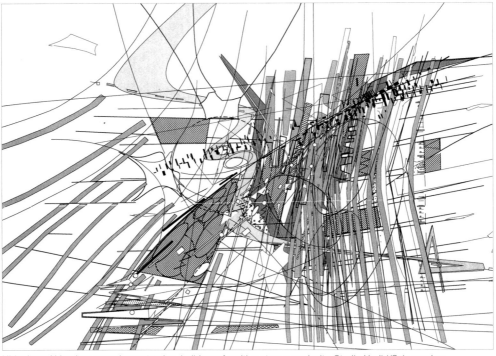

Ubiquitous Urbanism: generic masterplan, build up of multi-system complexity. Studio Hadid/Schumacher, Columbia University, 1993

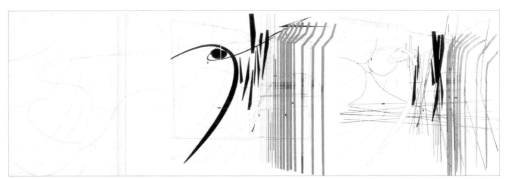

Ubiquitous Urbanism: layering process with adaptive distortion (action-reaction). Studio Hadid/Schumacher, Columbia University, 1993

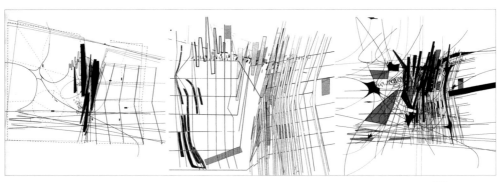

here. The strategic choice was made to translate the various fluids rather differently. The model contained four types of fluids driving four spatio-morphological systems. (The programmatic layers were stipulated as residential accommodation (two typologies), public/cultural facilities and landscape/park areas.) All transcodings display the fluidity of the original diagrams. This shared character assimilates the systems to each other despite their ontological difference. The shared, underlying fluid system thus ensures that these four systems are able to participate in a single, coherent, multi-layer urban field.

Parametric Semiology

This brief excursion into parametric urbanism serves only to set the scene for the task facing the semiological project under conditions of variety, density and complexity. The consistent mapping of four basic function types onto the four distinct morphological subsystems is only a crude beginning. Each of the spatio-formal subsystems is internally differentiated: these morphological differentiations then have to be correlated to their respective programmatic differentiations. An open-to-closed gradient in the domain of the signifier might be correlated to a public-to-private gradient in the domain of the signified. As Ferdinand de Saussure has taught us, a system of signification can only be built up as a system of distinctions, not via the positing of positive terms.[9] To be more precise, a system of signification (language) is established through the correlation of two systems of distinctions: one in the domain of the signifier (form) and the other in the domain of the signified (function). Through their correlation the two planes of distinction are mutually stabilising. The correlation is established through association. As Wittgenstein taught us, this association/correlation is constituted and reproduced through its use in social interactions. Saussure emphasises that language structures thought (action) as much as thought (action) structures the formal medium of language. This medium is the world of sounds in the case of spoken languages, and the world of spatial forms in the case of architectural languages. Both domains are in the first instance rather amorphous and open-ended: they only take shape through their correlation, as their mapped patterns of distinction find their stabilising scaffold in each other. Saussure illustrates the way linguistic order emerges by means of a diagram and explains:

So we can envisage the linguistic phenomenon in its entirety – the language that is – as a series of adjoining subdivisions simultaneously imprinted both on the plane of vague, amorphous thought (A), and on the equally featureless plane of sound (B). This can be represented very approximately in the following sketch. The combination of both a necessary and mutually complementary delimitation of units. Thought, chaotic by nature, is made precise by this process of segmentation … What takes place, is a somewhat mysterious process by which 'thought-sound' evolves divisions, and a language takes shape with its linguistic units in between these two amorphous masses.[10]

As indicated by the above example of an open-to-closed gradient, distinctions might involve a smooth spectrum rather than being restricted to hard-edged, discrete concepts. Thus parametric semiology involves the move from discrete logic to fuzzy logic – that is, it uses the logic of 'more or less', or probability, rather than the logic of 'either/or' and certainty. General distinctions such as open-closed or public-private may also be re-used across several function types, thus multiplying (rather than merely adding) determinations.

Potential briefs for the semiological project must be sufficiently complex, so as to enable the design of a system of signification. The task is to design an information-rich, dense built environment that orders and reveals the manifold social interactions to be expected within its spaces. The types of information to be encoded are the *function type* (interaction type: what is going on here?), the *social type* (the various status groups of the institution: who is to be expected here?), and the *location type* (facilitating navigation: how can I find the event I am looking for?). On the side of the signifier we can distinguish the following dimensions/registers of encoding: the positional dimension (distinguishing relative positions), the spatial shape dimension (distinguishing spatial shapes) and the dimension of surface treatment (materiality, relief/texture, colour, perforation, etc). These three dimensions are functionally equivalent and can substitute for each other. (Shape and surface articulation might be drawn together under the heading of morphology.) The designed semiological system should be conceived as a parametric system, ie the various distinctions and their correlations are subject to parametric variation. The programme domain, the domain of the signified, is best understood in terms of interaction patterns or communicative activities. These patterns are always patterns of a certain type, ie they adhere to a certain function type, although subject to parametric variation and open to programmatic intermixing and hybridisation. They can be modelled via programmed agents that respond to coded environmental clues. Each function type involves a typical social institution or interaction type unfolding in its relevant spatial setting. For instance, a lecture differs from a seminar (or workshop, or individual

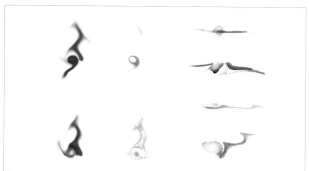

learning) in terms of the number of participants, their spatial constellation, orientation and pattern of action. A specific communicative interaction can only commence once the participants have been gathered, primed (mentally prepared) and ordered into the appropriate constellation. The specific spatial frames (organised and articulated territories) invite and structure such specific communicative situations. Architectural frames allow participants to find each other and to recognise and anticipate the communicative event. They help to define the situation. Without a shared definition of the situation no communication is possible. This is the societal function of architecture: the provision of an ordered system of situational definitions via spatial framing. The semiological project is thus at the centre of architecture's core competency.

1   Correlation is the third principle of parametricism's formal heuristics. See Patrik Schumacher, 'Parametricism – A New Global Style for Architecture and Urban Design', in Neil Leach and Helen Castle (eds), AD Digital Cities, *Architectural Design* 79:4 (July/August 2009). As an example of formal-spatial correlation one could refer to the correlation between the subsystems of a tower: skeleton, floors and envelope.

2   Mehdi Moussaïd, Dirk Helbing and Guy Theraulaz, 'How simple rules determine pedestrian behaviour and crowd disasters', in Proceedings of the National Academy of Science, 2011. See also Mehdi Moussaïd, Dirk Helbing, Simon Garnier, Anders Johansson, Maud Combes and Guy Theraulaz, 'Experimental study of the behavioural mechanisms underlying self-organization in human crowds', in *Proceedings of the Royal Society B*: Biological science, 2009. Although this kind of research is still in its infancy, relative to the challenge of phenomenal articulation, it ties in with the author's own concern with observer parameters as a crucial parameter type to be incorporated into the tool set of parametricism.

3   JM Allbeck, 'Functional Crowds', in Workshop on Crowd Simulation co-located with the 23rd Annual Conference on Computer Animation and Social Agents (Saint Malo, 2010). See also JM Allbeck and H Kress-Gazit, 'Constraints-Based Complex Behavior in Rich Environments', in *Proceedings of the 10th International Conference on Intelligent Virtual Agents* (Springer, 2010), 1–14.

4   Patrik Schumacher, *The Autopoiesis of Architecture, Volume 1: A New Framework for Architecture* (London: John Wiley & Sons, 2010).

5   Patrik Schumacher, *The Autopoiesis of Architecture, Volume 2: A New Agenda for Architecture* (London: John Wiley & Sons, 2012).

6   Niklas Luhmann, *Social Systems* (Stanford, CA: Stanford University Press, 1995).

7   The author joined Zaha Hadid in teaching an Advanced Architecture Studio at Columbia University in 1993. The work of the studio was published by Columbia University under the title Ubiquitous Urbanism.

8   Parametric Urbanism was the title of a three-year design research agenda at the AADRL (Design Research Lab) from 2005 to 2008.

9   Ferdinand de Saussure, *Course in General Linguistics*, fourth edition (London: Duckworth, 1995), originally published in French as *Cours de linguistique général*, Paris 1916.

10   Ibid, 110.

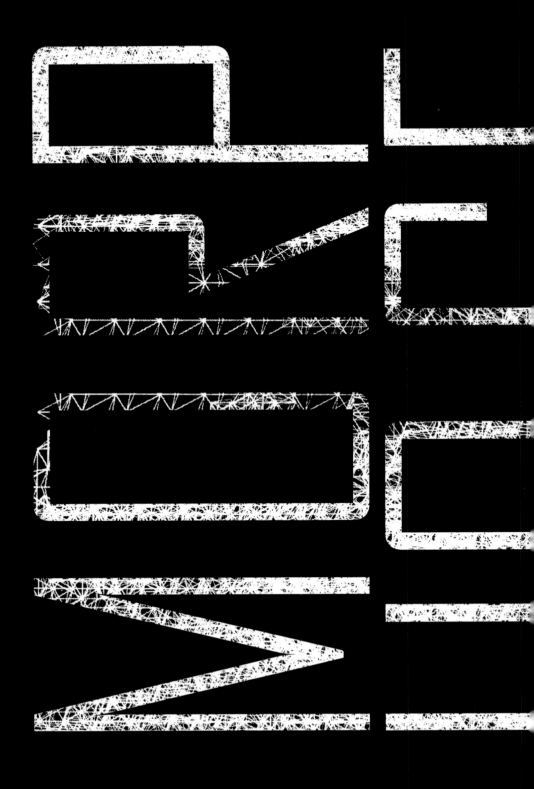

MORPHOGENETIC

Mangrove / Mangal / Polyp Growth / Colonial Form
Phyllotaxis / Seeding

MANGROVE: MANGAL

AADRL 2007-2008 / TEAM: CHIMERA
Pierandrea Angius, Alkis Dikaios, Thomas Jacobsen, Carlos Parraga

Morphogenetic design strategies enable an understanding of nature through constructs that actively couple singular and collective relationships, ordering the deployment of matter as a product of correlated interactions between the environment and each respective species. Within this natural world of metabolic balance the mangal – the plant community of the mangrove swamp – operates as a model of the social ordering of plants, demonstrating their migration and coevolution. A study of the mangal offers organisational strategies that afford an opportunity to consider population and performance as environmental drivers negotiating a force-deployed system that fosters adaptation and ecology.

This research project takes the mangrove–mangal relationship as a model of response in developing a housing proposal for Hudson Yards in lower Manhattan. Computational frameworks are used to integrate a dynamic structuring of bundled aerated roots that iteratively version options for optimising trajectory and path, moving towards a four-dimensional network of emergent organisations. These choreographies of thrust lines are informed as set out trajectories constructing an integrated urban system of ground and vertical housing typologies that extend the existing infrastructure through horizontal to vertical migratory populations of unit distribution. The emergent singular/collective constructs deploy a time-based sequencing of population engaging a model of development that allows unit-to-unit interactions to be understood and governed – in this case, through phyllotactic codification.

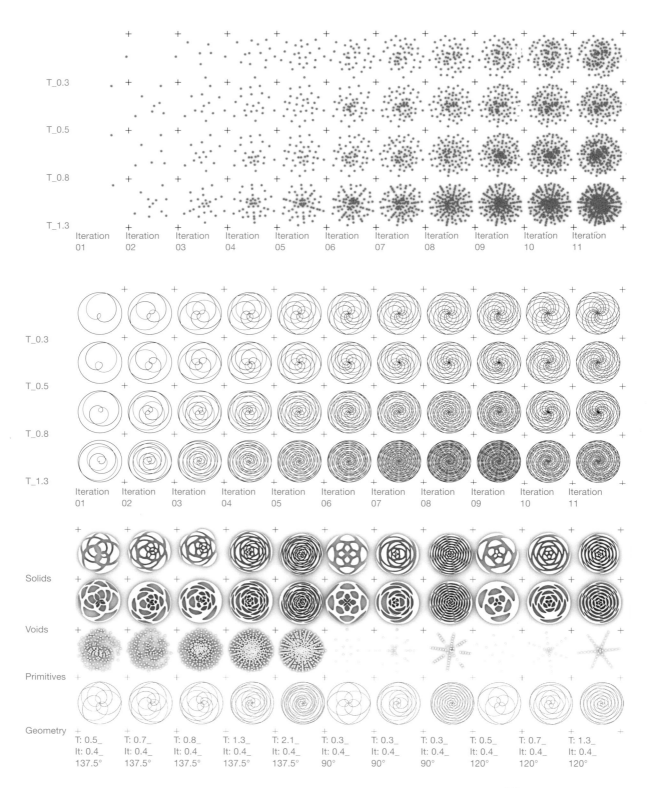

T_0.3

T_0.5

T_0.8

T_1.3

| Iteration 01 | Iteration 02 | Iteration 03 | Iteration 04 | Iteration 05 | Iteration 06 | Iteration 07 | Iteration 08 | Iteration 09 | Iteration 10 | Iteration 11 |

T_0.3

T_0.5

T_0.8

T_1.3

| Iteration 01 | Iteration 02 | Iteration 03 | Iteration 04 | Iteration 05 | Iteration 06 | Iteration 07 | Iteration 08 | Iteration 09 | Iteration 10 | Iteration 11 |

Solids

Voids

Primitives

Geometry

| T: 0.5_ It: 0.4_ 137.5° | T: 0.7_ It: 0.4_ 137.5° | T: 0.8_ It: 0.4_ 137.5° | T: 1.3_ It: 0.4_ 137.5° | T: 2.1_ It: 0.4_ 137.5° | T: 0.3_ It: 0.4_ 90° | T: 0.3_ It: 0.4_ 90° | T: 0.3_ It: 0.4_ 90° | T: 0.5_ It: 0.4_ 120° | T: 0.7_ It: 0.4_ 120° | T: 1.3_ It: 0.4_ 120° |

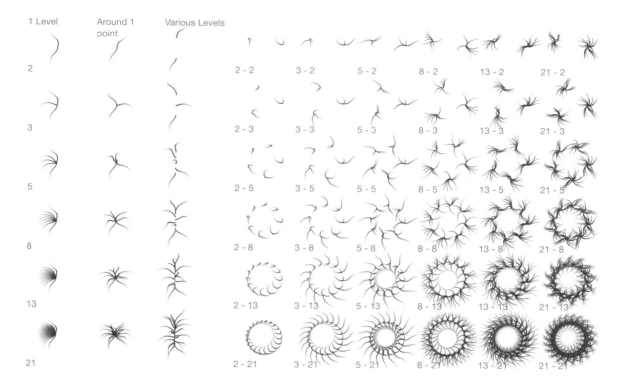

1 Level	Around 1 point	Various Levels						
2			2 - 2	3 - 2	5 - 2	8 - 2	13 - 2	21 - 2
3			2 - 3	3 - 3	5 - 3	8 - 3	13 - 3	21 - 3
5			2 - 5	3 - 5	5 - 5	8 - 5	13 - 5	21 - 5
8			2 - 8	3 - 8	5 - 8	8 - 8	13 - 8	21 - 8
13			2 - 13	3 - 13	5 - 13	8 - 13	13 - 13	21 - 13
21			2 - 21	3 - 21	5 - 21	8 - 21	13 - 21	21 - 21

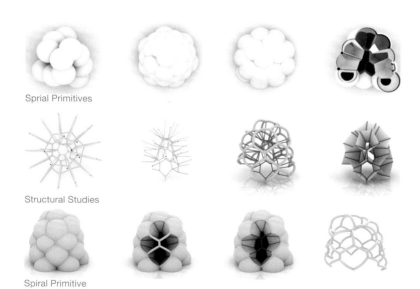

Sprial Primitives

Structural Studies

Spiral Primitive

(Opposite page)
Catalogue showing 2D geometrical iterations based on phyllotaxis principles

(Top)
Catalogue showing distributional schemes based on Fibonacci sequence

(Bottom)
Model showing volumetric studies of spherical primitives arranged following phyllotaxis principles

Floor 16 _____

Floor 15 _____

Floor 14 _____

Floor 13 _____

Floor 12 _____

Ramp 7% _____

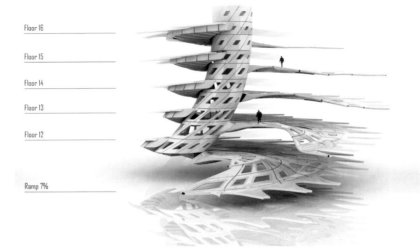

Mangal 2
1_aerial connective spaces
2_aerial massing connections

Mangal 3
2_aerial connective spaces
4_aerial massing connections

Mangal 5
0_aerial connective spaces
3_aerial massing connections

Mangal 6
5_aerial connective spaces
4_aerial massing connections

Mangal 8
1_aerial connective spaces
2_aerial massing connections

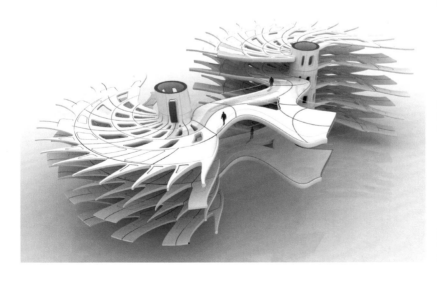

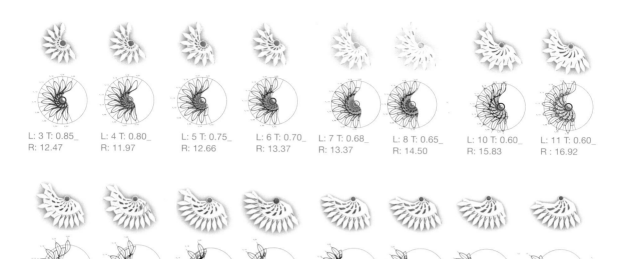

L: 3 T: 0.85_
R: 12.47

L: 4 T: 0.80_
R: 11.97

L: 5 T: 0.75_
R: 12.66

L: 6 T: 0.70_
R: 13.37

L: 7 T: 0.68_
R: 13.37

L: 8 T: 0.65_
R: 14.50

L: 10 T: 0.60_
R: 15.83

L: 11 T: 0.60_
R : 16.92

L: 12 T: 0.59_
R: 17.70

L: 13 T: 0.58_
R: 18.70

L: 14 T: 0.58_
R: 18.70

L: 15 T: 0.55_
R: 19.46

L: 17 T: 0.50_
R: 20.85

L: 18 T: 0.47_
R: 21.35

L: 18 T: 0.45_
R: 21.66

L: 19 T: 0.43_
R: 21.89

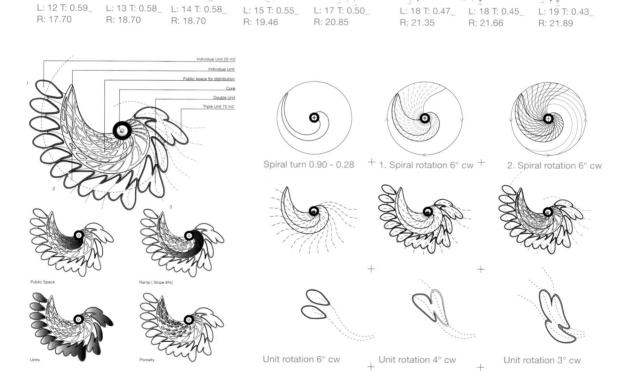

Individual Unit 25 m2

Individual Unit

Public space for distribution

Core

Double Unit

Triple Unit 75 m2

1

2

3

Public Space

Ramp [Slope 8%]

Units

Porosity

Spiral turn 0.90 - 0.28   + 1. Spiral rotation 6° cw +   2. Spiral rotation 6° cw

Unit rotation 6° cw   Unit rotation 4° cw   Unit rotation 3° cw

171

(Above)

Close-up of the urban massing highlighting
the connective spaces

172

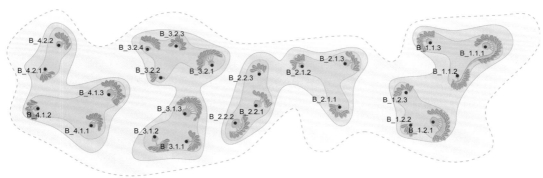

	STOREYS	UNITS
B_1.1.1	12	176
B_1.1.2	14	152
B_1.1.3	16	145
B_1.2.1	20	204
B_1.2.2	16	147
B_1.2.3	18	190
B_2.1.1	17	170
B_2.1.2	23	221
B_2.1.3	18	172

	STOREYS	UNITS
B_2.2.1	21	134
B_2.2.2	18	225
B_2.2.3	25	295
B_3.1.1	18	128
B_3.1.2	20	274
B_3.1.3	24	336
B_3.2.1	34	257
B_3.2.2	34	352
B_3.2.3	26	231
B_3.2.4	31	231

	STOREYS	UNITS
B_4.1.1	20	216
B_4.1.2	24	296
B_4.1.3	28	400
B_4.2.1	22	162
B_4.2.2	20	186
TOTAL UNITS		4972

(Above)

Urban massing highlighting the connective space between the buildings as well as building location and values in terms of storeys and unit deployment

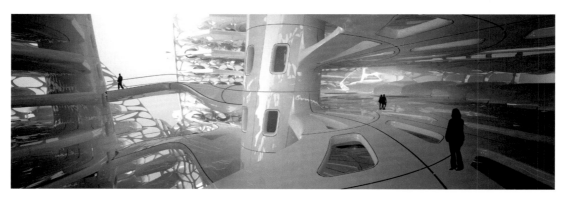

174

POLYP GROWTH: COLONIAL FORM

AADRL 2008-2009 / TEAM: SLASH
LeHa Hoang, Chia-Liang Huang, Jie Yuan, Subharthi Guha

Morphogenesis serves as a model for computational interrogation as it couples material and mathematical processes within genotype–phenotype distinctions and growth. Within this matrix of correlated interrelations, examples of social ordering enable a complex time-based network of singular/collective relations to demonstrate symbiotic and adaptive characteristics. These characteristics articulate features of an adaptive ecology. Coral, as s model of singular genetic versioning, is a responsive and simple creature. Its complexity arises from its internal ordering, which evolves growth patterns in response to environmental conditioning and the coupling of genetically identical multi-cellular organisms known as polyps. Local polyp interactions serve as the primary catalyst in the creation of collective reef ecologies that emerge as a product of growth over time.

This research project develops an organisational pattern language through formational strategies, exploiting rule-based growth strategies of polyps as models for housing unit distribution. Linear unit-to-unit parameters are coupled with the emergent concave and convex population-based growth constraints that underpin taxonomies of housing neighbourhoods. These high-density cluster formations are responsive to local environments, constructing patterns that are varied and formative. Neighbouring relationships allow for the unitary distinctions to be embedded within a coevolved time-based formation that reconsiders the typology of mat housing through an intimate fusion of units with a continuous circulatory network of interior and exterior urban systems.

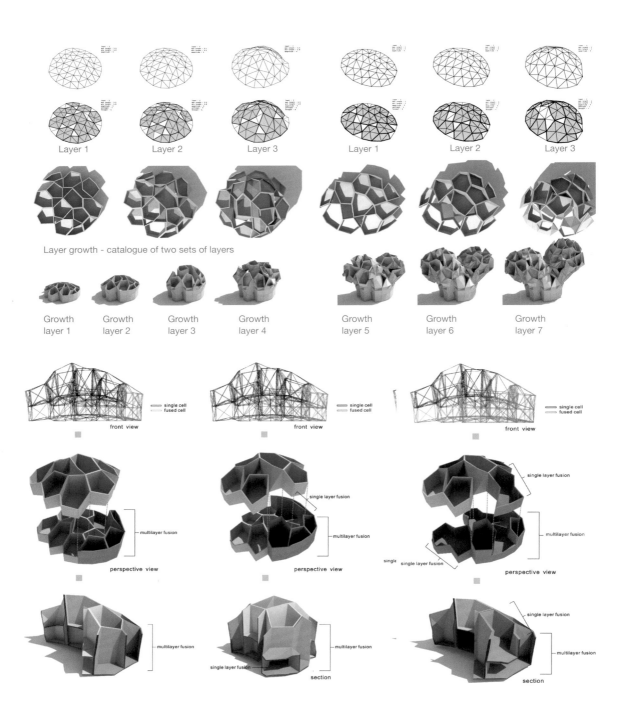

Layer 1   Layer 2   Layer 3   Layer 1   Layer 2   Layer 3

Layer growth - catalogue of two sets of layers

Growth layer 1   Growth layer 2   Growth layer 3   Growth layer 4   Growth layer 5   Growth layer 6   Growth layer 7

single cell
fused cell

front view   front view   front view

single layer fusion

multilayer fusion

perspective view   perspective view   perspective view

section   section

(Above)

Studies in organising and aggegating
housing units based on the cellular growth
logic exhibited by corals

Initial seeding branching system

First layer

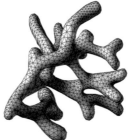

Second layer

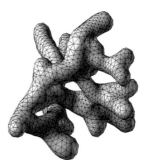

Third layer

The time-based growth shows
how housing incrementally grows
around initial seed units which
contain essential functions such
as circulation and services.

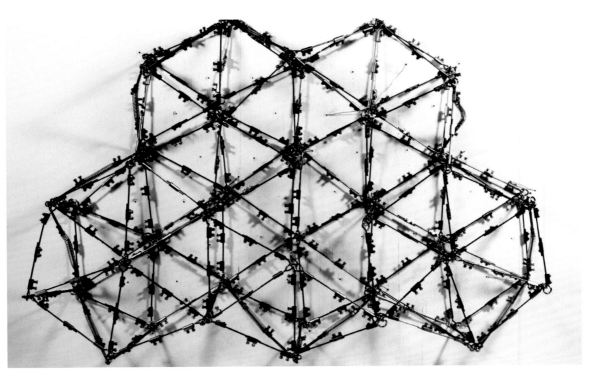

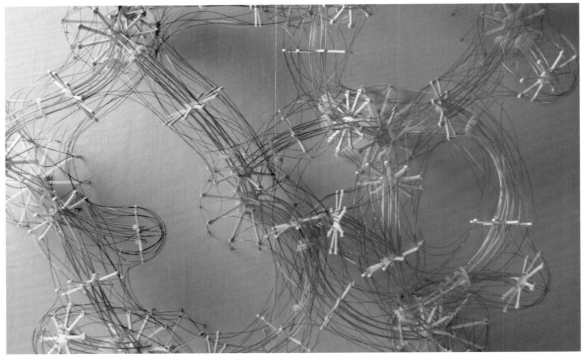

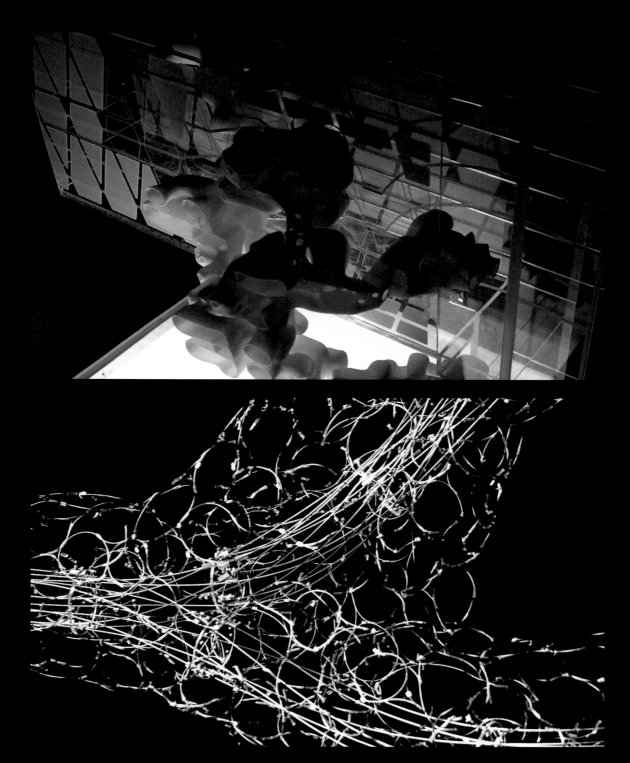

Studies in organising and aggegating housing units based on the cellular growth logic exhibited by corals

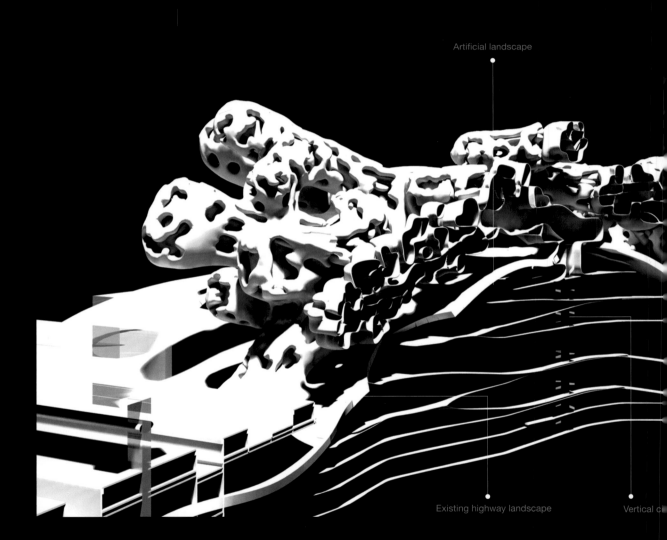

Artificial landscape

Existing highway landscape

Vertical ci

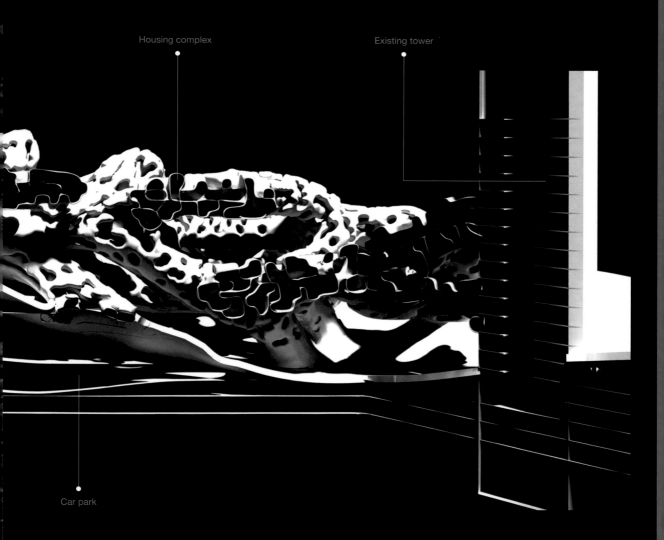

Housing complex

Existing tower

Car park

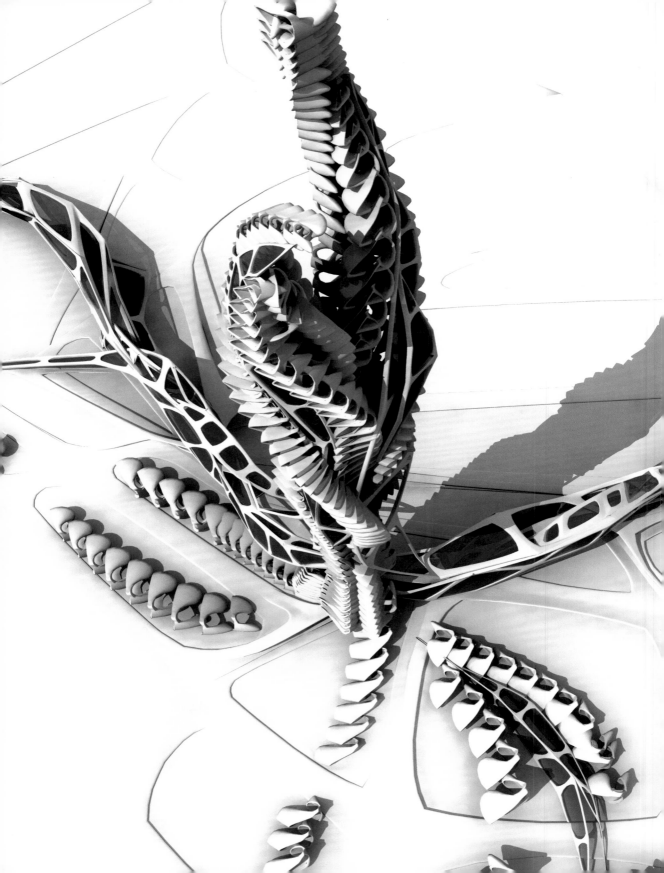

PHYLLOTAXIS

AADRL 2005-2006 / TEAM: RED.PDF
Dominiki Dadatsi, Eirini Fountoulaki, Eleni Pavlidou

Phyllotactic patterns emerge as self-organising processes in dynamic, self-propagating systems. Defined botanically as the arrangement of leaves on a branch, phyllotaxis serves as an operative model of computational enquiry through its responsive engagement with environmental stimuli such as sunlight and moisture. Within this linear distribution model a complex network of branching organisations construct pattern-sensitive correlations that allow for the emergence of a continuous soft veining infrastructure. As the primary objective in this system is solar exposure, orientation and population of branch networks are optimised through the structuring of networks, energy and material agency. The recursive arterial networks articulate circulation as an adaptive feature that operates as a metabolic sensory network within the regeneration of the plant.

Taking these principles as a model for housing distribution, this research project correlated sun exposure and natural ventilation as fundamental drivers for airy living spaces. Working within a field of tower topologies, the scenario-based proposal used phyllotaxis-driven systems to organise the distribution of housing units iteratively through linear cluster organisations. Cores and horizontal slab articulation were integrated within helical networks that propagated dynamically driven unit distributions nested within circulatory subsystems. Path-based optimisation and nodal network analysis informed transitional vertical to horizontal spatial transformations, allowing for the creation of common spaces between clusters of living units.

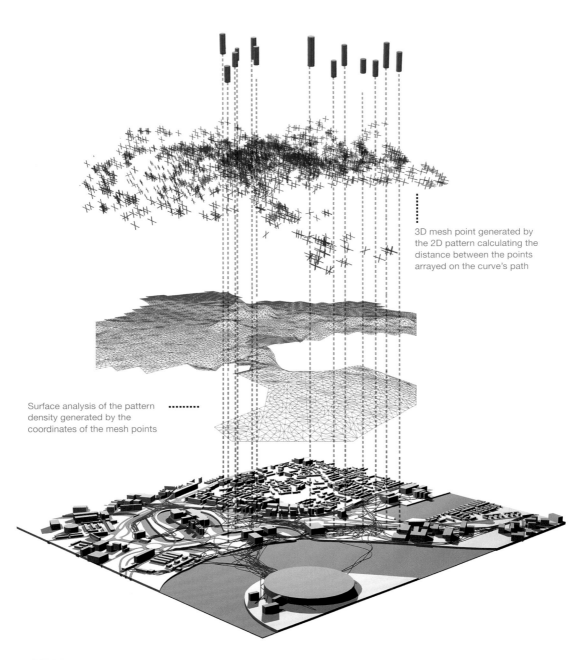

3D mesh point generated by the 2D pattern calculating the distance between the points arrayed on the curve's path

Surface analysis of the pattern density generated by the coordinates of the mesh points

(Above)

Layered diagram of the generative process indicating agent-based pattern formation translated to 3D mesh points along with a density analysis showing the location of tower cores

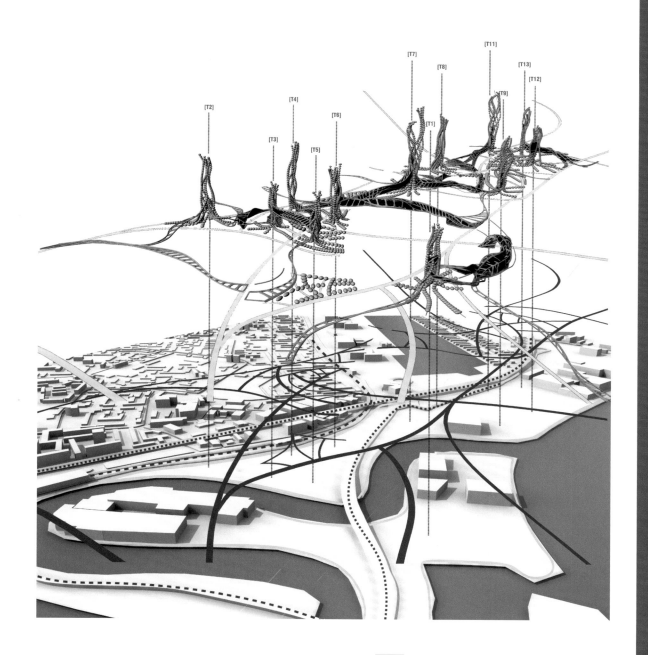

[T2] [T4] [T7] [T11] [T8] [T13] [T12] [T9] [T3] [T6] [T1] [T5]

(Above)

Full urban proposal including vehicular
and pedestrian circulation

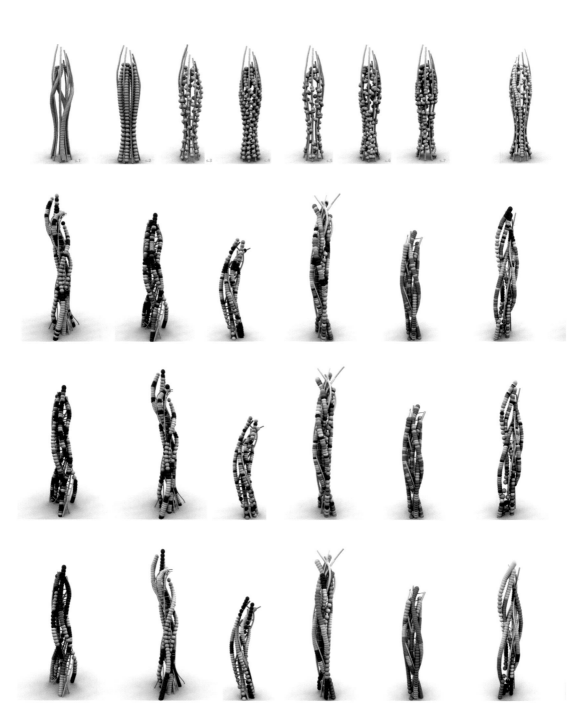

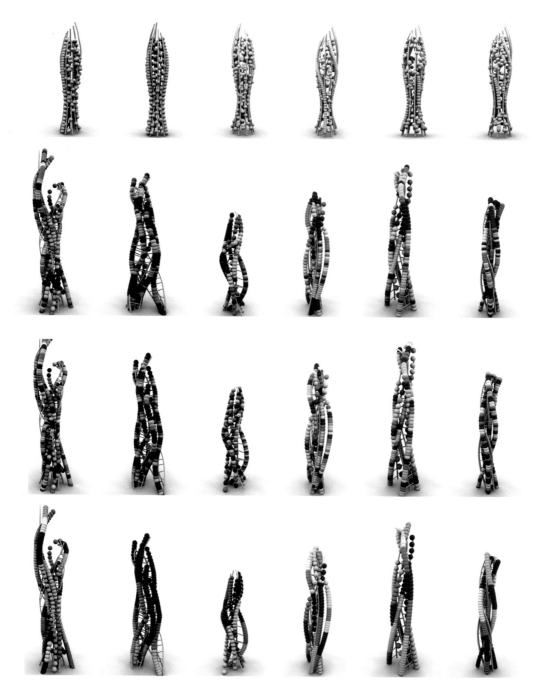

Catalogue of parametrically generated and controlled towers showing organisation and distribution of five different typologies based on phyllotactic organisation

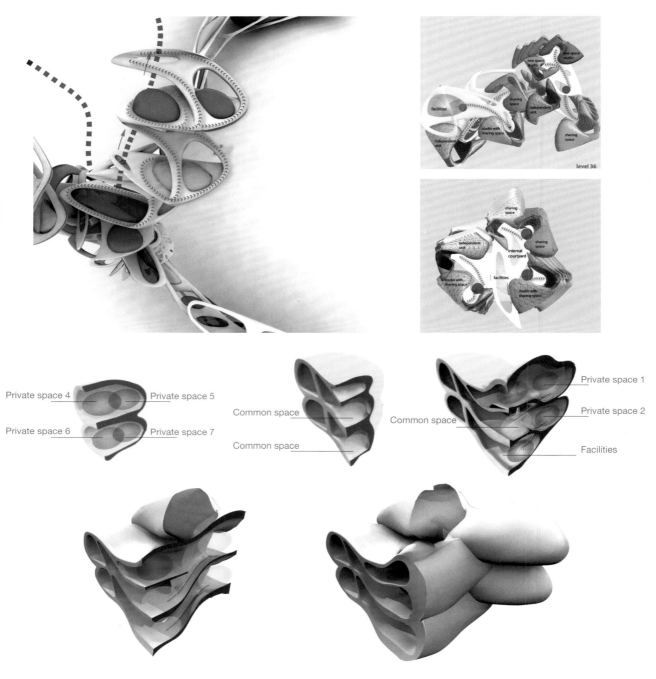

one space studio

one space studio

facilities

sharing space

independent unit

independent unit

studio with sharing space

sharing space

level 36

sharing space

independent unit

sharing space

internal courtyard

facilities

studio with sharing space

studio with sharing space

Private space 4 — — Private space 5

Private space 6 — — Private space 7

Common space

Common space

Private space 1

Common space — — Private space 2

Facilities

(Above)

The organisation of internal spaces in an individual unit employs back-to-back aggregation and vertical stacking

190

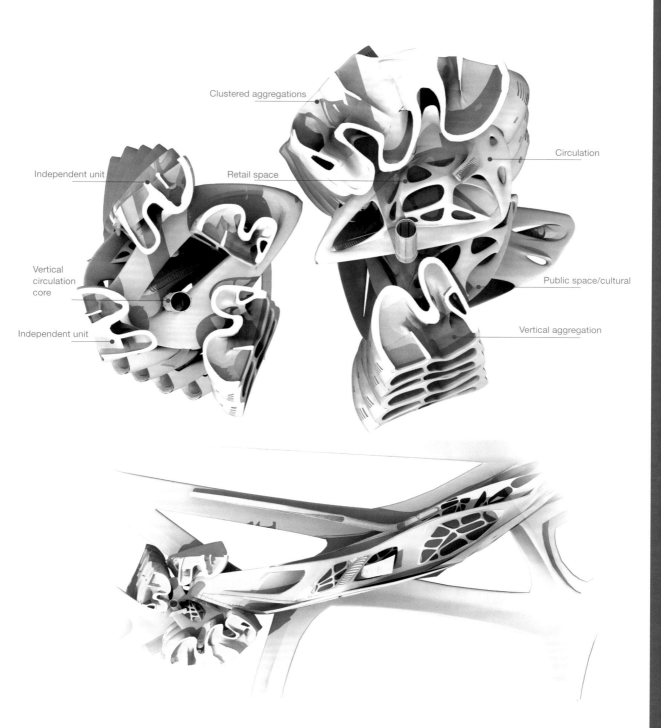

Clustered aggregations

Circulation

Independent unit

Retail space

Vertical circulation core

Public space/cultural

Independent unit

Vertical aggregation

(Above)

Horizontal sections through the towers showing the spiralling phyllotactic organisation of the complex connection between housing units, cores and public spaces.

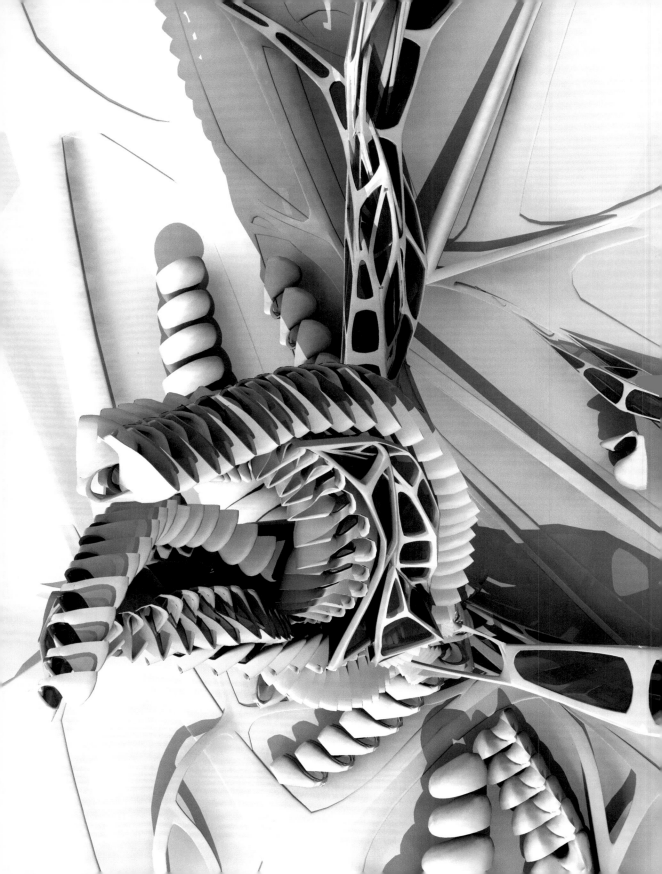

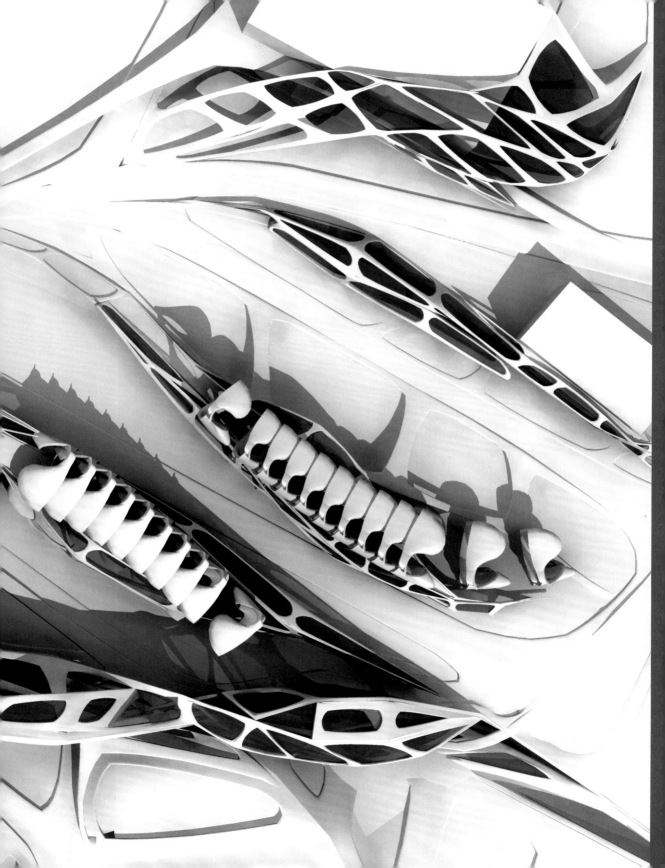

SEEDING

AADRL 2005-2006 / TEAM: ARCHITECTA
Danilo Arsic, Yoshimasa Hagiwara, Hala Sheikh

As in an agricultural context, the process of seeding is designed to foster growth and production within the natural cycles of a given ecology. Serving as a deployment scenario for urban massing, computational drivers are articulated through growth models that operate through signals and boundaries. Unlike organisational models that are top-down linear or radial, seeding-based organisations are relational allowing for time-based parameters to drive development. Unlike grid-based systems, seeding logics are polycentric and accommodate hyper-specific versioning that can address large-scale urban infill strategies over time. Scenario forecasting within this sequential development is an important feature of how adaptation within the genetic parameters of distribution can inform a model for time-based urbanism.

This research project explores computational seeding strategies as urban nodes that address development through the construction of signals and boundaries, producing a varied urban fabric as a model for density and land development. The project proposed a flexible lattice-based framework that would allow units to be embedded within coupled radial core networks. The tower typologies within these prototypical formations emerged as serial and vertical fields of housing. This distribution scenario is strongly related to Japanese metabolist strategies, and in particular Kiyonori Kikutake's Marine City.

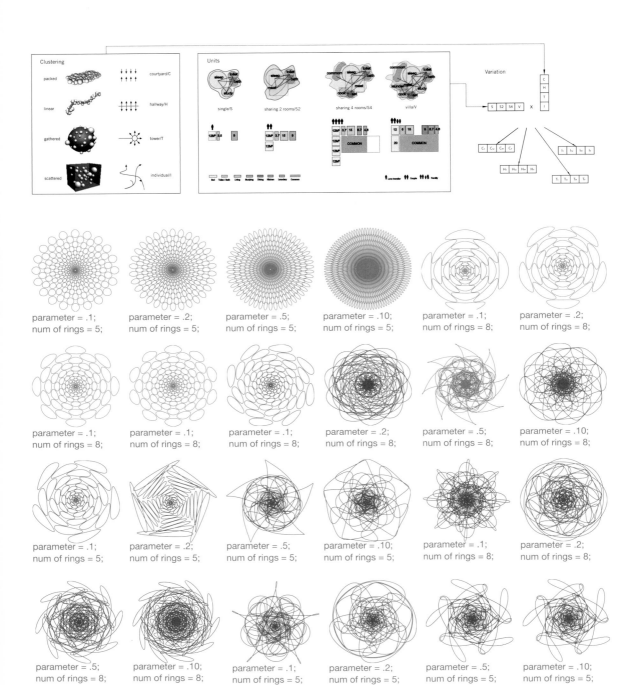

parameter = .1;
num of rings = 5;

parameter = .2;
num of rings = 5;

parameter = .5;
num of rings = 5;

parameter = .10;
num of rings = 5;

parameter = .1;
num of rings = 8;

parameter = .2;
num of rings = 8;

parameter = .1;
num of rings = 8;

parameter = .1;
num of rings = 8;

parameter = .1;
num of rings = 8;

parameter = .2;
num of rings = 8;

parameter = .5;
num of rings = 8;

parameter = .10;
num of rings = 8;

parameter = .1;
num of rings = 5;

parameter = .2;
num of rings = 5;

parameter = .5;
num of rings = 5;

parameter = .10;
num of rings = 5;

parameter = .1;
num of rings = 8;

parameter = .2;
num of rings = 8;

parameter = .5;
num of rings = 8;

parameter = .10;
num of rings = 8;

parameter = .1;
num of rings = 5;

parameter = .2;
num of rings = 5;

parameter = .5;
num of rings = 5;

parameter = .10;
num of rings = 5;

(Above)

Diagram showing the parametric relationships
between seeds, cores, unit typologies and unit sizes

196

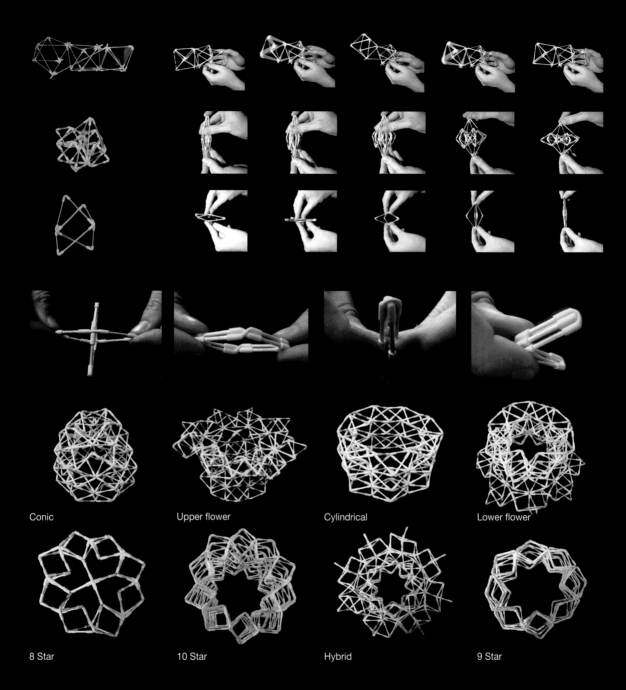

Conic   Upper flower   Cylindrical   Lower flower

8 Star   10 Star   Hybrid   9 Star

The rubber joint allows for 360° rotation –
a connection logic that provides a differentiated
array of spatial and formal organisations.

Catalogue of the bundling system. Operating on the principles of branching and subdivision and transforming between rigid and soft states, the system is global and local.

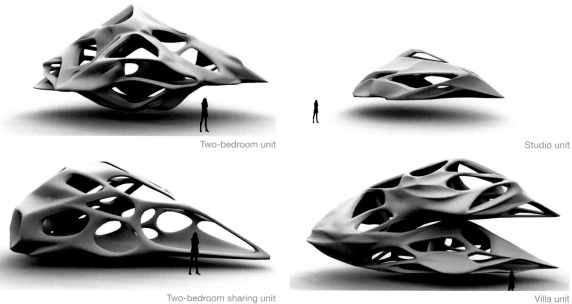

Two-bedroom unit

Studio unit

Two-bedroom sharing unit

Villa unit

Digital translation of the analogue models with the corresponding housing type

199

Catalogue of radial tower clusters showing the relationship between vertical cores and inhabitable units

The central elevator core is the main vertical circulation connecting the groundscape to the inhabitable units

Studio1_30 degrees

Villa_60 degrees

Studio2_30 degrees

Share2_60 degrees

Villa2_90 degrees

Share2_90 degrees

Share4_60 degrees

Villa3_90 degrees

Share4_90 degrees

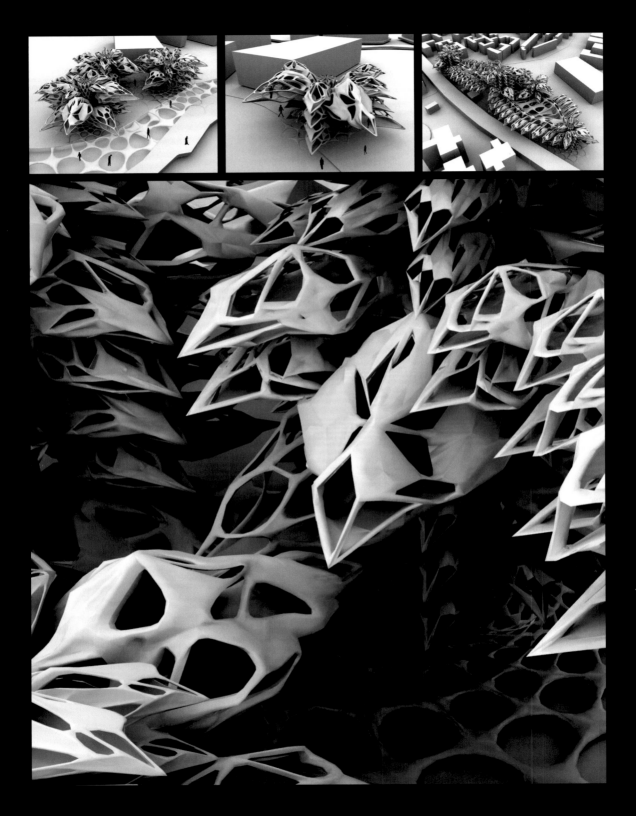

INDUCTION DESIGN VERSUS THE HUMAN BRAIN
COMPUTER PROGRAMS VERSUS FREEHAND
WHAT CAN WE DO NOW, WHAT CAN'T WE DO YET?

Makoto Sei Watanabe

This text provides a contrasting look at freehand sketches and some of the INDUCTION DESIGN/ALGODesign programs. However, the intention is not to show them in competition with each other. Both sketches and programs are valuable and necessary design methods. Instead of one or the other, we need both.

Depending on the project, an image that relies on direct intuition may ultimately turn out to be the means to solve every problem. In other cases, it may be impossible to satisfy all of the required conditions manually, regardless of how many times you try. The best approach is to select and combine according to the particular situation. Compared to sketches, programs benefit more from progress in technology. Eventually they will cover more areas than they do today and become far more useful. Sketches will probably not benefit from that kind of evolution. Those who possess the skill will use it, more or less as they do today. But this does not mean that technology will evolve while human skills stand still. Programs supplement human skills. When friendlier interfaces appear and program themselves to become more capable, people will gain the ability to sketch while interacting with programs. This should represent an evolution in humans' intuitive capacity. The aim of the Induction Cities and KeiRiki programs is to enable that kind of design methodology for a new era. Instead of allowing us to work more efficiently, the aim is to allow our skills and operations to evolve to a new and higher level.

Sketches and Programs: Giving Form to Mental Objects, and Giving Form to Thinking

Drawing by hand is the most low-tech methodology. Even a three-year old with a stub of crayon can do it. Tens of thousands of years ago, when humans lived in caves, they drew sketches on walls to give form to the images in their minds. Since then, the only notable technical progress in sketching has been the invention of perspective. Over tens of thousands of years, the act of sketching has not changed.

In those early times, humans had probably acquired the ability to convey their thinking to others through the medium of speech. They taught each other how to escape from wild animals and the steps in hunting procedures. Those procedures were algorithms. Then a technological revolution occurred – the invention of writing. Writing made it possible for humans to record (fix) their thinking, and this was followed by printing, communications and a series of other technologies to transmit this fixed thinking.

But there was no tool capable of creating form out of fixed thinking. That had to wait until much later, until the twentieth century – until the appearance of the computer program. Sketching as a tool to give form to mental objects, and programs as a tool to give form to thinking: for the first time in human history, both are becoming available together.

Algorithms: The Logic Required of Architecture

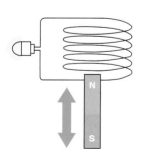

Electromagnetic induction

There are always conditional problems that must be solved by architectural design. In the normal design process, conditions are solved by bringing experience and intuition to bear. If that process could be clarified, revealing how solutions are found, then condition-solving methodologies could be established, possibly opening the way to solutions that are better than the solutions found through intuition. Constructing these methodologies is the goal of INDUCTION DESIGN/ ALGODesign. (The name 'Induction Cities' was derived by analogy from electromagnetic induction, in which an electric current is induced in a distant coil by bringing a magnet closer. It refers to a design method in which the desired design is 'generated' without manipulating the results directly.)

Sketches: The Images Required of Architecture

Architecture is expected to deliver one other thing – the creation of images. The emergence of something that does not yet exist, something that has never been seen, a visible aspect of reality that surpasses imagination. This is more than simply a solution. A solution is sufficient if it meets the requirements, but an image must deliver results that exceed expectations. Logic cannot be applied here. This is exactly where human capabilities excel. Conversely, those human capabilities must be free to concentrate on where they excel without being distracted by other tasks. This is where INDUCTION DESIGN can provide effective support.

Programs and Sketches

The sketches accompanying this text do not directly envision objectives or functions as architecture. Liberated from those necessary conditions of normal architectural design, they are free images drawn by hand of spaces and forms and arrays. Looking at the results, it should be possible to imagine functions and applications. This is the reverse of the normal architectural design process. First there is form, first there is space, then we conceptualise the kinds of functions that should be assigned to these shapes and spaces, and how large they should be. But let's think about that. If you take a conch shell that you pick up on a beach, create a 3D model, expand and deform the model, and assign an appropriate function, it may turn out to be excellent architecture. A Roman temple can be remodelled and turned into a building with a different function, such as an art museum. In some situations, form, structure and function can be switched in or out. It is not the case that the set cannot be changed once one of them is decided. But INDUCTION DESIGN using programs is a logical process. The objective is clear from the start. The program operates on the basis of an explicit value (what is wanted, what is better) and standards to measure that value in order to achieve a state where the value is maximised. There is no trace here of a process that works for unknown reasons. Everything works though deliberately constructed logic. Even when the project contains an element of the indeterminate, it is included as planned indeterminacy.

If this is so, does it mean that programs cannot produce images? And does it mean that sketching from intuition cannot produce solutions to conditions?

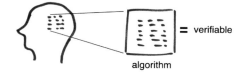

writing down the design process in brain

= verifiable

algorithm

ALGODesign= verifiable: design as science

The Meaning of Drawing by Hand: Living Lines, Momentum of Lines

One of the most powerful features of freehand sketching is its momentum:
the momentum of lines. A drawn line varies its curvature as it moves
along a vector. It speeds up as it traces a path, varying smoothly and
continuously. But a computer graphics line lacks this kind of momentum.
Where does the line want to go? How much force has been applied, and
how is it distributed – stronger in some places, and weaker in others?
This cannot be captured by digital pen pressure detection. Spirit, arm,
fingertips and pencil move as a single unit to produce... a line. The human
eye can decipher the various kinds of ancillary information contained in
the line. It can sense the momentum of the line, its movement, and the
intention that underlies it. Metaphorically, we say this kind of line 'has life'.

What does the momentum of the line produce? There is no guarantee
that momentum will result in a draft that solves a problem. But a line with
life is beautiful. The impression that it induces calls up another image. A
wave-like propagation of images, a chain of associations. The value of
momentum probably lies in the ripple effect of this vibration. In the normal
design process, the designer creates many so-called studies. He draws
sketches that approach a problem from a certain direction, and makes
models. He checks the results with his own eyes, and tries again with
another approach. Then, at some point, the designer feels certain – this
is it, let's go with this idea. When that feeling comes, the sketch or model
solves all problems and appears as the beautiful form that the designer
wanted. Out of the residue of a long process of trial and error, a shining
crystal is plucked.

The Circuitry of Intuition: The (Possible) Shortcut to an Answer –
Zen Enlightenment

During the trial-and-error search for a beautiful solution to the problem,
circuits to process the problem are no doubt constructed in the brain

of the designer. It seems that when the brain reiterates a particular action, it constructs nerve circuits dedicated to that action. Unconscious examination of the problem proceeds in the shadow of conscious searching and thought. Eventually this unconscious processing yields a great idea, which then rises to the level of consciousness. From below the world of consciousness, a small bubble rises up. As it nears the boundary of that realm, the bubble grows larger and finally bursts as it breaks into consciousness, making an inexpressible sound. It is a great idea. This is similar to the way that enlightenment is achieved in Zen, by sitting quietly and emptying the mind until it arrives. When asked how one achieves enlightenment, all one can say is: by practising Zen.

A designer who can achieve enlightenment is an exceptional architect. Runners run fast because they are fast runners. Composers compose beautiful music because they can. If we want a deeper explanation, what would it be? We do it because we can. It is a black box. Or it might be better to call it a magic box.

Brute Force Programs: The Longest but Surest Path – Scientific Experiment

INDUCTION DESIGN is an attempt to shine a scientific light on that magic box. The way that processing circuits gradually form in the brain through training in manual trial and error may resemble the programming technique known as neural networks. Of course, it is not possible to replicate the complicated processes that take place in the brain. But we can do things that the brain cannot do. One of those is the drawn-out but untiring processing of large volumes of data. Without errors, moreover. Repetition of the same kind of task, over and over and without errors, is something that the human brain cannot do. But this is what programs do best. Or rather, all that they can do. Instead of enlightenment achieved through rigorous spiritual training, we have the result of a logical process. Instead of discoveries made through trial and error, systematic searching. Instead of irreproducible singularities, verifiable reproduction. Not literature, but science.

ALGO(rithmic)Design/INDUCTION DESIGN: What Becomes Better with Programs?

So, what can science do? Just because there is a system to create form = an algorithm, it is not necessarily a good thing. (Of course, it is not necessarily a bad thing either.) What is important is the objective – what the algorithm can accomplish. A tool without an objective is like a car without a driver rolling down a mountain road. No one knows where it will go. For example, if a degree of randomness is incorporated into a program that creates form according to rules, automatically it becomes possible to create any number of variations of the form. In the case of this method, the program is not solving any problem.

It is also possible to create intricate shapes by fractal or chaos formulas. By varying the parameters, an infinite number of variations can be drawn. It is virtually impossible to manually draw a form like those that we can create with a Julia set or a recursive procedure. Methods like those are an effective class of techniques, but the question is how to use them and for what objectives. Determining that is the core function of INDUCTION DESIGN.

It is also possible to create simulation programs that display the results of behaviour under specified conditions. A gravity simulation could extract the shape of water scattering as it falls. But here as well, a shape-generating algorithm alone is not enough. A condition of INDUCTION DESIGN is that the algorithm solve some kind of problem.

From the Programs of the Natural World

For example, ShinMinamata-MON resembles a tree. But no one needs a program to design a shape that resembles a tree. From ancient times, the shapes of living things have been a treasure house of quotations for architecture. They are often used metaphorically, as in metabolism. But a quoted shape is nothing more than a quotation. A metaphor is only a metaphor, something like literature.

The KeiRiki-1 program used for ShinMinamata-MON utilises a method that is close to how living organisms generate skeletons, making it available for use in architecture. The resemblance in the resulting forms is a superficial effect, due to the fact that the generating principles are similar. There is a decisive difference between programmatic generation and conventional quotations or metaphorical allusions to living things. Form is not imitated, but rather acquired by learning the principles.

But how will architecture become better by learning from organisms? It will become better by acquiring the rationality that organisms possess as

ShinMinamata-MON generated by KeiRiki-1 program (Minamata, 2005)

part of their nature. What is that rationality? It is what allows organisms to acquire forms that meet a certain set of required conditions in a certain environment, with the minimum expenditure of resources and the minimum risk.

The advantages of this rationality go beyond simply using resources without waste. If there is no need to make anything wasteful, the result is just that much more leeway in total resources. That leeway can be invested in making other things better. There is another important point

Forms with this kind of rationality are often beautiful (although not always). In this case, 'beauty' does not mean pretty or lovely. It refers to an overall intuitive judgement that 'this is good'. It is a comprehensive kind of beauty that includes impressions, function and structure, including aspects like amazing, cool, just right although we don't know why, extreme, balanced and harmonious.

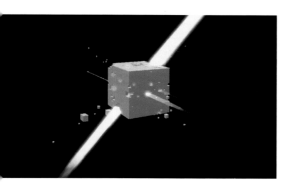

Concept of SUN-GOD CITY program
(1994)

Programs for Artificial Objects

Another advantage is being able to satisfy required conditions in a way that cannot be done manually.

The complex forms generated to satisfy the specified conditions of neo SUNGOD CITY would be impossible to create manually, no matter how hard we try.

In the WEB FRAME project, if we wanted to create a completely different form that satisfied the specified conditions manually, then every time a single location was changed we would have to begin again and satisfy the conditions again, starting from zero. If this had to be repeated with every change, the design would never be completed. To complete the project, a program is needed.

Designs that are impossible with manual sketches and computer graphics become possible with INDUCTION DESIGN.

Eventually – *Concordia res parvae crescunt*

Eventually, programs and sketches, logic and sensibility will come together to complement each other, enabling what neither can accomplish alone. Approaches from both areas will resonate in concert to create beautiful music. By utilising programs, sensibility will be liberated from laborious tasks and allowed to spread its wings to fly more freely. Guided by sensibility and imagination, programs will become able to create beautiful forms. This graceful cooperative relationship has still not been established. But it should be possible. That day will come when the 'versus' in the title of this text changes to 'in concord with'.

WEB FRAME (Tokyo, 2000)

WEB FRAME (Tokyo, 2000)

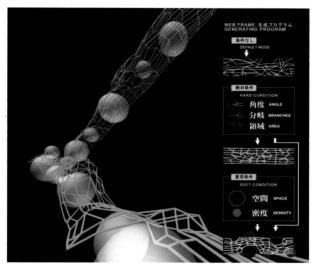

WEB FRAME program

WEB FRAME

WEB FRAME (2000) is probably the first work of architecture in the world with a form that was generated by a computer program that solved a set of required conditions. WEB FRAME took shape below ground at the Iidabashi station of the Oedo subway line. It is a framework with a networked configuration, and was generated from two types of conditions: absolute conditions, which must be satisfied, and the intentions of the designer, which should generally be satisfied. The generative process resembles the growth of a plant, as roots emerge from a seed planted beneath the ground and extend themselves according to the rules of gravity, while searching for water and soft soil.

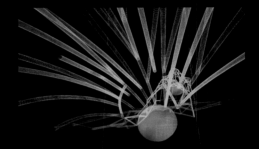

WEB FRAME-II (Tokyo, 2011)   WEB FRAME-II program

WEB FRAME-II

WEB FRAME-II (2011) was designed ten years after WEB FRAME. Curved lines were generated along the surfaces of the rotating ellipsoids, beginning from the end point of the existing WEB FRAME. There was a need for these curved lines to satisfy specified branching conditions. The new program was used for this generative process.
The generative starting point was the end point of the existing section around the rotating ellipsoids. From there, multiple curved lines extend along the ellipsoid surfaces. Physical fabrication and construction restraints limited the number of intersections and their branching angles. It was not enough for the lines to simply trace the ellipsoids. The number and positions of branches and intersections are linked, so that it was not possible to decide them independently, one by one. This program made it possible to simultaneously generate curved lines and intersections that satisfied the limitations.

Flow of KeiRiki-1 program

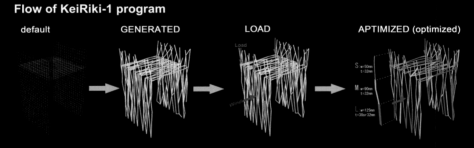

Process of KeiRiki-1 program

KeiRiki-1,-2

The purpose of the KeiRiki series is to generate form and to aptimise (optimise) structure. In addition to creating forms, it ensures that they are rational in terms of structural mechanics, ie that they have the minimum total mass of members required to configure the form. ShinMinamata-MON was created with KeiRiki-1. Members are selected from among three types (SML) according to stress. This is probably the first work of architecture in the world that was designed using a program that generates form at the same time as ensuring structural rationality.

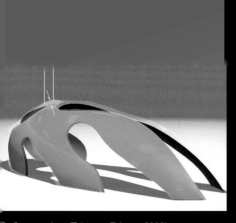

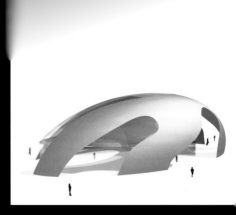

CoCoon project (Tai-tung, Taiwan, 2008)   CoCoon project (Tai-tung, Taiwan, 2008)

KeiRiki-3

As structural members, KeiRiki-1 and KeiRiki-2 use straight materials like beams and tubes. Mechanical rationality is ensured by automatic selection of the sectional size of members according to stress. These programs envision mainly structures with steel frameworks. KeiRiki-3 handles shell structures. It automatically varies the thickness of the shell according to the amount of stress to which it is subjected, as having the minimum total mass of members. Practice of KeiRiki-3 program: to optimise structure varying the thickness of the shell as having the minimum total mass of members.

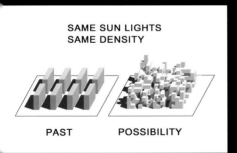

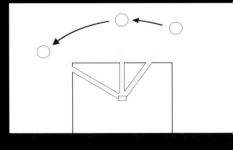

SUN-GOD CITY program (1994)   Concept of SUN-GOD CITY program

SUN-GOD CITY

SUN-GOD CITY was created in 1994. It was the first program in the Induction Cities series. Under the condition that all units receive at least a certain amount of sunlight, the program generates a multi-unit housing complex where

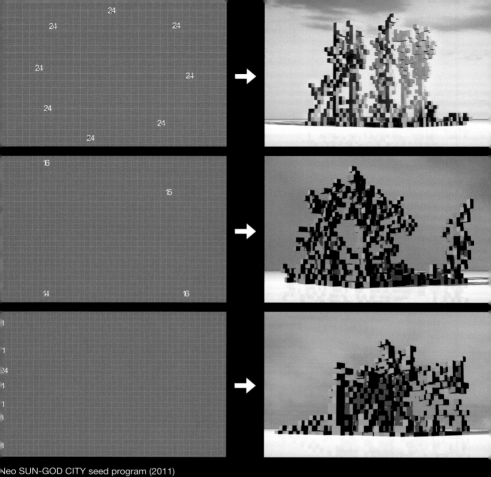

Neo SUN-GOD CITY seed program (2011)

Neo SUN-GOD CITY seed

Neo SUN-GOD CITY seed is the 2011 version of this program, with some new features. In neo SUN-GOD CITY seed, it is possible to 'induce' results to a certain extent by distributing initial units in freely chosen locations before starting. With this method, initial values are freely chosen and the growth of the whole is left up to the program. It is like selecting locations to sow seeds and then watching as plants grow. What kind of flowers will bloom, and where?

MOON GODDESS CITY: More light, or more darkness

Some may say that in Europe, unlike Japan, sunlight is not such an urgent requirement for housing. But think about it. SUN-GOD CITY allows housing to receive light efficiently. When all of the materials used in exterior walls and windows acquire the function of solar cells, then it will become possible to reduce the total amount of energy consumed.

Receiving more light or less light, in other words SUN-GOD CITY or anti-SUN-GOD CITY = MOON GODDESS CITY. That choice depends on whether light is viewed as a resource to be exploited or as a heat load to be avoided. The

K-MUSEUM (Tokyo, 1996)

Shi
(Mi

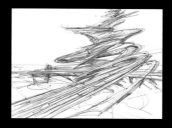

K-Z / history museum project
(Astana, Kazakhstan, 2010)

RIB

ShinMinamata Station
(Minamata, 2004)

WE
(Tok

Sketches: with no going back

Here we see the order of the sketching process. All sketches, not only on this page, a
Once a line is drawn, it is as it is. It is alive. These sketches were not drawn as part of
architectural works with which they appear. They are individually drawn sketches that
relationship to the actual works of architecture. These sketches are not the parents of
from a group of images that developed alongside the design, a network that crosses t
call them brothers, sisters and grandparents, or clones with slightly different genes. T
mutations generated by genetic algorithms. Each of the sketches harbours the possib
Sketches are the seeds of architecture. They may grow to become buds and then fully
not yet time for them to germinate. These seeds are asleep and dreaming. Can we loo
on the other side of the screen?

SELF-ORGANISATIONAL

Stigmergy / Hair-Optimised Detour Networks /
Cellular Automata / Swarm Behaviour

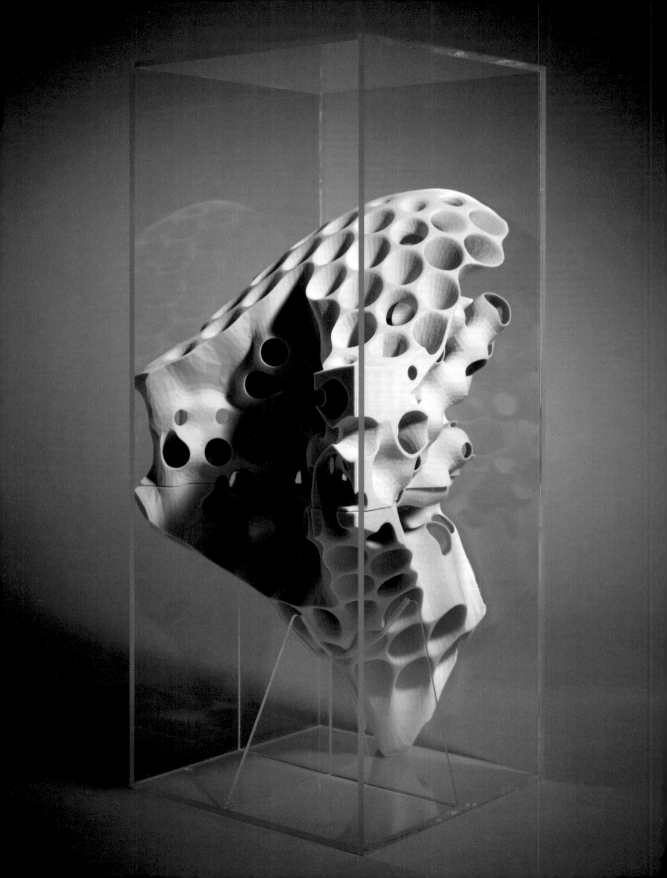

STIGMERGY

AADRL 2007-2008 / TEAM: FARM
Marga Busquets, Sebastien Delagrange, Iain Maxwell

Stigmergic behaviour is demonstrated in eusocial creatures that construct their complex habitations through simple decentralised rule sets. A network of complex relations built up through the use of pheromones creates an adaptive model of agent-based communication. A primary example of stigmeric patterns can be seen in termite ecologies, which are co-constructed through indirect, self-organised and spontaneous coordination structures. Pheromones stimulate individual agents through complex networks of trails that enable local rule-based deposition sequences – one mud deposit attracts others next to it. From an initial procedure set in play through randomness, emergent dynamic patterns construct architectures of great complexity. The architecture is not a product of set blueprint or plan, but an evolving structure that correlates local agency within an evolving environment.

This research project develops its housing-based strategies by creating a playpen of multi-agent systems that are programmed through local subsets of depositional rules. Population-based agency is designed to negotiate the spatial parameters necessary for habitation and circulation. From abstract systems of stigmergic spatial sequencing, housing templates such as Le Corbusier's Unité d'Habitation serve to construct models of corridor-to-unit distributions that are correlated by the agent formations. Long central corridors deployed every third floor give access to bi-level unit types. Through a scenario-based versioning of this template, a complex matrix of programmable distribution patterns emerges as the agents operate as sequential spatial pattern enablers. Beyond organisation this programmable agent-based model implicates embedded construction and production practices that operate within the depositional methods found in 3D printing.

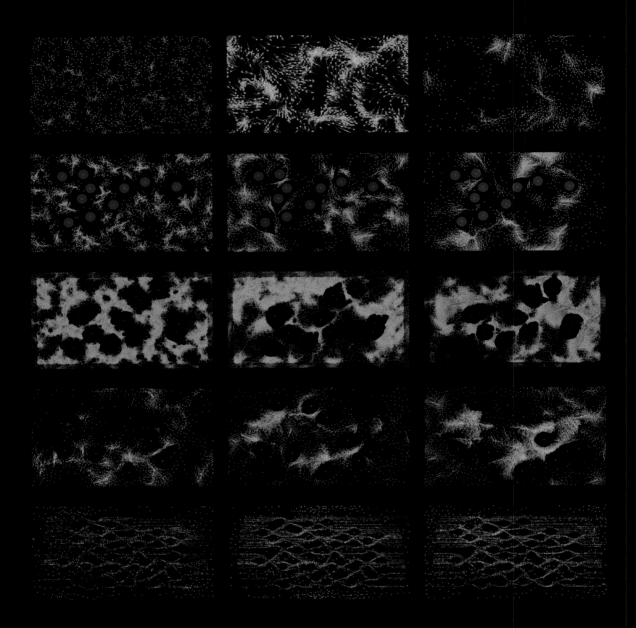

Agent-based systems respond to local conditions, be
it agent-to-agent interactions or agent-to-environment
interactions, to produce emergent organisations.

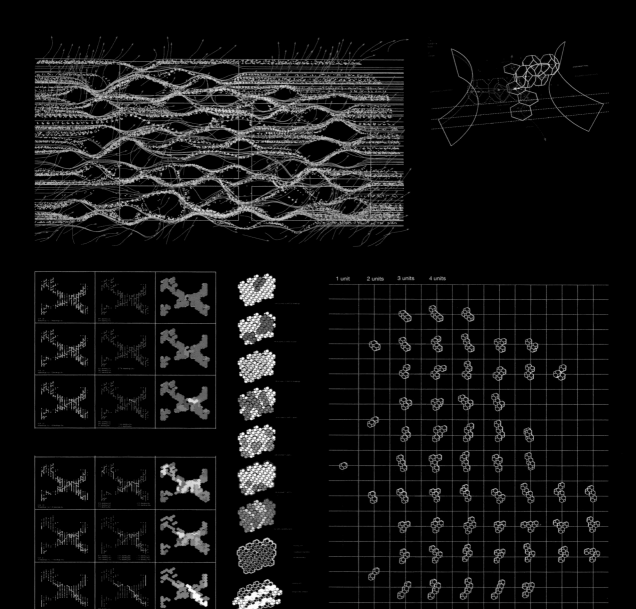

FARM developed an agent-based system premised
on the organisational and spatial strategies of the
Unité d'Habitation to explore the potential of these
systems to proliferate difference between the units.

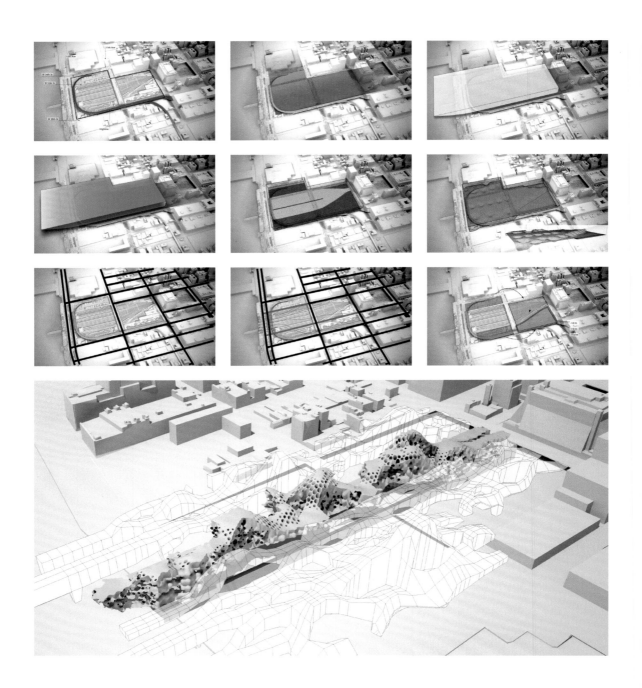

The development of a prototypical strip helped in
developing key programmatic and site responses that
can proliferate throughout the whole site.

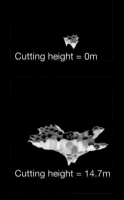 Cutting height = 0m

 Cutting height = 3.2m

 Cutting height = 6.8m

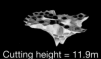 Cutting height = 9.3m

 Cutting height = 11.9m

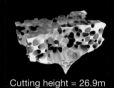 Cutting height = 14.7m

 Cutting height = 16.8m

 Cutting height = 19.5m

 Cutting height = 21.8m

 Cutting height = 24.5m

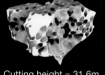 Cutting height = 26.9m

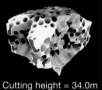 Cutting height = 31.6m

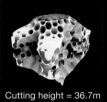 Cutting height = 34.0m

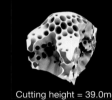 Cutting height = 36.7m

Cutting height = 39.0m

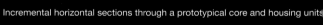 Incremental horizontal sections through a prototypical core and housing units

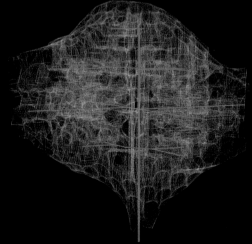

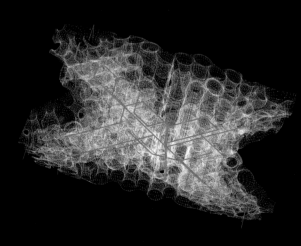

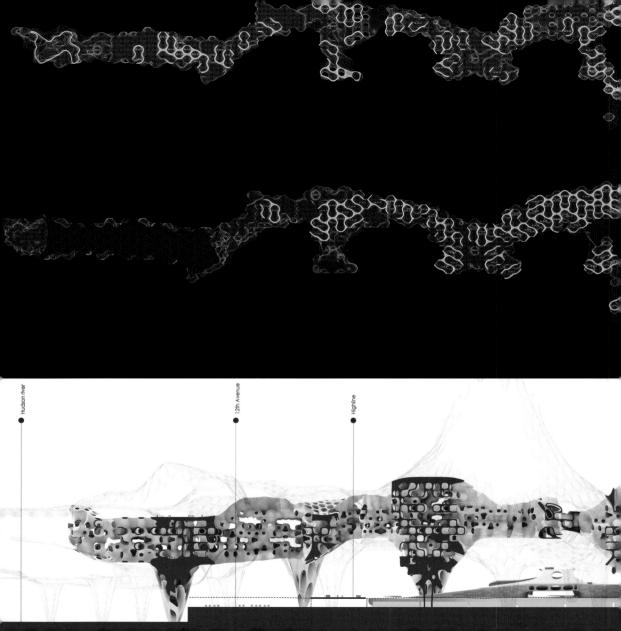

Hudson river

12th Avenue

Highline

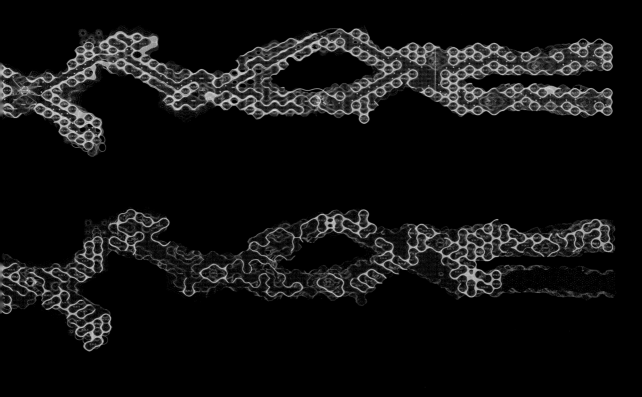

11th Avenue

10th Avenue

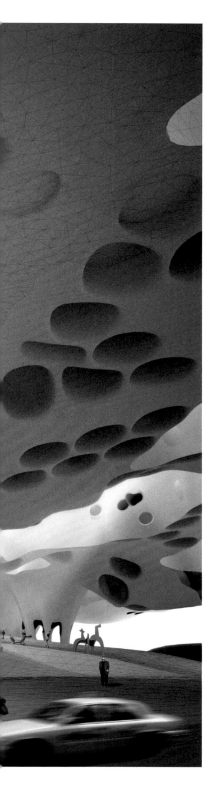

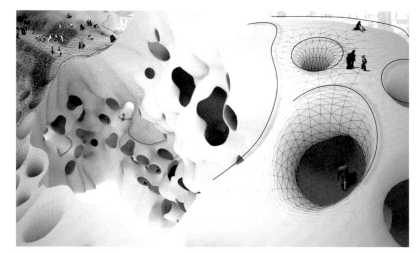

HAIR-OPTIMISED DETOUR NETWORKS

AADRL 2007-2008 / TEAM: SHAMPOOO
Alexander Robles Palacio, Irene Shamma, Konstantinos Grigoriadis, Pavlos Fereos

One of the seminal experiments developed by Frei Otto at the Stuttgart Institute for Lightweight Structures used a radial ring apparatus of slack wet wool strands to articulate computable path networks through cohesive forces. As part of Otto's continued interest in settlement patterns and processes, these models formed an operational design research that speculated on and distinguished between direct path, minimal path and minimising detour networks. Each analogue experiment would self-calculate an optimised solution that was unique though behaviourally equivalent.

This research project took these early analogue setups forward by developing a digital version enabling an operational fibre network distribution to be explored. Using Maya hair dynamics, correlated setups were iterated and developed with a sensitivity to dynamic stability and higher resolution fibre articulation. The digital model afforded design opportunities that went beyond the proof of concept of the wool threads example. It also opened the way for 4D experiments that deployed a fibre network to synthesise circulation, structure and unit distribution. These recursive hair networks allowed for a seamless interface of dynamic line trajectories, creating 3D networks that were spatialised as public connective urban tissues that extended local landscape features within an ecology of interconnected mid-rise tower topologies.

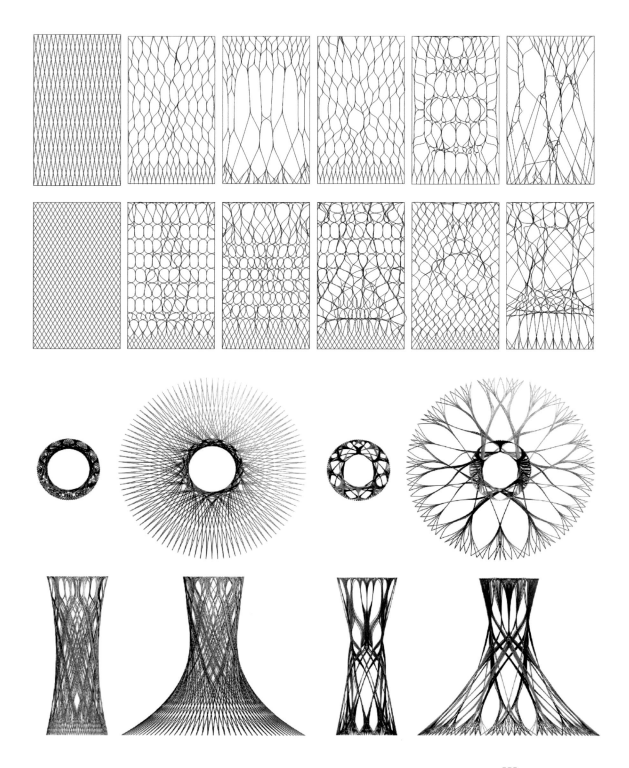

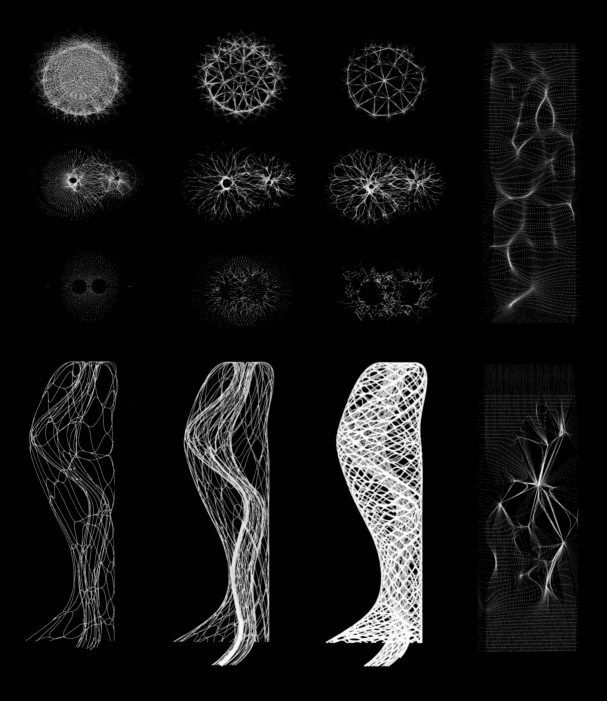

Dynamic hair systems allow for the exploration of ideas of structural bundling and optimised connectivities

On-site infrastructural node locations

Setout for AM pedestrian count

Optimised AM count network

Urban massing scenario 01

Pedestrian count locations/numbers

Network setout for total count

Optimised total count network

Building cluster selection

Setout for PM pedestrian count

Optimised PM count network

Urban massing scenario 02

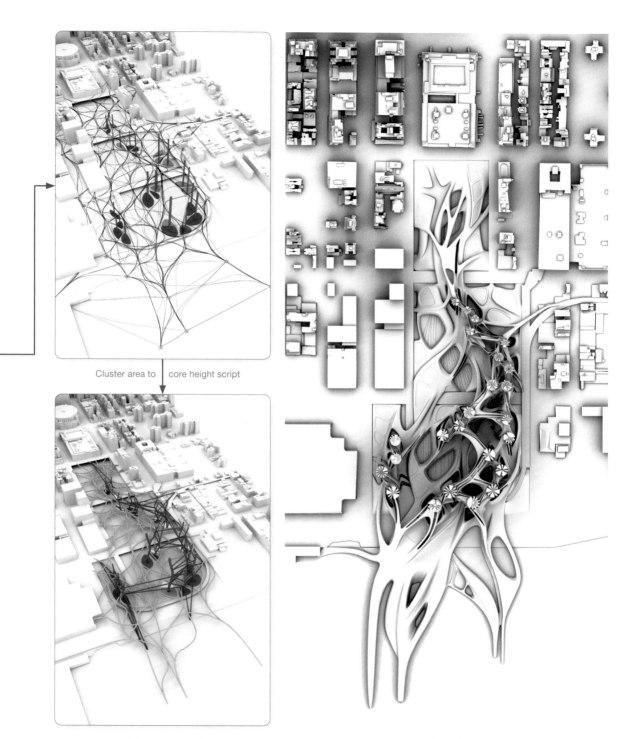

Cluster area to | core height script

Horizontal connection script and
vertical core optimisation

Final massing

235

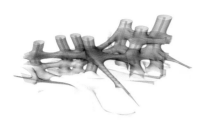  

Number of vertical cores: 7
Number of branches: 15
Housing: 25,594m²
Mixed-use (green space/housing): 49,560m²

Number of vertical cores: 6
Number of branches: 14
Housing: 121,334m²
Mixed use (green space/housing): 219,950m²

Number of vertical cores: 4
Number of branches: 7
Housing: 51,082m²
Mixed use (green space/housing): 121,330m²

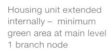

Housing unit with internal balcony – minimum green area at main level
1 branch node

Housing unit extended internally – minimum green area at main level
1 branch node

Housing unit extended internally at main level

(Above)
Prototypical unit organisation showing the complex network of vertical and horizontal connectivity

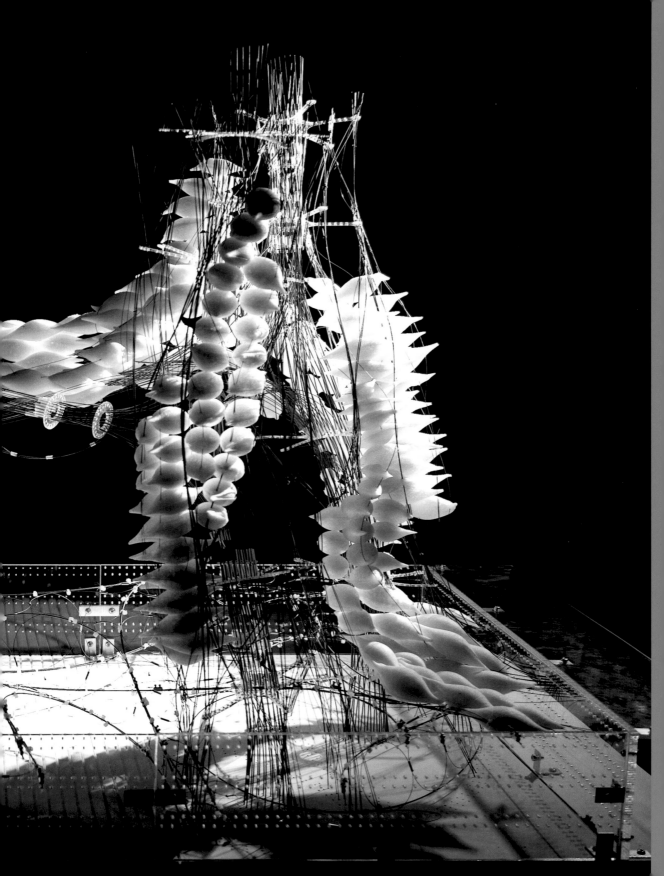

CELLULAR AUTOMATA

AADRL 2006-2007 / TEAM: CHECKMATE
Sofia Daniilidou, Nuno Rosado, Selahattin Tuysuz

Simplified rule-based cellular automata offer a discrete model that consists of a matrix of cells interacting with one of a finite number of states. John Conway's Game of Life is an example of this model of computability, which was discovered by Stanislaw Ulam and John von Neumann in the 1940s and has been studied in mathematics, biology and complexity science. Stephan Wolfram has continued this research in self-replicating systems, formulating a concept for a science of intrinsic randomness that is extensively articulated in his book, *A New Kind of Science.*

This research project attempts to articulate generative parametric features through drivers that include seed location, unit proximities, direction of growth, unit scaling and overall dimension properties of housing density. Using developer-driven programmatic features such as number and type of housing units, a rule-based growth model offered a generative solution space of distribution while maintaining a quantifiable control on the overall housing units deployed within each plan (numbers ranged between 30,000 and 50,000). The use of computation to manage and codify this distribution greatly increased scenario planning options.

Density checks are correlated with controlled depth of floor plate to limit deep nested spaces and introduce porosity within the system. Rather than serving as a proxy grid-based model, the cellular automaton was articulated as a housing type generator whose orthogonal geometry was interfaced with continuous circulatory landscapes at the ground that articulated and codified entries and way-finding.

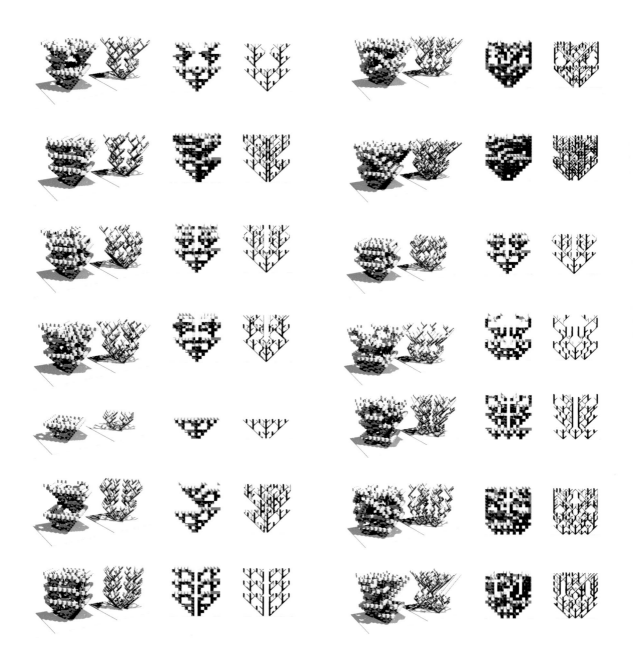

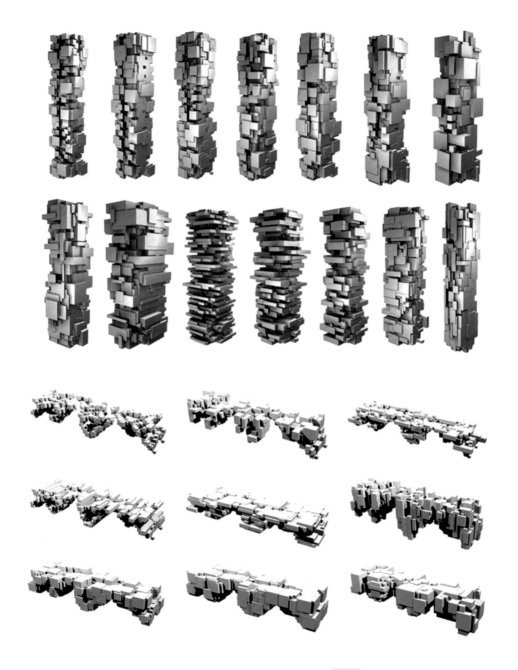

(Above)

Rule-based growth model developed to organise housing units through a parametric model. Parameters included seed location, unit proximities, direction of growth, unit scale and overall dimensions of the housing clusters.

243

Rule-based growth model deployed
on the urban site

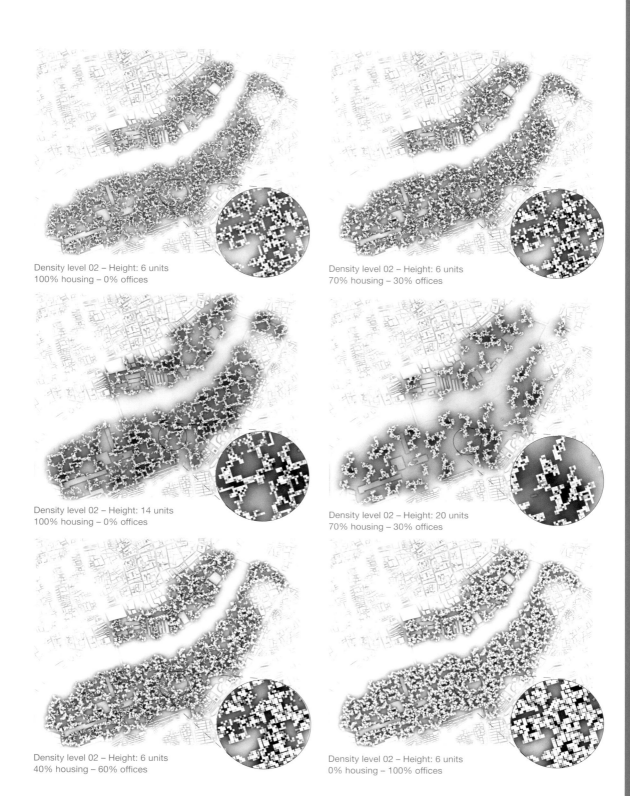

Density level 02 – Height: 6 units
100% housing – 0% offices

Density level 02 – Height: 6 units
70% housing – 30% offices

Density level 02 – Height: 14 units
100% housing – 0% offices

Density level 02 – Height: 20 units
70% housing – 30% offices

Density level 02 – Height: 6 units
40% housing – 60% offices

Density level 02 – Height: 6 units
0% housing – 100% offices

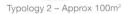

Typology 1 – Approx 50m²   Typology 2 – Approx 100m²

Typology 3 – Approx 150m²   Typology 4 – Approx 200m²

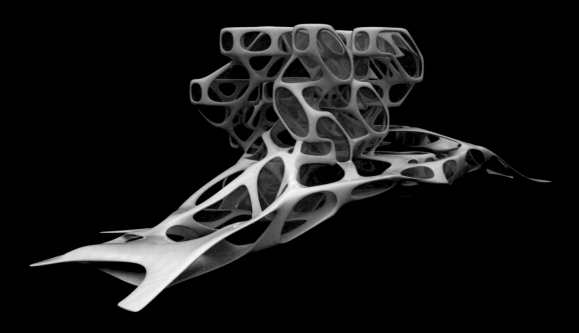

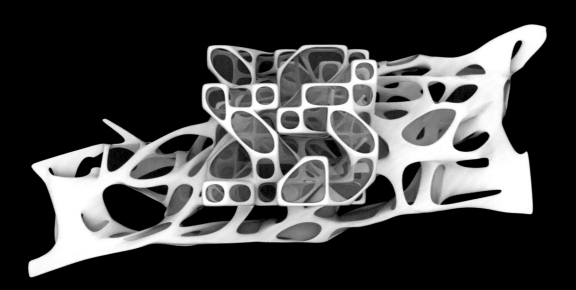

Geometric articulation of the housing clusters
based on creating continuous structural members
and introducing porosity

SWARM

AADRL 2005-2006 / TEAM: CXN-REACTION
Sangyup Lee, Luis Fraguada, Nantapon Jungrun, Shu-Hao Wu

Swarm systems exhibit emergent collective behaviours through local rule-based interactions. Population-dependent swarm organisations exhibit migratory behaviours (such as flocking and herding) that are commonly found in social animals. These self-organised systems can be classified as natural or artificial, interacting and exhibiting features that are intelligent and task-oriented. Rather than programming explicit command and control algorithms, swarm systems evolve characteristics through local and global signalling. Contemporary research in artificial intelligence and robotics explores swarm systems to forecast and construct emergent relationships with the environment.

This research project explores how multi-agent systems could be deployed to create path systems that would augment existing infrastructural networks. Through the creation of generative path-based setups, agent organisations construct relational models that negotiate the existing ground within the urban fabric – such as vehicular routes, pedestrian routes, train and tube access points – and embed these systems as generative drivers for building networks and density distribution. In addition, generative techniques within these swarm setups allow unit clusters to be developed within the trajectories. The units themselves are further detailed to operate as collapsible systems. Flexibility is enabled through temporal and evolving features, as individual units are designed to flat-collapse, allowing for a pop logic that can offer multifunctional public spaces and support event-based programming.

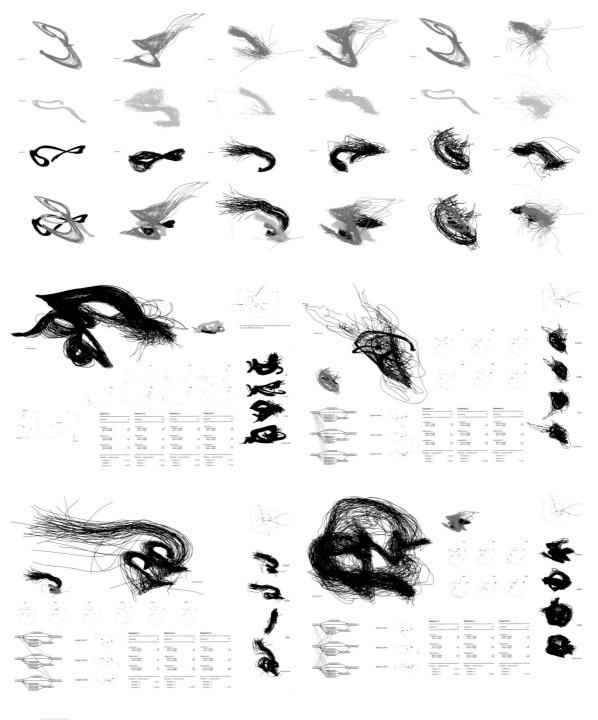

(Above)

Pattern formations produced by tracking the
collective movement of agent-based systems

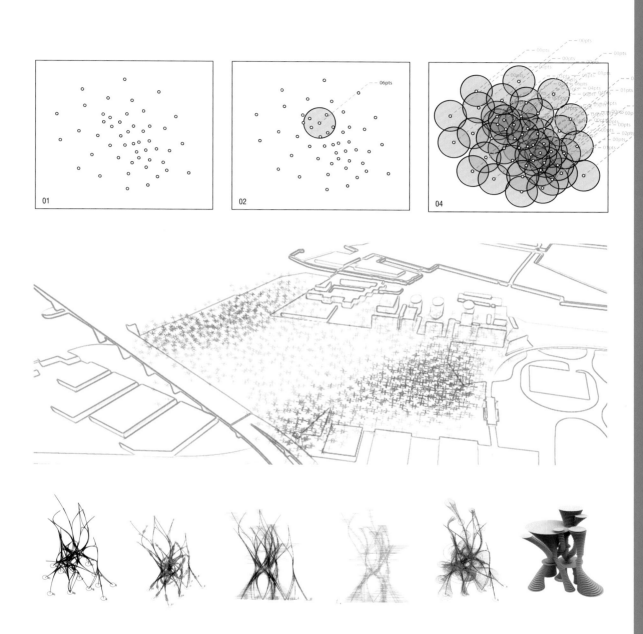

01

02

04

06pts

(Above)

Agent-based tower core development. Here,
agents are programmed to respond to particular
structural specifications.

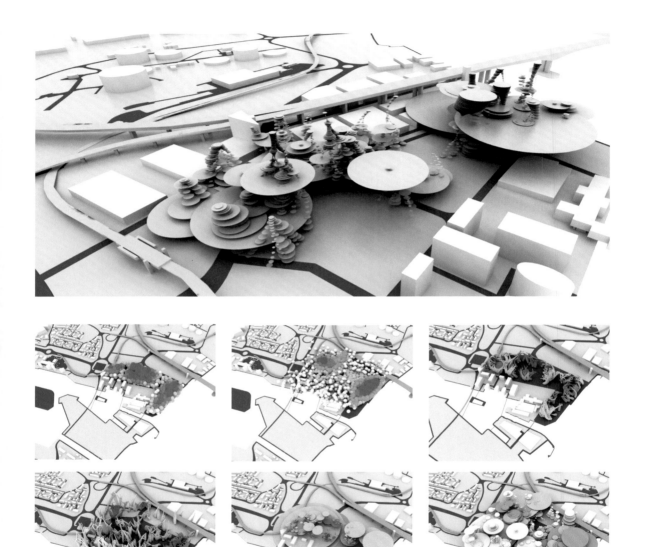

(Above and Opposite)

By integrating the agent-based organisational
strategy and the core generation, multiple site-
specific applications can be achieved.

252

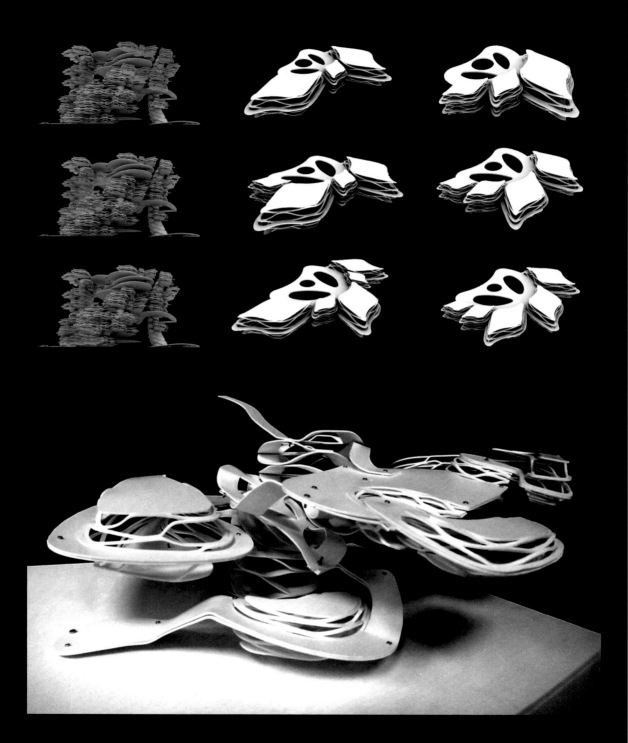

degree 019 degree 039 degree 058 degree 078 degree 097 degree 019 degree 039 degree 058 degree 078 degree 097

degree 135 degree 155 degree 175 degree 194 degree 213 degree 135 degree 155 degree 175 degree 194 degree 213

degree 252 degree 272 degree 291 degree 310 degree 329 degree 252 degree 272 degree 291 degree 310 degree 329

degree 019 degree 039 degree 058 degree 078 degree 097 degree 019 degree 039 degree 058 degree 078 degree 097

degree 135 degree 155 degree 175 degree 194 degree 213 degree 135 degree 155 degree 175 degree 194 degree 213

degree 252 degree 272 degree 291 degree 310 degree 329 degree 252 degree 272 degree 291 degree 310 degree 329

(Above)

The tower clusters are generatively designed through an integration of curvature analysis, major structural members and a combination of convex and concave structural skins.

254

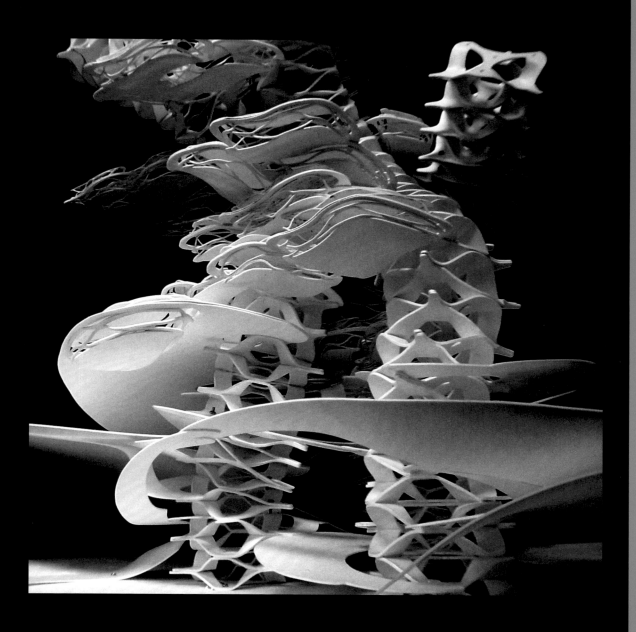

The recursive line generation process creates a dynamic negotiation and relation between the curved vertical paths and clusters in the urban field.

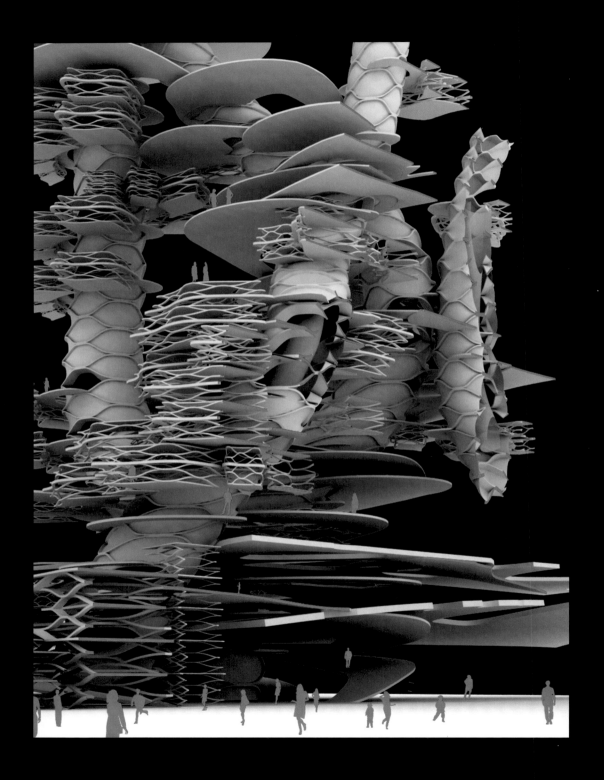

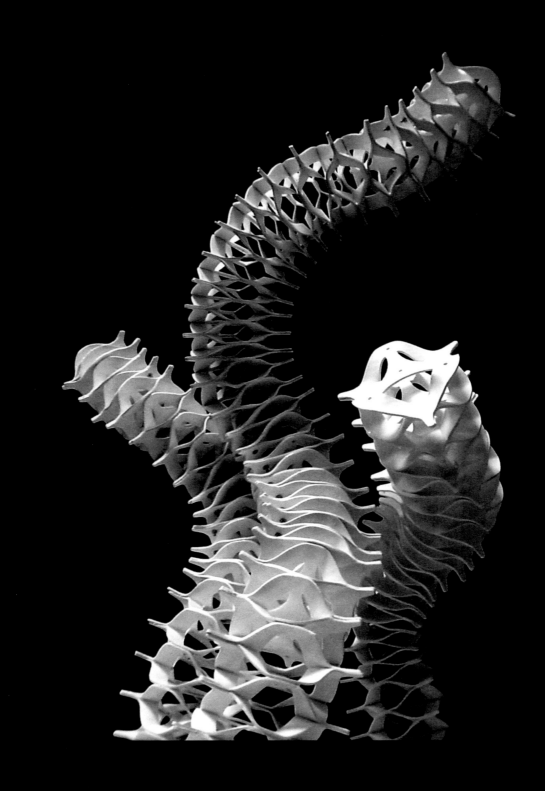

CELLULAR AUTOMATA

AADRL 2006-2007 / TEAM: JUNGLE
Yiota Goutsou, Diego Perez and Rob Stuart-Smith

Cellular automata (CA), as described in Stephen Wolfram's *A New Kind of Science*, construct a ruled-based algorithmic model of nearest neighbour conditions. Evolving through time, cells exhibit binary states – on or off – as one-dimensional, elementary automata that play out 256 possible rules. Constructing an abstract array of cells that are relational to neighbouring conditions gave an opportunity to use local associative rules to develop a model of generative urbanism that was able to incorporate variable densities over time. Enabling a quantifiable model of cell-to-cell deployment allowed iterative versions of complex programming to be understood as three-dimensional spatial subsets.

The research project was developed through scenario planning focused on Shanghai's accelerated projections of pre- and post-2010 expo development. This approach necessitated computational models that are adaptive to change. Typically urban organisations of this magnitude are rendered as generic and stratified tower-based distributions within the city. Here, by contrast, systemic deployment strategies computed through CA were used to generate a diverse typology of landscape urbanism. This alternative high-density model constructed a framework for developing the city as a complex three-dimensional horizontal spatial field, thereby enabling an integrated and dynamic programming plan for the proposed cultural district.

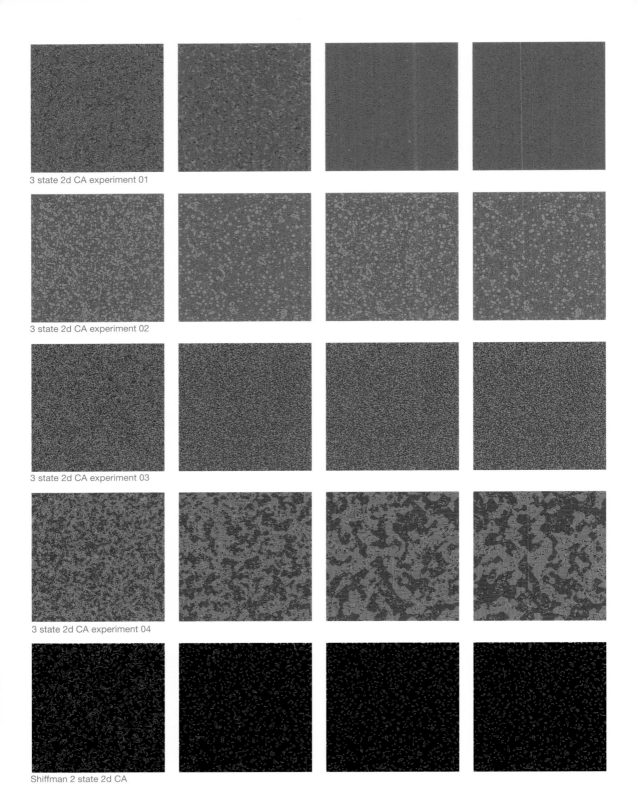

3 state 2d CA experiment 01

3 state 2d CA experiment 02

3 state 2d CA experiment 03

3 state 2d CA experiment 04

Shiffman 2 state 2d CA

(Above)

Various studies exploring various
parameters and relationships afforder
by Cellular Automata.

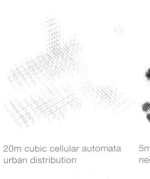

20m cubic cellular automata urban distribution

5m cubic cellular automata neighbourhood organisation

5m cubic cellular automata neighbourhood organisation programmed

Neighbourhood scale unit-housing distribution and circulation-collective space

Seeding locations and Swarm Pointgrid definition

Seeding locations and Swarm Pointgrid interface with adjacent structures

Individual trajectories seeded from collective space follow targets in an agent logic

Unit-space swarm embedded in the environment created by the trajectories

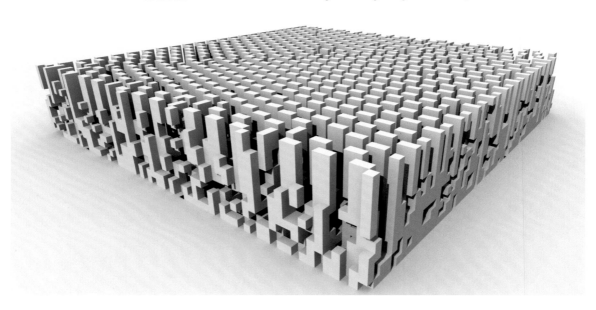

(Above)

Polyscalar organisation of housing units within the urban blocks using neighbourhood logics

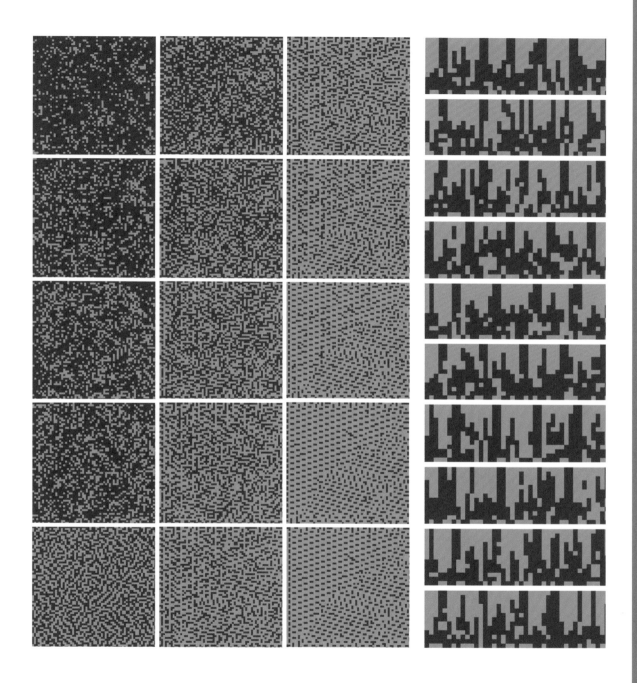

(Above)

Plans and sections of studies in density and occupancy values. The ability of the cellular automata to mitigate between built and unbuilt space is critical in developing an urban-scale organisation.

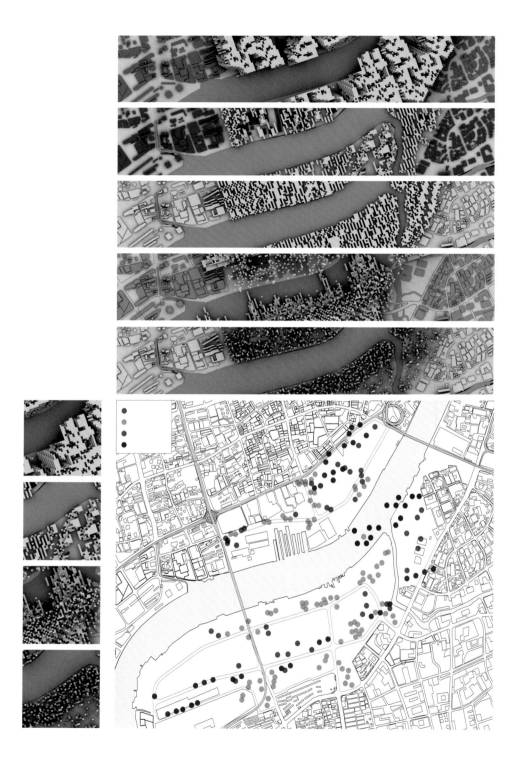

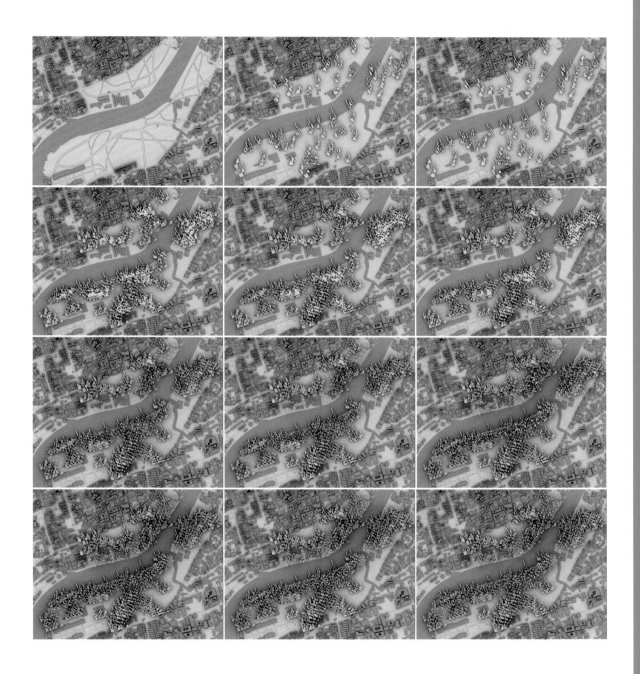

(Above)

The dynamic growth model is instigated by a
seed logic, negotiating existing urban conditions.

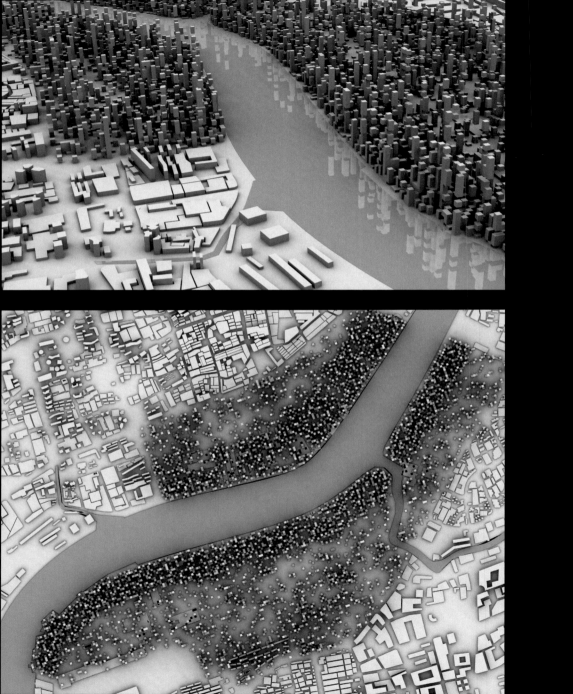

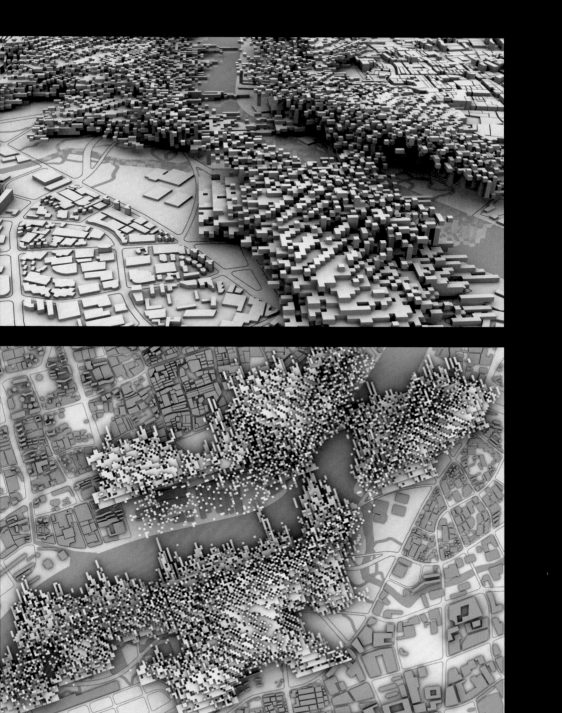

RETURNING TO (STRANGE) OBJECTS

David Ruy

Since the mid-1990s, the discourse of architecture has increasingly moved away from the architectural object towards the architectural field.[1] The architectural object, with all its vicissitudes, has lost its uncanny appeal, and recent work is more often than not circumscribed by the mental image of an underlying global network of relations that is deep, dynamic and somehow more real than the object itself. A manic effort to interface with this network now seems to be the ordinary response to the anxiety that architecture is perpetually on the verge of being left behind by a constantly accelerating and interconnected world.[2] In retrospect, popular paranoid fantasies such as The Matrix and The Wizard of Oz were reasonable depictions of the deep suspicion that reality is not what it seems. We celebrate the hero who sees the network for what it is and share a common desire to discover the secret reality behind the veil of appearances.

Architects today approach architecture as a by-product of socio-cultural milieus, as a conditional component of technocratic systems and networks, or even as the provisional end calculation of measurable parameters within the literal or construed environment. Even those who are primarily interested in form and aesthetics have had a peculiar tendency to search for external parameters and constraints with which to couch the legitimacy of the architectural object in relation to a projected external milieu. Like Janus, the transition from object to field has more than one face, but shares a single body moving towards the virtual.

These days, it seems perfectly natural to think of architecture as a consequence of its context, however that is defined. The coordination of external forces (sometimes measurable, sometimes hypothetical and sometimes downright imaginary) is understood to be a central concern of contemporary practice. Those who love architecture remain ambivalent about this state of affairs. On the one hand, there is an earnest – clearly sincere – desire for engagement in the conditions of the world, which has resulted in a new emphasis on the application of architectural intelligence to a wider field, at the expense of the architectural object. On the other hand, expanding architecture's field of operations has made the authority of the architect more vague, ambiguous. What exactly is meant by 'architectural intelligence' – and whether or not such intelligence is actually needed in a world replete with so many other forms of expertise – is open to debate. The mysterious power of the architectural object is rarely spoken of today without embarrassment, but still the loss of architecture's significance and influence seems to be an ever-present source of lament.[3]

If we take the longer view of architectural history, however, this shift from object to field seems odd, because architecture has consistently been presented as a thing in the world, largely independent of external influence.[4] This shift from architecture as a practice of embodiment (of values, idealities or of the universe itself) to architecture as a practice of coordination is a peculiar feature of the modernist legacy.[5] The contingency of architecture on external conditions seems to have become a default assumption, while considerations of the architectural object itself, independent of its context, now seem esoteric. The prevailing desire is for architecture to avoid being insular, to form larger networks of relations, and, in general, to be more engaged in the conditions of the contemporary world.[6]

It is worth studying this shift in more detail because there are some profoundly problematic assumptions in theories of the architectural field from an ontological point of view.[7] But perhaps more tangibly, this shift has unexpectedly reshaped expectations concerning the authority of architects and the power of architecture. Both of these concerns (and they are surprisingly linked) need to be addressed in order to assess the current state of the discipline and develop an alternative to the gloomy forecasts for the practice. But before this, it is necessary to mention the relation between nature and architecture, as it is the most urgent contextual concern today – although it often plays a subsidiary role to the expression of cultural values and the integration of architecture with urban fabrics. Nature is the ultimate milieu, the all-encompassing field of material phenomena. In this respect, the examination of architecture's move from object to field is also an examination of architecture's move towards nature, one that will perhaps culminate in the involuted erasure of the architecture/ nature divide.[8]

It is important to consider this move from the two standpoints of architecture as a discipline and architecture as a practice. The problem of nature is deeply embedded in the history of the discipline, and nature has often been a source of architectural innovation. Starting in antiquity, accelerating through the Renaissance, and going underground in modernism,[9] we see architecture looking to nature for aesthetic inspiration, formal models and proportional constraints. Even in instances where architecture deliberately avoided nature in favour of developing an explicitly rational theory, nature was always the sublime 'other' bracketed by such rationality. Geometry and proportion, form and function, and structure and ornament are some of the major disciplinary territories that have revolved around the problem of nature. Nature has ceased to be a mythical source of design inspiration, but continues to be mined for architectural knowledge with investigations into such things as nonlinear dynamics, self-organising systems, genetic algorithms and biological morphogenesis. While many of these investigations have their origins in science, they are still aimed at the design of significant architectural objects, and are rarefied experiments by a relatively small group of experts who are primarily interested in the discipline, and not the practice, of architecture.

By contrast architectural practice, until recently, revolved around the endless logistics of the building itself, and had little concern for nature beyond the basic pragmatic issues of manipulating the ground, keeping out the rain, or making sure the interior has enough light and air. This has changed dramatically. Faced with the spectre of global warming and environmental collapse, architectural practice has been forced to contend with the even more impossible logistics of the environment itself. To cope with such demands, it has necessarily embraced ecological theory. This theory, and its extension into the ethics of architecture's material practice, outline the imperative of sustainable practice today, largely replacing the disciplinary investigations of nature that were dominant in the academy prior to modernism.

Though the words 'nature' and 'ecology' seem interchangeable in contemporary discourse, it is important to make a critical distinction between them, insofar as ecological thought involves a very particular way of understanding nature. Ecological theories predominantly project systems that describe a field of discernible relations,[10] the individual constituents of a given ecological system being of less concern than the relations themselves[11] – so much so that even the constituents of an ecological system are themselves theorised as ecological systems in their own right (the internal ecological network of a particular human body, for example). Nature, seen through the ecological telescope, is a grand network of relations where the appearances of objects (rock, tree, frog, cloud, human, etc) are superficial, and the network of relations is understood to be the deeper reality. The grand finale of architecture's movement from object to field may very well be the collapse of the architectural object into a field of relations that then dissolves into a general ecological field of relations that constitutes the world. And thus, architectural practice unintentionally becomes subsumed into ecological practice. Though it is difficult (and perhaps unethical) to contest the perceived sustainable imperative of the early twenty-first century, there is cause for hesitation before the prospect of architecture's disappearance as it becomes an entirely new form of practice based on ecological thought.

Sustainable politics have become forceful and monolithic in recent years, resulting in new codes and protocols for all material practices, including architecture. But what exactly is being sustained in sustainable practice? One aim is generally understood to be the equilibrium of human material practices in relation to nature. This desired equilibrium is an extension of the widely held belief that nature itself would be in balance, except that human beings keep throwing it out of sync. Nature is seen as some kind of grand calibrated clock that requires thoughtful maintenance by enlightened caretakers to keep it running.[12] To put it more bluntly, nature is good while humans are bad. Laws and protocols are seen as necessary in order to promote good behaviour, because good behaviour apparently does not come 'naturally'.

As an alternative to the caretaker model, perhaps the darker scenario from the standpoint of individual liberty is the idea that the world is a single ecological system or network. In such a case, maintaining the equilibrium requires everyone to play their part in the machine – in other words, to be a cog within the clockwork of nature. You cannot break the machine

271

if you are part of the machine;[13] and like a cog in a clock, you cannot change your relationship to the system. This is politically problematic. In response, recent ecologists have made a concerted effort to theorise emergence and change in the hypothetical systems of nature, incorporating such principles as feedback and nonlinearity to face what appears to be an obvious need to address change, novelty and a politically necessary condition of indeterminacy in human action. However, these theories are still problematic, and the sentimental, mythological image of nature in equilibrium continues to be a dominant cultural mindset.

Yet all observable evidence indicates that nature is not so much in equilibrium as in a perpetual state of change. Because nature itself is not stable, the stability sought by sustainable practice has to be forced – an artificial equilibrium constructed with an eye to the maximum benefit for human occupation over the long term. Once you eliminate the sentimentality associated with the mythological image of nature, the aesthetics of gentle stewardship and bias against artifice evaporate too, leaving nothing but impossible questions regarding what exactly constitutes the maximum benefit for human occupation, and the even more difficult questions regarding how to construct and enforce such conditions.

The flux and instability of nature is an astonishingly problematic condition because ecological system theories, despite their many successes, have never been able to fully account for change in networks of relations. In this regard the philosopher Graham Harman observed that 'relationism' leaves no room for conditions in excess of those relations (by its own definition) and therefore provides an inadequate account of how change comes about.[14]

To quote Harman:

'All of these positions overmine the object, treating it as a useless substratum easily replaced by direct manifestations. Though we claim to be speaking of objects, they are really nothing more than palpable qualities, effects on other things, or images in the mind. But there are problems with relationising the world in this way. For one thing, if the entire world were exhausted by its current givenness, there is no reason why anything would alter. That is to say, if there is no difference between the I who is what he is and the I who is accidentally wearing a yellow shirt from India at this moment, then there is no reason why my situation should ever change. An injustice is thereby done to the future.'[15]

Having fired off this salvo, Harman goes on to advocate a greater focus on the development of an ontology of objects – and objects alone, abandoning ontologies of the mind in relation to the world (eg Husserl's phenomenology, among many others). In this new object-oriented ontology, the human being is a being like any other (an object like any other). The provocative extension of this line of thought is the necessary conclusion that objects withdraw from one another. To explain this initially cryptic idea, it is necessary to be briefly reminded of the problem previously pointed out concerning relationism. If an object could be completely exhausted by a summation of its relations, there could be no way for the object to change its relations. Therefore, there must always be something about the object that is in excess of its qualities and relations: there must always be some 'dark nucleus of objects' (as Harman puts it) that is withdrawn from access by other objects. The being of the object is always more than its relations. By extension, the architectural object is always more than any summation of its internal relations. Like any other object, it always has that 'dark nucleus' that cannot be exhausted by a list of its qualities. Going further, this object-oriented ontology necessarily throws the being of any relational model into doubt. Though networks and fields may continue to be eminently useful models of understanding, they carry with them a flawed ontology. In the end, the field is not real in the same sense that the object is. While none of this suggests that all field models should be abandoned, we can conclude that they cannot be legitimised as a deeper way of understanding the thing in front of us. We may continue to incorporate field models for their usefulness, but should never forget that they are artificial constructions.

Perhaps the most astonishing aspect of this object-oriented ontology is that two terms that have been used liberally throughout this discussion – 'nature' and 'world' – are themselves not real objects. What we refer to as 'nature' or the 'world' may be comprised of real objects (this frog, that tree, this river, that building) but they themselves – the hypothetical super-containers of all these things – are not actually real objects (but false unities). In this respect, Harman's object-oriented ontology opens up a unique possibility of rethinking the peculiar problems associated with the problem of nature. A return to the object would have to be understood as a turning away from a mythological or sentimental understanding of nature and a turn towards the particularities and the essential strangeness of the objects themselves. In the same way that Timothy Morton sees the need to investigate the possibilities of an 'ecology without nature',[16] we may also want to investigate the possibilities of an architecture without nature.

It must be emphasised that this does not mean abandoning all interest in current environmental problems. Quite the reverse, in fact: abandoning idealisms of nature would leave us with a greater interest and focus on the objects of nature themselves. We would start to think that the particularities of the objects are not meaningless accidental features, but imbricated with their being. There would also be a productive indeterminacy in our consideration of objects, because we would recognise that objects are always to some degree withdrawn and strange.

While thinking about this object-oriented ontology, it is fascinating to finally consider how the architect is to be understood. Assuming, for a moment, that the architectural object is unified as an object, what exactly is the architect doing in making such objects? Remember that the architect is also an object in this ontology – not an enlightened mind outside of the world of objects giving form to formless matter. The making process is something very different in this scenario than what we're used to – perhaps 'making' is not even the appropriate word anymore.

It is impossible to do full justice here to this emerging movement in contemporary philosophy, but I hope to indicate possible alternatives to the idea of architecture as a field of relations, and describe some initial speculations about what it might mean to return the focus to the architectural object itself. A return to the architectural object as a disciplinary priority cannot be a nostalgic return to pre-modern academic preoccupations with character, propriety and the idealities of compositional balance. Nor is this return to the object a simple return to figuration and detached massing. 'Object' here should not be understood in a literal sense. Much of what has been learned through modernism is now invaluable, or at the very least, indispensable to architecture's possibility of being in the world. Even if the world is not a real object, the projected world remains the locus of contested values still essential to survival. A call to return to the architectural object, strange as it may be, is not a call to rewind the tape of history, but instead a plea to avoid what might be unproductive dead ends in current directions. A renewed focus on the architectural object itself should not fetishise the discipline's history, but instead be a recognition of what is withdrawn and strange in the architectural object's interaction with other objects (including the human being).

A return to the architectural object would refocus interest on the thing itself. This may seem obvious enough, but it is not so obvious given architecture's tendency to illustrate theory through practice. In other words, architecture has a tendency to consider theory as somehow being more important (or real) than the project through which it manifests itself. A return to the architectural object suggests that theory is always retroactive to the architectural object, and is itself another form of making. Architectural theory would always have to be retroactive, because if indeed the architectural object is real there will always be something about the architectural object that will be withdrawn from theoretical access. However, as a form of making in its own right, the production of architectural theory may be less constrained and more creative than it has been of late. By relaxing hang-ups over primacy, the interaction between the architectural theorist and the architect might possibly be more promiscuous and produce more offspring.

For the maker of the architectural object, the idea of the muse continues to be absurd, but muse-like ideas of intuition or phenomenal sensitivity persist because creativity continues to be perplexing and mysterious. In the language of object-oriented ontology, the strange, withdrawn interaction between objects sometimes brings forth a new object. However, the new object is not a simple Boolean operation of adding objects together. New objects come into existence through a strange interaction between objects where new relationships are formed but without the qualities of the originals being exhausted. To apply it to the problem at hand, in the interaction between the architect, as object, and other objects (be it a place, a material, a piece of software, or a preexisting theory) an architectural object sometimes comes into existence. What exactly happened in this interaction will be occluded. In other words, a successful object-making event cannot be completely encapsulated by a methodology that might repeat the success. Good architects have known this for a very long time. Perhaps object-oriented ontology might simultaneously open radical territories while rediscovering or affirming some very old insights of the architectural discipline.

It would also have to be recognised that there is a lot more to craft than is generally thought. As a non-theoretical interaction between the maker (as object) and the various objects of the making process, 'craft' is the ambiguous word that has, in the past, identified the unique expertise of the maker. Here, the authority of the maker does not originate out of a certification according to generalised standards, but from the strange individuality of the maker. There is something about the master craftsman, as object, that cannot be reproduced or reduced to a set of qualities.

If the architect, as object, were to be reduced to a set of qualities, the authority of individual instances would naturally be undermined. In that case, in fact, why not go ahead and implant all of those qualities into an artificial intelligence and have as many architects as we want? Is it just a technical problem of programming the artificial intelligence? Or, more likely, is it a fundamental problem of never being able to completely encapsulate the architect (again, as object) through a list of the architect's qualities? As difficult as it may be to accept, the individuality of the architect, on a deep ontological level, needs to be recognised in order to claim more authority, because then every maker is one of a kind.

Finally, with regard to the power of architecture, the manifold meanings and conflicting interpretations of the architectural object need to be recognised not as undesirable misinterpretations and accidents of perception but as strange but real interactions between objects. Because the interactions between objects are irreducible to a finite set of discernible relationships, the interactions are unpredictable and strange.
The multiplication of signification through the interaction of strange objects again highlights what may be considered a very old thought – that the mysterious power of the architectural object persists beyond individual readings or individual interpretations.

The undermining of the architect's authority and the diminishing of architecture's power through the dissolution of the architectural object into a field of discernible relations seem to be an accidental, self-inflicted wound. Through the sincere desire to be more in the world, architecture may have accidentally turned away from the very real objects right in front of it, including the architectural object itself. The full implications of this nascent ontology are yet to be considered. At the very least, however, there appear to be strong reasons for considering the significance of the architectural object once again, and to reflect upon its strangeness.

1   Stan Allen's concept of the 'field condition' was a seminal moment in this regard. See Stan Allen, *Points + Lines, Diagrams and Projects for the City* (New York: Princeton Architectural Press, 1999), 92-103.

2   See Sanford Kwinter, 'Virtual City, or the Wiring and Waning of the World', *Assemblage* (April, 1996), 86-101.

3   At recent lectures Rem Koolhaas has been regretfully pointing out that architects never feature on the cover of *Time* magazine anymore. The implication is that to have more authority and influence, architects need even more engagement with the contemporary situation. But it is hard not to wonder if the reverse might be necessary, since this is already the prevailing tendency and the architect's predicament seems to be getting even worse.

4   Without a doubt, there has always been a degree of contextualism in architecture. But I would like to make a distinction here between pre-modern practices with those modernist methodologies where architectural form was determined and constrained through rational measuring of external factors (zoning envelope becoming architectural form, for example). However, this is a general tendency. Many exceptions can be identified.

5   Throughout the past two decades Sanford Kwinter has made an invaluable contribution in documenting and critiquing the modernist legacy in contemporary urbanism and architecture. His speculative theories have had a profound influence on the current generation of architects. See Sanford Kwinter, *Far from Equilibrium* (New York: Actar, 2008).

6   The most well-known and explicit exception to this rule would be Peter Eisenman. Throughout his career, Eisenman has emphasised the autonomy of the architectural discipline.

7   See Levi Bryant, Graham Harman, Nick Srnicek, *The Speculative Turn* (Melbourne: re.press, 2011).

8   See Jeffrey Kipnis, '/Twisting the Separatrix/', *Assemblage* (April, 1991), 30-61.

9   Detlef Mertins has written extensively on the lesser known organicist strains of early modernism. See Detlef Mertins, 'Bioconstructivisms,' in *Machining Architecture*, ed Lars Spuybroek (London: Thames & Hudson, 2004), 360-69.

10   This is not a stable observation. Timothy Morton and others working in the field of ecocriticism are actively contesting the intellectual frameworks of ecological theory. Ecological theory will likely undergo radical transformations in the twenty-first century.

11   An extreme version of this is the systems dynamic model of Jay Forrester constructed in 1970 while a member of the Club of Rome, a think-tank currently based in Winterthur, Switzerland. The attempt was to model the entire world as a single interrelated system. His model predicted environmental collapse in the early twenty-first century.

12   See Daniel Botkin, *Discordant Harmonies* (New York: Oxford University Press, 1990).

13   See Adam Curtis, 'All Watched Over by Machines of Loving Grace, part 2: The Use and Abuse of Vegetable Concepts', DVD (BBC, 2011).

14   Graham Harman concisely presents a critique of prevailing ontologies (relational ontologies and materialism is of particular interest here) through his denial of 'undermining' and 'overmining' philosophies. See Graham Harman, *The Quadruple Object* (Alresford: Zero Books, 2011), 7-19.

15   Ibid, 12-13.

16   See Timothy Morton, *Ecology without Nature* (Cambridge MA: Harvard University Press, 2007).

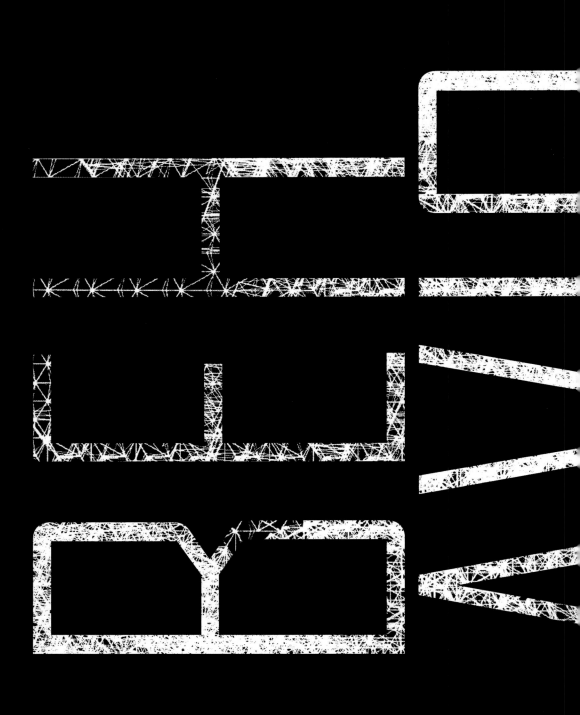

BEHAVIOURAL

Surface Tension / Hele–Shaw Cell / Siphonophora
Cymatics / Soft Cast

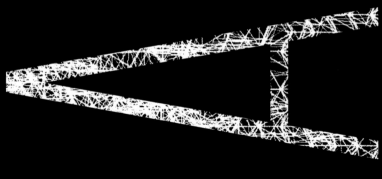
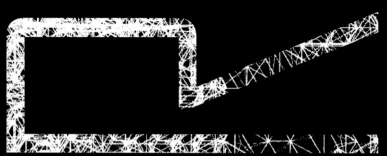

SURFACE TENSION: HELE-SHAW CELL

AADRL 2006-2007 / TEAM: EGLOO
Pankaj Chaudhary, Jwalant Mahadevwala, Mateo Riestra, Drago Vodanovic

Behavioural models have the capacity to organise matter dynamically through internal restructuring as a response to environmental stimulus. Hele-Shaw cell models examine properties of cohesive forces of surface tension where viscous fluids are placed between two pressurised parallel plates demonstrating properties of connective micro-flows. This flow-based connective structuring allows a systemic understanding of fluid networks to emerge as each nodal deposition reconfigures the overall network as one continuous flow-field. Hele-Shaw cell experiments open the way for a form of digital materialism, as the analogue computational attributes can be simulated through the interdependence of nodal and boundary thresholds.

This research project sets out to harness the connective behavioural attributes found within this signal and boundary model by programming algorithmically a multi-nodal framework that operates through evaluation frequency and threshold tolerance. Proposed as a connective neighbourhood model, this generative design system allows networks to recursively operate in a polyscalar manner. Unlike traditional fractal systems, it is boundary sensitive and self-evaluating, weighing line networks through real-time analytical synthesis. This synthesis is achieved through the integration of flow analytics developed by Space Syntax, which uses pattern-sensitive colour mapping to evaluate network connections. The network analysis can identify nodal patterns within high-resolution fields that could serve as potential locations for high streets and other organisational planning features. As a result the proposed model can construct connective neighbourhoods that allow for high integration of complex living patterns within a time-based framework.

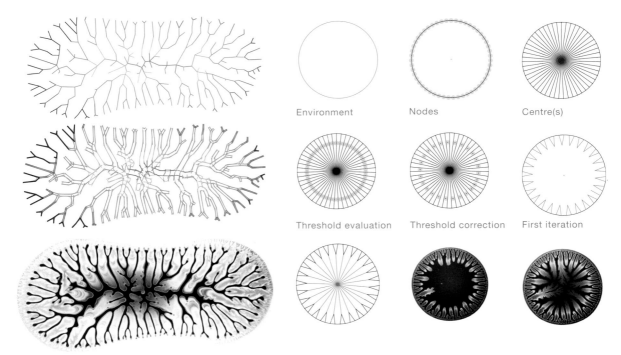

Environment

Nodes

Centre(s)

Threshold evaluation

Threshold correction

First iteration

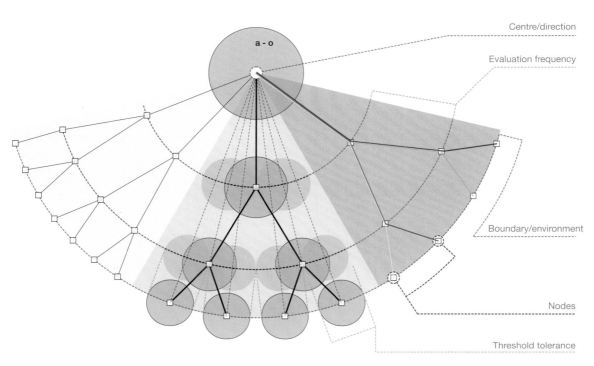

Centre/direction

Evaluation frequency

a - o

Boundary/environment

Nodes

Threshold tolerance

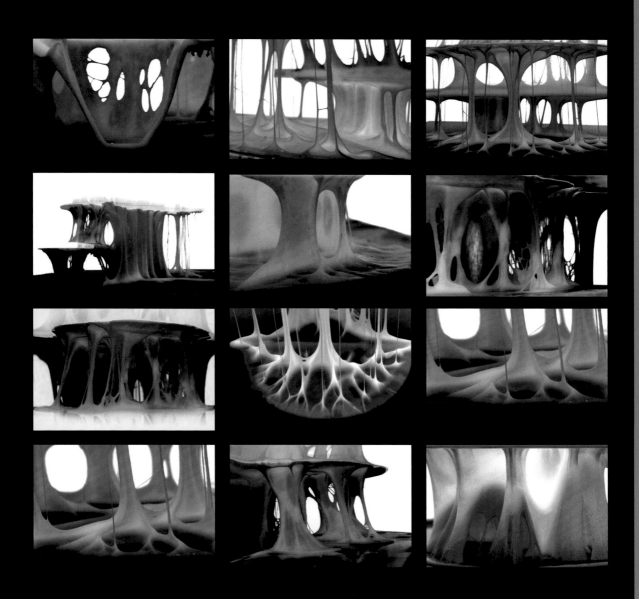

Surface tension generative diagram showing
the parameters studied in the glue experiments.
Material Experiments. Drops of glue were
subjected to surface tension between two parallel
plates. The experiments show differentiated
material build-ups.

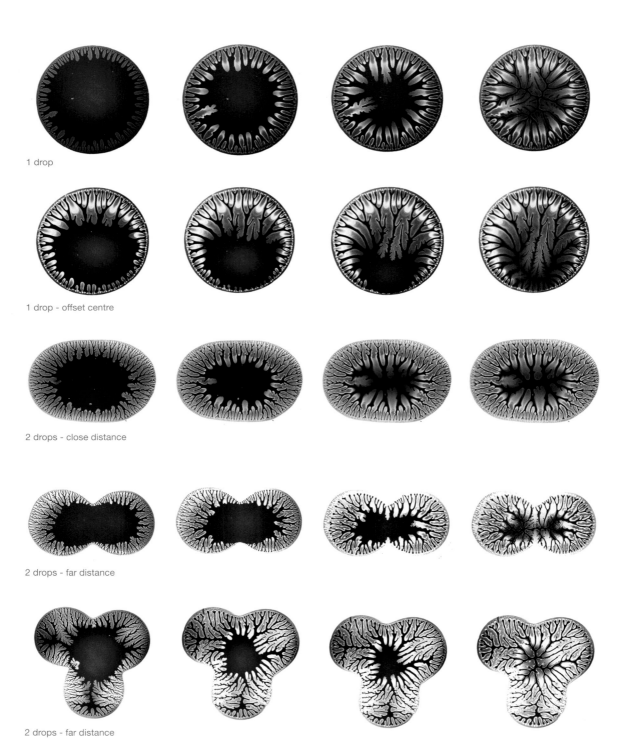

1 drop

1 drop - offset centre

2 drops - close distance

2 drops - far distance

2 drops - far distance

284

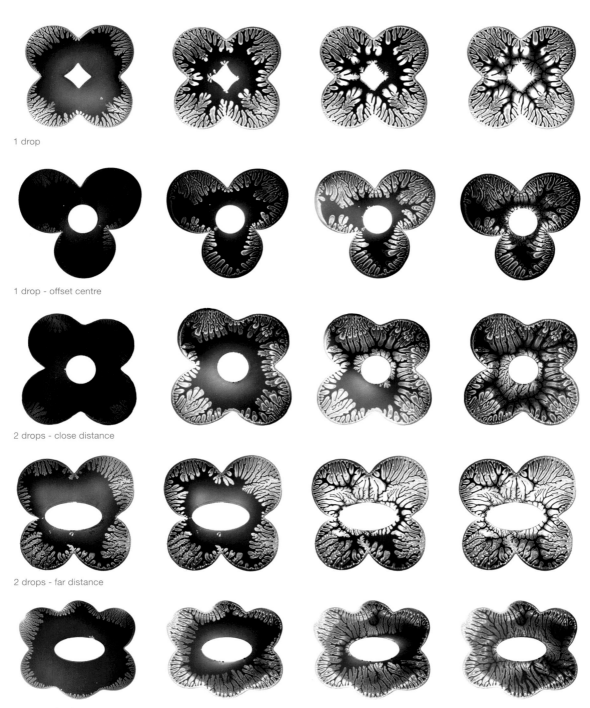

1 drop

1 drop - offset centre

2 drops - close distance

2 drops - far distance

2 drops - far distance

285

NODE COUNT 250M RADIUS
LOCAL COMMERCE VS HOUSING

NODE COUNT 1000M RADIUS
CORPORATE VS HOUSING

NODE COUNT 5000M RADIUS
EXPO VS HOUSING

NODE COUNT 500M RADIUS HIGH
STREET VS HOUSING

(Above)

Programmatic differentiation across
the masterplan

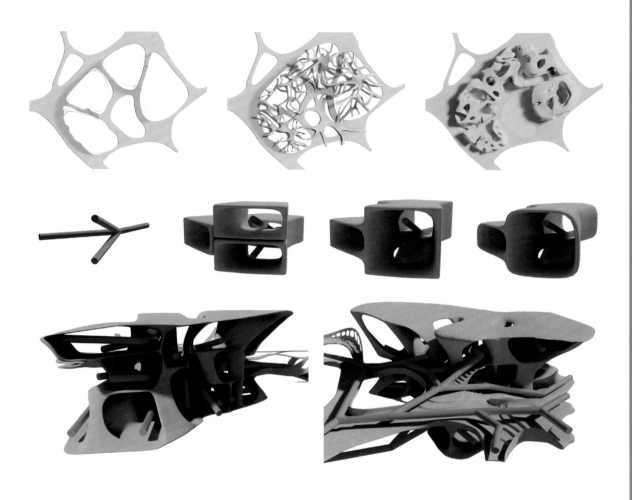

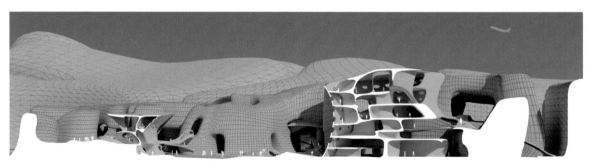

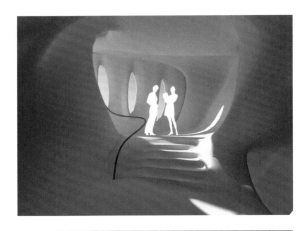
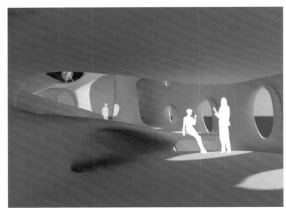

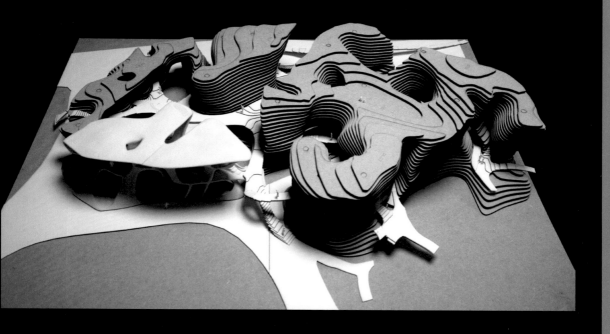
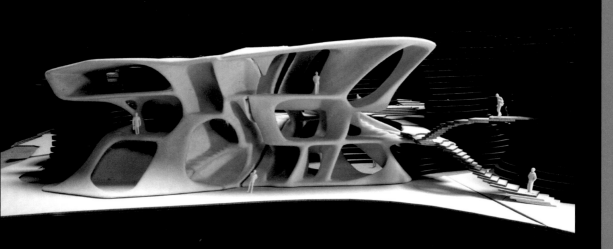

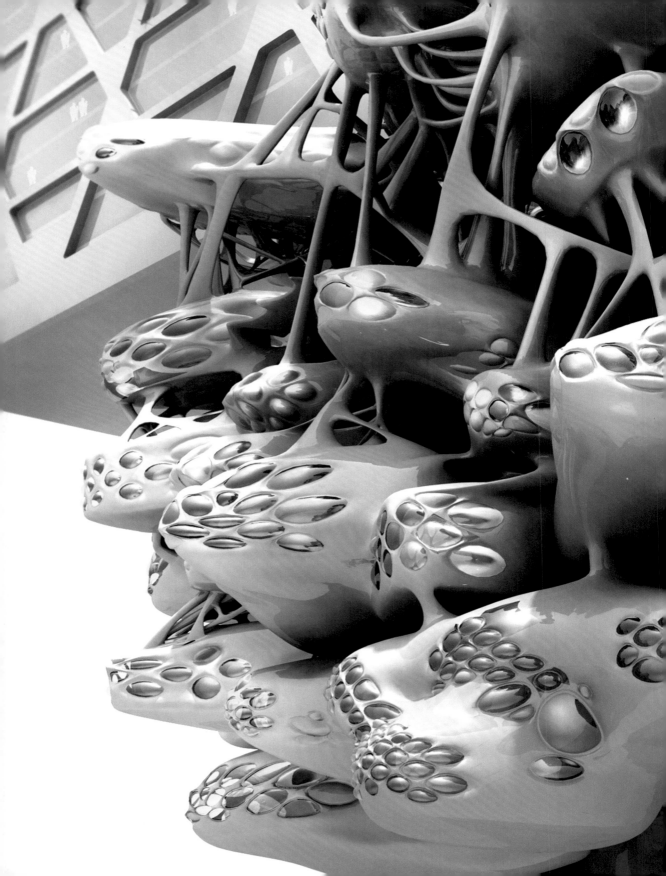

SIPHONOPHORA

AADRL 2008-2009 / TEAM: SYPHONOPHORE
Alicia Nahmad, Elizabeth Leidy, Paul Wintour, Riccardo Sosa

Operating as a model of colonial and complex multi-cellular organisms, siphonophora consist of specialised populations of singular zoids that evolve symbiotic relationships and hyper-specific functions as part of an emergent ecology. As an integrated model of dynamic singular / collective relationships, siphonophora are morphologically and functionally distinct although they operate within a symbiotic and metabolic collective. For this reason, as a behavioural model, the organisational body plan for such collectives introduces redundancy and genetic variation as a product of its adaptive ecology.

This research project examines agent-based computational systems that develop time-based growth models through genetic refactoring. Nested radial and linear unit interactions construct organisational patterns coupling structure, circulation and unit distribution. This generative population-based system was tested through scenario deployments within Kenzo Tange's Tokyo Bay proposal. Through augmenting the segregated programming environments of the original proposal, the research aimed to achieve spatial models that could evolve flexible programming and living environments within the megastructural framework. Unit-to-unit interactions constructed emergent body plans that allowed for varied spatial organisations to integrate themselves within the infrastructural networks of Tange's core and ground territories.

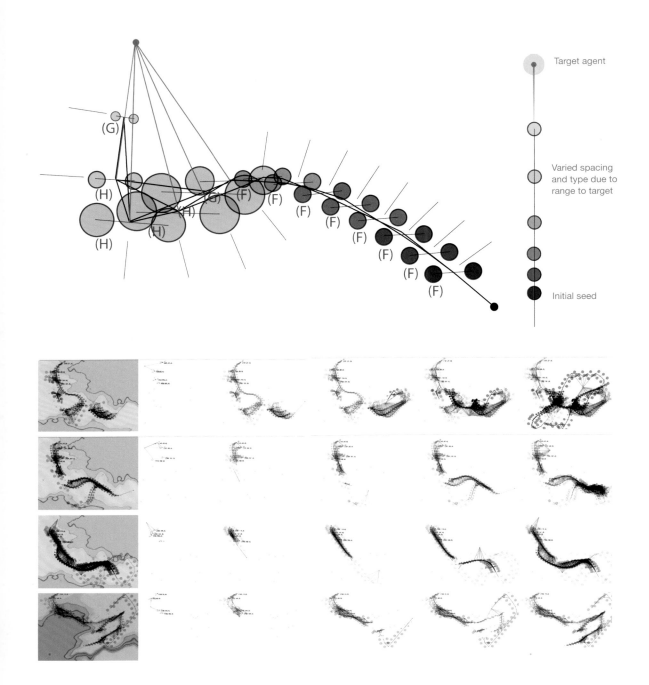

Target agent

Varied spacing
and type due to
range to target

Initial seed

(Above)

The growth model, based on the non-linear growth
of the Portuguese man-of-war, was first developed
prototypically outside the site but within given
boundary conditions.

292

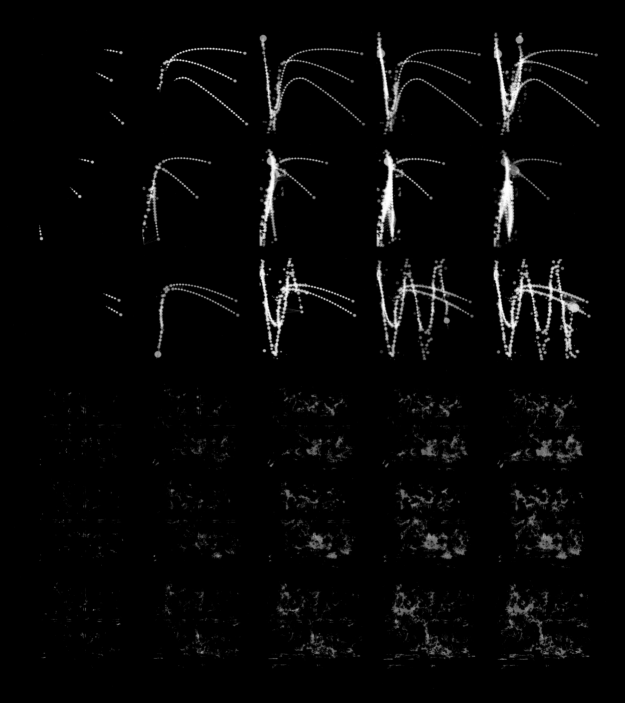

Time-based deployment of the growth model produced dynamic organisations that respond to local relationships and boundary conditions.

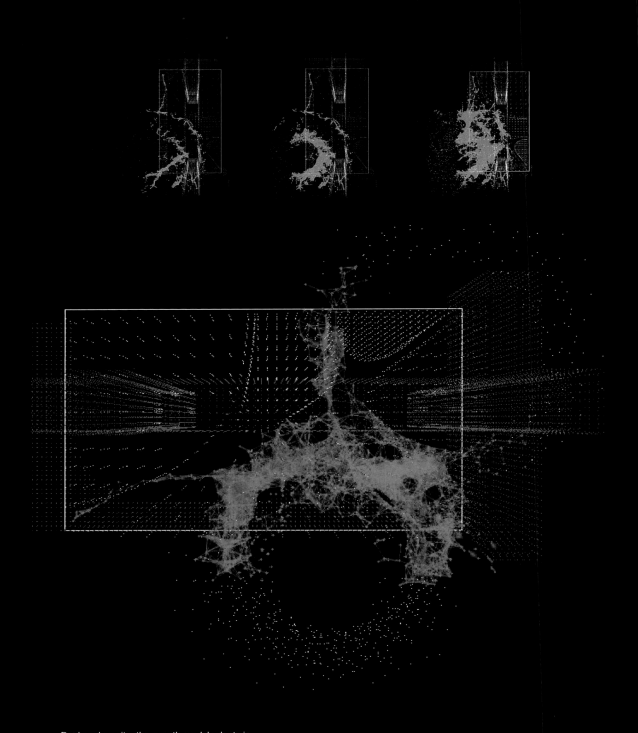

Deployed on site, the growth model adapts in
response to the main cores of the Tokyo Bay
scheme and develops housing neighbourhoods
that have varying degrees of density, public/private
space and unit sizes

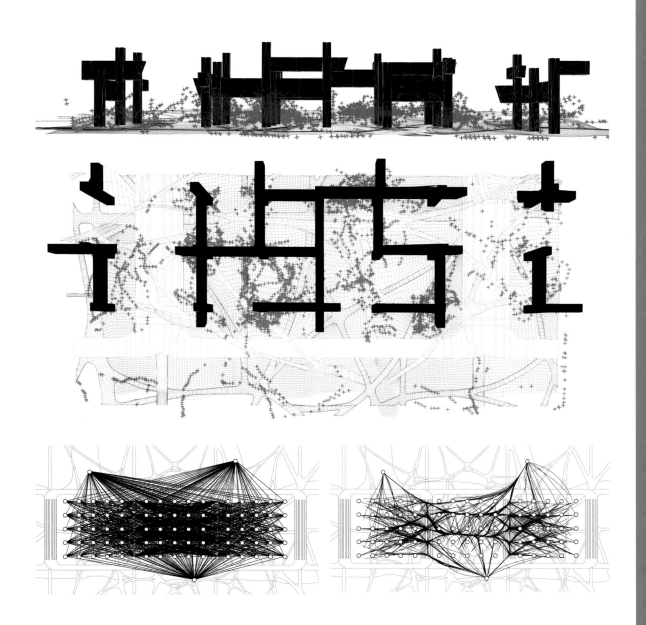

In order to transcode the growth model's data into geometry, a point cloud becomes the setting out for geometric articulation. The overall site organisation was developed out of an exploration of optimised networks.

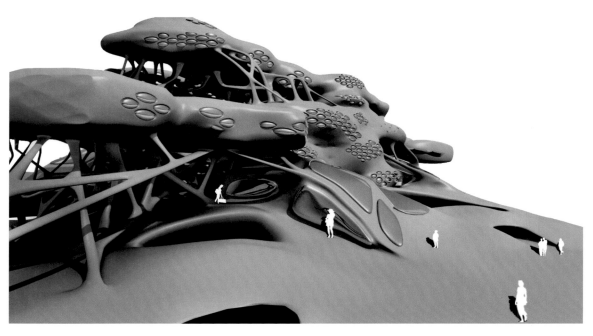

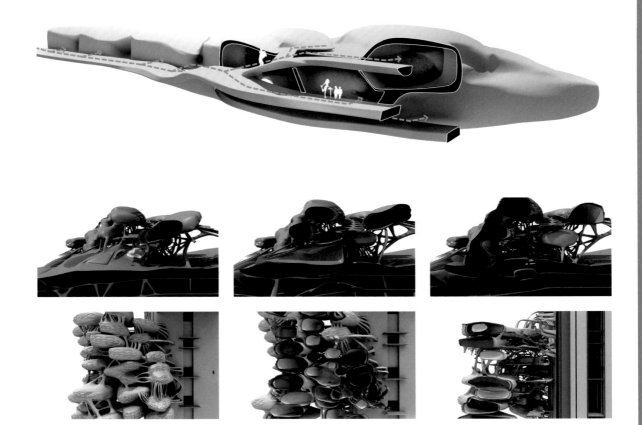

(Opposite and Above)

The generative process resulted in nested and clustered housing units.

CYMATICS

AADRL 2008-2009 / TEAM: CYMATITTUDE
Maryam Mohammad Sadeghi, Puja Shah, Manya Uppal, Natalie Wong Chauvet

Modal phenomena, or cymatics, to use the term coined by Hans Jenny, denotes the periodic effects that sound and vibration have on matter. Pattern-sensitive formations driven through frequency construct a model that organises and amplifies matter as a dynamic sorting machine. Pattern behaviour is amplified with observable effects through the use of granular aggregate or viscous material such as non-Newtonian fluids like cornstarch. The organisational properties of this phenomenon shape matter into complex patterns that are highly controlled, exhibiting parametric symmetries. Observable resonance fields allow matter to behave with life-like attributes, reconfiguring and adapting to obstacle interventions in a seamless and coherent manner.

This research project explored cymatics as behavioural model for constructing a computational platform to speculate on urban morphologies that create seamless mat-like building urbanism. Voxel-based field simulations allowed the research to develop a continuous notational field with identifiable unit distributions. Operating within fluid networks, the periodic effects could be sequenced in multi-wave configurations embedding distinct urban features within the sinuous ground formation. Time-based accretion allowed for a delineated path formation, enabling a polyscalar approach within the deployed voxel network.

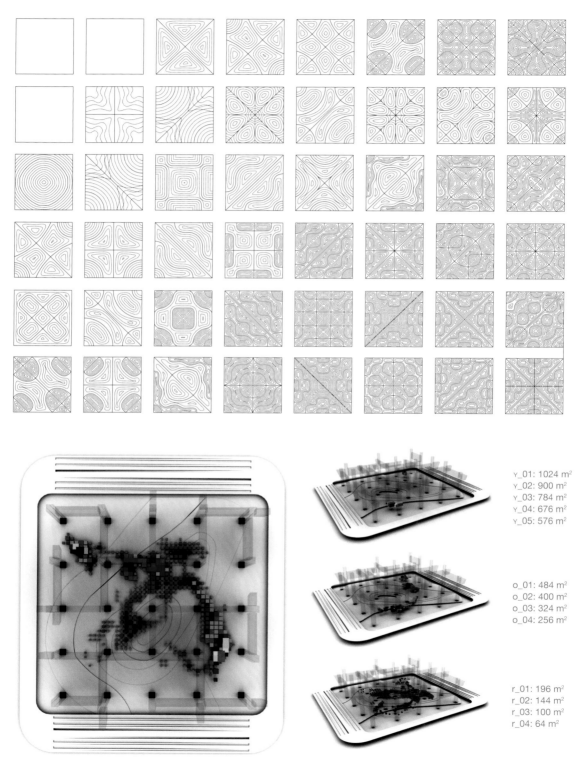

Y_01: 1024 m²
Y_02: 900 m²
Y_03: 784 m²
Y_04: 676 m²
Y_05: 576 m²

o_01: 484 m²
o_02: 400 m²
o_03: 324 m²
o_04: 256 m²

r_01: 196 m²
r_02: 144 m²
r_03: 100 m²
r_04: 64 m²

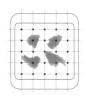

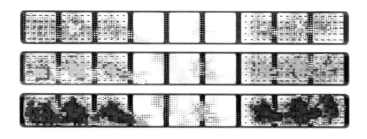

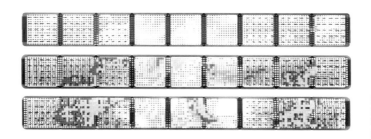

Emitter Position:
Centralised Cores
Dens / Vox / Sec:
Incremental
Emitters / Ring: 4

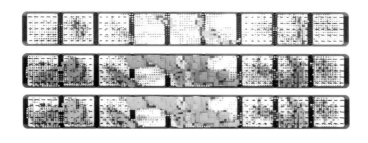

Emitter Position:
Four Corner Cores +
Centre Core
Dens / Vox / Sec:
Incremental
Emitters / Ring: 5

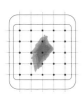

Emitter Position:
Centre Core
Dens / Vox / Sec:
Incremental
Emitters / Ring: 1

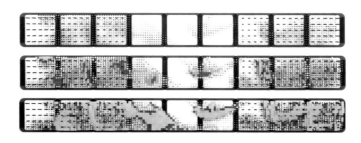

Emitter Position:
2 Corner Cores
Dens / Vox / Sec:
Incremental
Emitters / Ring: 2

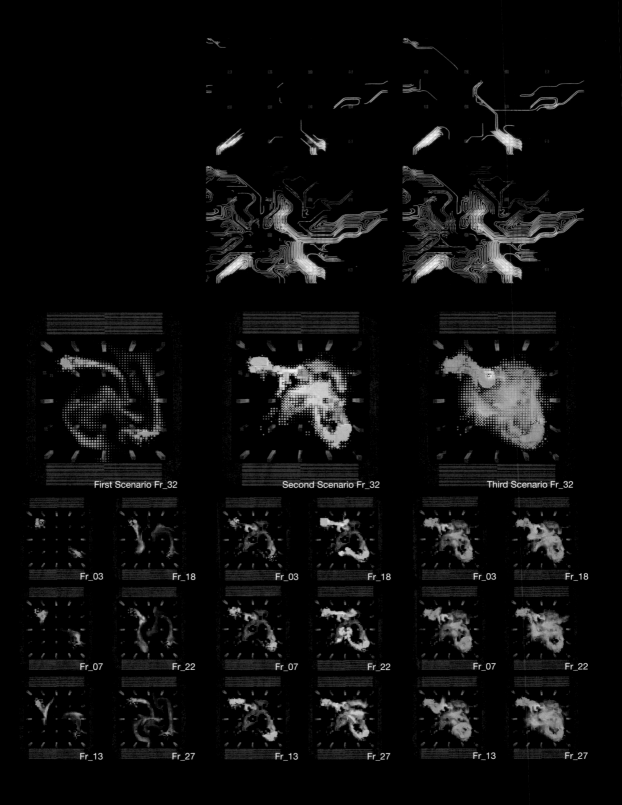

First Scenario Fr_32

Second Scenario Fr_32

Third Scenario Fr_32

Fr_03

Fr_18

Fr_03

Fr_18

Fr_03

Fr_18

Fr_07

Fr_22

Fr_07

Fr_22

Fr_07

Fr_22

Fr_13

Fr_27

Fr_13

Fr_27

Fr_13

Fr_27

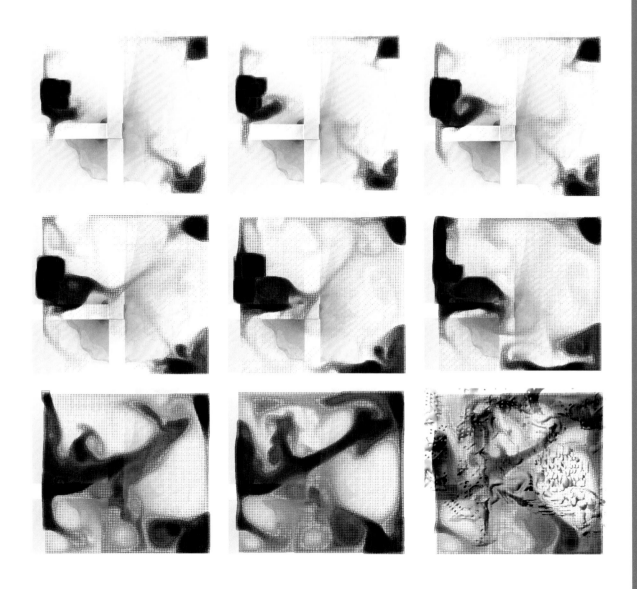

(Above)

Growth logic starts from Tange's cores and interacts with the voxel field to define circulation trajectories and time-based accretion, generating an array of prototypical voxel fields.

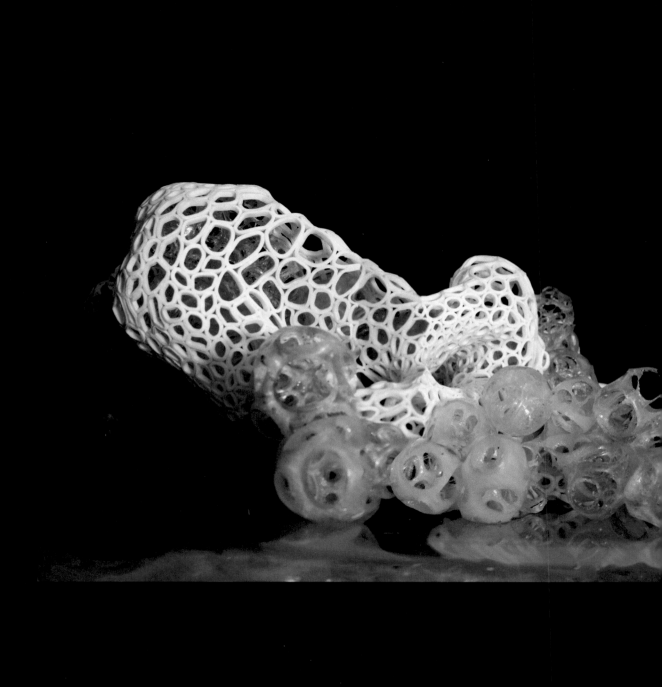

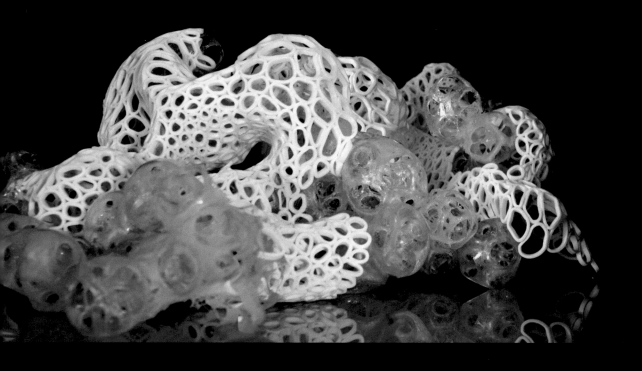

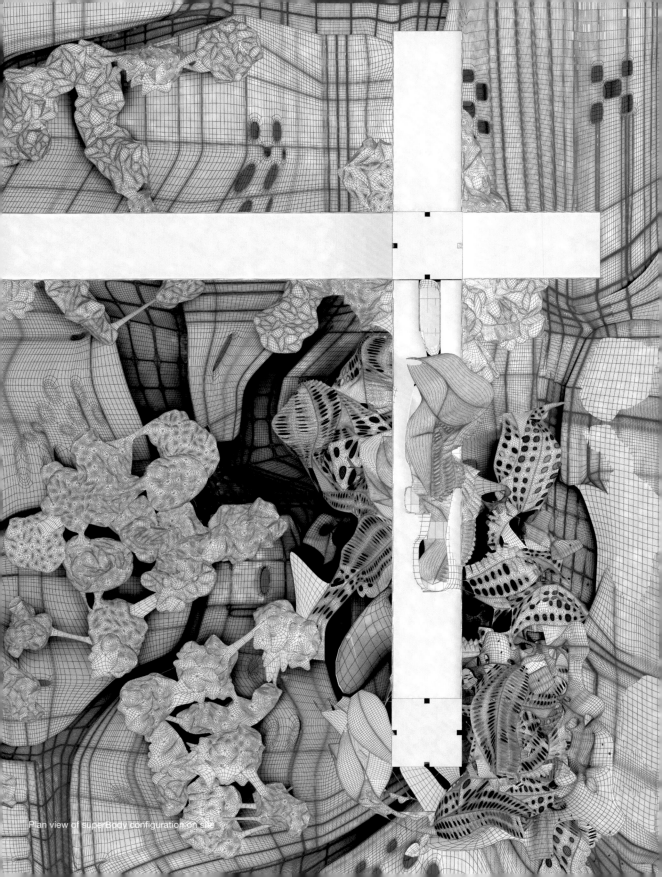

Plan view of superBody configuration on site

SOFT-CAST

AADRL 2008-2009 / TEAM: ANON
Omrana Ahmed, Musatafa El Sayed, Sara Saleh and Nick Williams

Artificial ecologies born out of synthetic playpen environments afford generative organisational frameworks that can develop behaviours as a product of their adaptive interaction. Within this genetic soup emergent body plans organise themselves, evolving unit-to-unit relations that construct super (organisms) bodies. This genetic versioning employs Karl Sims's bodybuilding computational environments, evolving relations that include body plan delineation, locomotion and social interaction attributes. The interaction within a given population over time builds taxonomies of varied species, constructing an evolutionary computational ecology.

This research project exploited the genetic versioning of synthetic body plans by further constraining agent interactions through material phase change and physics-based parameters. Utilising phase change through pattern management, elastic textile properties allowed a process of formation that constructed a digital materiality of soft-cast formwork. Behaviour within this context articulated organisational subsets that offered varied and expressive living environments. The proposed model coupled adaptive spatial organisation with material computation, enabling an integrated and computational approach that addressed latency and uncertainty through self-aware forecasting.

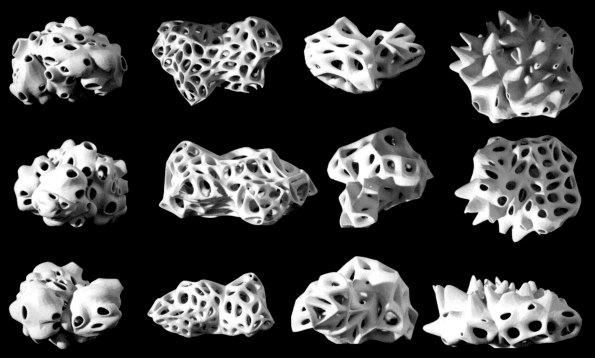

SuperBody configurations according to formal parameters that are triggered due to the site constraints and neighbours

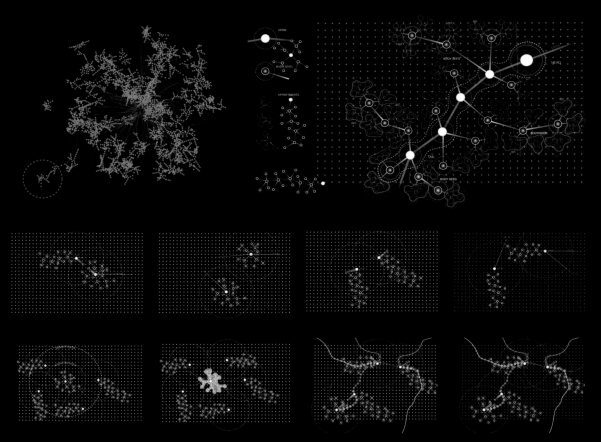

Depicting the superBody's different abilities and search conditions, and an example of deployment

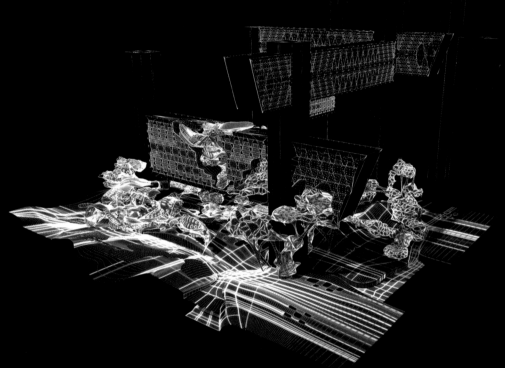

Render of superBodies inhabiting the host – Kenzo Tange master plan

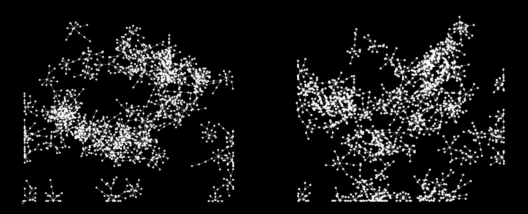

SuperBody deployment that displays the effects of neighbourhood parameters

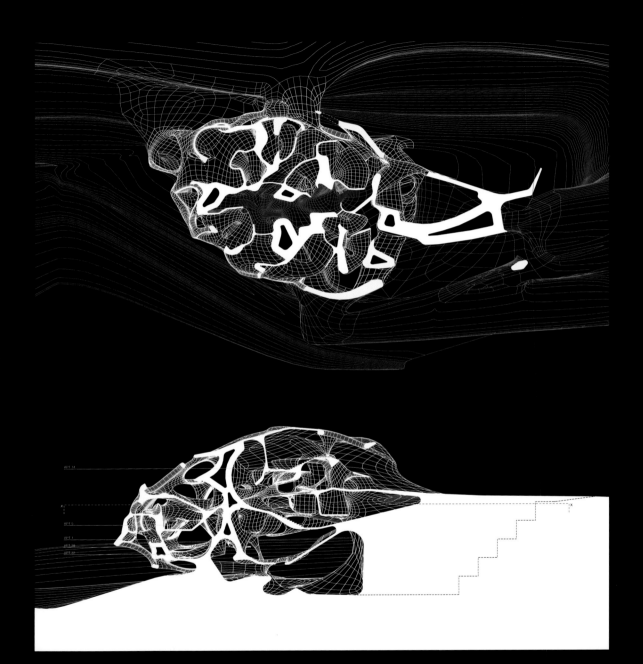

Plan and section of prototypical superBody within the ground

Exploded axonometric of programmatic layout within the superBody and rendering
of the ground-inhabiting superBody type

Overall catalogue of analogue computation models

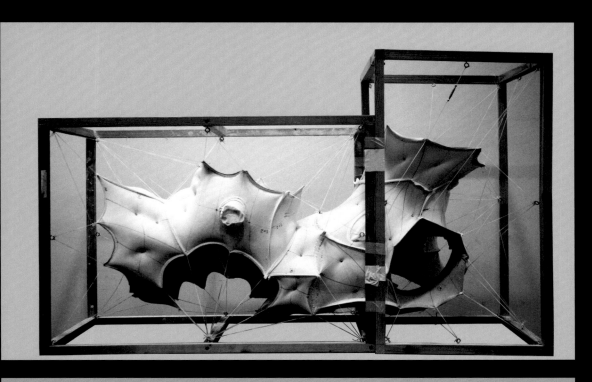

Example of multi-frame cast

Night render of superBody neighbourhood on site

IDEAS AND COMPUTATION IN CONTEMPORARY URBAN DESIGN: ADDRESSING THE DISCONNECTS

Mark Burry

'They [cities] aren't made very well today; urban design is a craft in peril. Physically, too much urban design is homogeneous and rigid in form; socially, modern built forms frequently take only a faint imprint of personal and shared experience. These are unfortunately familiar complaints.'
Richard Sennett, 2012

If our ability to envisage bold new outcomes is unmatched by an equal skill in envisaging the corresponding means of production, then each step forward in a credible visionary project risks generating an equivalent step in the opposite direction, taking us further away from achievability. In this text I am contending that developments in *computation and visualisation* over the last two decades have progressed far more rapidly than developments in *computation and realisation*, and the widening gap between the two suggests all sorts of unintended consequences, not least the possibility that designers will be relegated to a back-seat role in the teams shaping the urban environments of the future. I believe that this gulf particularly affects urban design, and to illustrate my point I will refer to a radical urbanisation project that commenced in 1859 and, as an adaptive ecology, continues to grow in status and impress from all points of view: Barcelona. Looking at this case-study of a successful adaptive ecology gives us an example of an urban development where the visionary postulation of a city fit for the future tallied with a corresponding level of technical invention and achievement. I will draw indicators from this pre-digital example and align and contrast them with future digital design research trajectories in an effort to draw back a little from the rhetoric. Doing so might help limit the risk of the divide between design speculation and material capability becoming ever more unbridgeable.

Barcelona as an Adaptive Ecology Paradigm

Plan Cerdà is the name of the area surrounding Barcelona's Gothic (and earlier) quarter, with its characteristic grid with octagonal intersections. It is more commonly known locally as the *Eixample* or *Ensanche*, respectively Catalan and Spanish for 'extension', referring to the nineteenth-century expansion of a city hitherto confined to the boundaries of its ancient walls. Commerce and industrial development during the first half of the nineteenth century placed considerable pressure on the already overcrowded medieval city. In 1859 Ildefons Cerdà, an engineer, was tasked with surveying the outlying area for the purposes of a possible expansion of the city. As part of his contribution he also studied the conditions of the working class in detail and in 1867 produced his three-volume *magnum opus*, 'General theory of urbanisation and application of its principles and rules for the reform and amplification of Barcelona'. His coining of the word '*urbanización*' in Spanish preceded its equivalent in English by two decades. While Cerdà's general theory included coloured plans of his proposal for Barcelona's extension it principally took the form of tables presenting an extraordinary quantity of data. Cerdà's thorough statistical approach to the issue established a clear link between overcrowding and ill health, leading him to propose a less dense urban fabric.

Cerdà was able to anticipate issues such as the radically different approach to transportation required by the greatly expanded cities of the industrialised world. The invention of the railway pointed the way in this regard, but whereas London, for example, cleared a path for the trains with wholesale slum clearances and arched embankments that snaked across the urban skyline, Barcelona's expansion began at exactly the same time as the railways were being established. Cerdà accommodated them along principal axes in his grid in open-cut trenches, which were covered over with the advent of smokeless electric trains. The characteristically chamfered corners to each block forming the octagonal intersections were partly a response to horse-drawn and later electric trams: the configuration allowed for unconstrained future routing. The chamfered corners were also more conducive to impromptu encounters or gatherings than right-angled intersections, where any dallying impedes the flow of pedestrians. Cerdà's plan was based on a principle of *polycentric egalitarianism*.

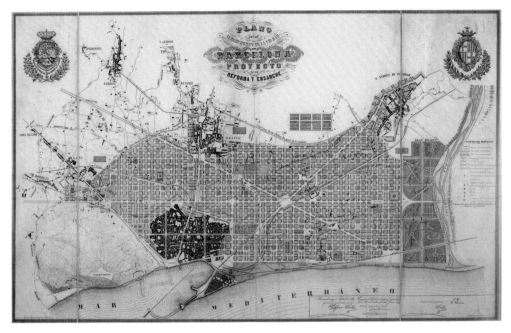

Plan Cerdà

Plan Cerdà

He anticipated the risk that an expanding city would give rise to a peri-urban condition that would attract only the less well-off, who would find it more and more expensive – as the physical separation increased – to access the services traditionally offered in the city centre. His solution to this was a polycentric development. Applying the ratios derived from his statistical analysis of the ills of the congested city and the rules for a viable expansion, he worked out optimal distances between neighbouring hospitals, schools, markets and civic administration nodes. This calculated placement of principal public resources underpinned his *polycentric approach*, while the concomitant *egalitarianism* sought to offer equal opportunity of access for all.

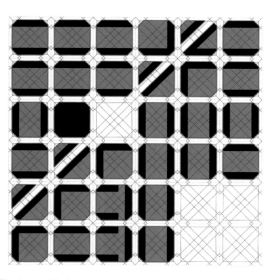

Closing the blocks

There were, alas, two limits to the viability of this approach, one natural and the other economic. Barcelona's expansion was physically contained by the sea to the east, the mountains to the west, and the flood plains of the Rivers Besòs and Llobregat to the north and south. Economic forces, however, meant that the grid was corrupted even before these natural constraints fully took effect. Part of the brilliance of Cerdà's plan was to separate pedestrian infrastructure as far as possible from road traffic. The typical urban block was originally set out to have buildings only on two opposite sides, leaving the space in the middle, open at both ends, for public use as a park with pedestrian routes filtering down the middle. These paths or passages connected with adjacent blocks, providing pedestrians with a relatively peaceful thoroughfare. Inevitably the open ends of the blocks were seen as lost real-estate opportunities, and so were developed as housing with small businesses accommodated at ground level. This factor, combined with crafty regulation-dodging rooftop extensions, increased the height of the buildings around the central open spaces, which evolved as light-industrial spaces in the main. Today there are only two vestiges of the 'passages' surviving in the whole of the Cerdà grid.

This particular adaptive ecology is a supreme example of a strategy of a seed growing within a basic armature, leading to a development that is both self-propelled and self-organising, unconstrained by regulations steering it in a particular direction. Extreme market forces put paid to the more open distribution of buildings of the original plan and ultimately the grid petered out into more ad hoc development, some pre-dating the plan, some contemporaneous but from neighbouring municipalities. The result was a clumsy fusion, especially in the area where the *Eixample* meets the medieval quarter and the village of Gracia further inland. Though the plan was ultimately corrupted by commercial reality, the ideas behind it continued to be valued, particularly by all those who did not stand to gain materially from the plan's derailment. In other words, this visionary approach to the new city did not necessarily lose its vigour once its chief protagonist was out of the picture. Fifty years after the inception of Cerdà's *Eixample*, an international competition was launched to reactivate its more important aspects, especially those that had not been wholly satisfactory from the outset. The competition of 1907 was won by the French architect Léon Jaussely, whose project set out boldly to form major new boulevards with grand intersections, corniches and generous avenues. In fact very little of his winning project was realised, but efforts to soften up the grid's unyielding quadrilateral insistence can be seen at Avinguda Gaudí, which runs diagonally from the Sagrada Família Basilica to the extraordinary Hospital San Pau. Thirty years later another initiative led by Le Corbusier – the Pla Macià – formed the second attempt to update Cerdà's initiative, this time with larger blocks anticipating the growing impact of the motor car. To date there have been at least three further waves of 'urbanisation' applied to the existing city. During the 1980s Oriol Bohigas et al received international attention with their necklace of tiny (for the most part) interventions strung throughout the inner city and outer suburbs. The 1992 Olympic Games hosted by Barcelona acted as a further stimulus for rethinking the city's overall infrastructure. An inner and an outer ring road were constructed with one part running invisibly beneath the city's waterfront. New sports facilities were set up in such a way as to create long-lasting zones of activity. Most recently, Europe's longest underground tunnel (Metro Line 9) has begun to wrap around the city, while the high-speed train line connecting Madrid to Paris via subterranean Barcelona is nearing completion at the time of writing. From the moment that the constraints of Barcelona's medieval city walls were removed, the city began to grow and mature as an adaptive ecology, its effective aspects far exceeding market-driven shortcuts.

In terms of vision this case-study is not surpassed by the scale, modality and fixations of contemporary digital speculative design research, nor is its outcome constrained by the use of analogue methodologies. Essentially my proposition is that the more real the results of envisioned new urban environments appear to be, in light of formal experiment and advances in visualisation, the more distant the prospect is of fulfilling these dreams using the available technology, and this risks marginalising designers from other urban decision-making groups. Imagined future technologies never seem to be as deep reaching as the imagined future urban environments in which these yet-to-be-invented technologies will be called upon to manufacture and build. In essence this principal issue of unrequited desire was manifest even before the recent global financial crisis led to a rapid evaporation of confidence in western-style capitalism. The benchmarks of achievability in the current climate rest shakily on the extremes of unembarrassed consumption developed over three decades and characterised by the opportunities offered in the boom cities, principally in the oil states, and by the politics of necessity and exigency in China and its more prosperous near neighbours.

Design Computation and 'What Problem? – There is No Problem!'

If our design computation capability is substantially ahead of our ability to frame the problems we seek to address technically, we are not equipped to provide credible and convincing physical outcomes through real, as opposed to virtually simulated, outcomes. Like the jilted partner on the night of the prom we could be all dressed up but not too sure what our next move might be. Given that we have far too few admirers external to the design process to be truly confident that we are making a major difference (let alone dent planners' complacency about their own *savoir-faire*), it seems that, with a few notable exceptions, we may not even have properly identified how we might be more effective in showing our work to those who commission and use it. I refer to the potential for developing computational tools to describe possible new urban environments at every imaginable scale. It is telling that in an age of extraordinarily convincing 3D and 4D representations of possible futures we still plan the city as a 2D construct. Here I hypothesise that our potential to contribute positively to urban design through advanced computation is far greater than our ability to influence decision-makers to look enthusiastically on our unique combination of skills and insights. At best demonstrations of visual prowess are greeted with polite amazement, at worst such demonstrations are irritably dismissed as over-optimistic or even irrelevant. My examples of such failure are drawn principally from an Australian set

Barcelona
Data from the US Geological Survey

Melbourne
Data from the US Geological Survey

San Fernando de Henares
Data from the US Geological Survey

of adventures. Like many arid countries with vast areas of desert, Australia is both wealthy, with huge mineral resources, and dangerously poor in terms of water and soil fertility. It is an extremely edgy environment, especially outside the cities, subject to a worryingly wide spectrum of natural disasters – heavy snowfalls and earthquakes might be the only ones missing from the list. It is the most urbanised country in the world: that is to say, it has the greatest proportion of its total population living in cities (eighty per cent). Australia also has some of the oldest geology in the world and is home to the world's oldest indigenous populations, yet its cities are among the newest. The states are bigger in area than many countries and, to newcomers especially, they and their capitals are more like city-states with relatively small regional centres in the hinterland.

Several international indices, such as the Mercer scale, place cities such as Melbourne and Sydney, both with populations of over four million, at or near the top of liveability league tables. Each announcement of this sort becomes tub-thumpingly good news on the front pages of our national newspapers. When a designer tries to voice publicly their concerns about the loss of opportunity that our poorly designed cities represent for the broader population, the consistently high scores in the liveability league tables are cited as evidence of there being no problem at all. Indices such as the Mercer scale are important mechanisms for attracting executives to 'successful' cities, with their focus on access to private schools and advanced medical facilities clustered around the centres. However these priorities may not be shared by the wider working population, who mostly live in the vast urban sprawl, keeping at least one eye on a public infrastructure that is failing to keep up and petrol prices that can only rise. It seems that the extra pressure placed on existing infrastructure by a bulging urban periphery hardly impacts on the international benchmarks, but is only too evident to the local population. Many cities in the United States have similar problems. Asia, of course, presents an entirely different dimension, but given the mistakes that are already being made there, the disconnect between the bold visions of new types of city and the timid actuality of the outcomes is just as relevant.

This outward appearance of civic comfort in Australia is just one of the obstacles facing any designer attempting to convince decision-makers of the inherent flaws in our conceptual framework for cities. In a supposedly spacious and urbane city (such as Melbourne, for example), in a 'new world' country that has had every chance to invent the egalitarian and workable new city, it is an uphill struggle to break the curse of being so firmly established as an automobile city: we have a lot in common with the United States in this regard. What's more, we cannot even the draw on the vestiges of historic centres pre-dating post-industrial revolution transport systems. Referring to successful pedestrianised precincts in Europe tends to inflame passions rather than inform strategy. (Melbourne was developed almost simultaneously with Barcelona's Plan Cerdà, and the differences between the two cities offer much food for thought.) It is doubtful that Australia has much to offer the rest of the world in terms of design excellence at the urban scale, regardless of the many world-class architectural gems that individually make exciting contributions to our city centres and elegant inner suburbs. Individually there is abundant talent to draw on, as we can see from studio work and avant-garde publications, but its uptake at a political level is minimal, as we collectively struggle to find a voice that others can listen to, comprehend, and be persuaded by. Those architect grandees who do have wider political influence are not working with all that we have to offer as designers, but nevertheless they're still the ones calling the shots. The critique that follows details eight dimensions of difficulty – effectively a collective impasse preventing contemporary urban designers from including their generative thinking as robustly in their design processes as I believe we should be able to do. Other designers will claim their own set of frustrations, but this list of stumbling blocks is offered in an attempt to move the debate forward and seek fresh ways to engage with the decision-makers we hope to influence.

Eight Dimensions of a Creative Impasse in Urban Design

1. What is Design Today?

For a long time we have been able to debate design among ourselves, almost hermetically sealed from the views of other related non-design disciplines such as anthropology, sociology, politics, economics, planning and business. From the creation of the guilds onwards the skill of the designer has remained something of a mystery to the layperson, a situation we have taken advantage of. However, 'design thinking', as a newly defined intellectual strategy, is now elbowing its way to the fore, offered as a possible panacea for every strategically focused discipline lacking its own set of creative thought processes and traditions. An increasing awareness of challenges too great in scale and complexity to be solved in a simple way is coupled with the realisation that traditional approaches to solving complex problems have failed.

Designers have always applied a knowledge acquired through 'action-based design thinking' to their practice, so it is a little unnerving to see this promoted beyond *designing itself* – that is, beyond actual design practice. 'Design thinking', as embraced by governments and large organisations, presumes a clean (mis)appropriation of design's iterative processes, adopting novel 'left field' approaches and profiting from 'hybrid left side–right side brain engagement' without any of the *messiness* that typically accompanies the design process in practice. If 'design thinking' turns out to be more than a passing fad, how might designers lead the process rather than be further demoted – reduced to the level of experienced operatives working to order for upscale 'design thinkers'?

2.   Scale

Computation is scale-less and I believe an increased cognitive distance is emerging between what we conceive and what we make as a result. At first it is liberating to work conceptually uninhibited by real space and Cartesian dimensions, but it can become a trap, making it more difficult to move from the conceptual model into a more practical domain. Often in avant-garde creative thinking there is no expectation that anything more than conceptual experimentation will result; in which case, how does the design proposition move beyond an internal conversation? Unconstrained, undimensioned and scale-less conceptual thinking needs an elegant software route to a greater plausibility than common 3D software currently allows.

3.   Complexity

The great strides we have made in engaging with sophisticated computation seem to have made us a little intoxicated with the opportunities we now have to be more credibly complex. But could it be that this complexity has the opposite effect on the decision-makers we most want to impress? Simplifying the complicated might be a sufficiently complex strategy in itself, and all the more credible for its potential to put a design into action, beyond the realm of discussion.

4.   Originality

Putting aside the semantic debates around the definition of design, we might at least agree that design is a creative act leading to an outcome that goes beyond simply making an alternative to something we already have. Design is not mimesis or versioning; it implies an originality of purpose, to challenge prevailing archetypes. Design is utopian in the sense that it aims to improve on the existing situation. Being original by creating a successful design ought to be in itself a sufficient goal, but the fertile opportunities offered by our digital computational and fabrication tools encourage us to be original for originality's sake.

We need to be clear about what we are undertaking, and work harder to distinguish design from art. Computation, through genuine engagement with the instrument (computer) through scripting, for example, forces us to break down the problem in terms of logic, sequence, etc. The alternative to engaging with a problem or situation in this way is the *tabula rasa* approach, which accommodates unconstrained creative freedom. Cerdà almost had this opportunity in 1863 when his plan was accepted. Exciting as such liberation might be to the designer, it seems to appeal much less to those who are in a position to commission our 'original work'. Culturally it seems harder for the designer to enjoy the degree of transgression afforded to artists. Should designers engage more closely with artists?

5. Transdisciplinarity

The 'designer as (sole) author' paradigm might need to be re-examined in light of enhanced computation and the opportunities to link data inputs to possible urban future thinking in real-time decision-making. The sequential nature of information inputs from so many rich sources, including public censuses, transport and service engineering, social work and police, health and recreation, agriculture and commerce, has the potential to influence design decision-making during the design, as opposed to design being iteratively reconditioned to end-user and implementation inputs. Urban designers of the future might benefit from a more robust transdisciplinary approach, whereby each discipline works within its area of expertise, contributing positively to the overall process; but they would not necessarily be able to presume leadership of this process, as was the case during the twentieth century, especially in the postwar reconstruction of European cities and the new cities of rapidly developing economies. This more inclusive modus operandi obviously requires a considerable re-education of all the parties involved, and not just the designers. Even more than speaking each other's language, what is needed is a fundamental level of understanding and respect for the contributions of individual disciplines. In treating urban design as an adaptive ecology we can perhaps remove the label of 'master planner' from the mix and replace it with the concept of a diverse team working with a multidimensional symbiosis. Computation is a perfect and neutral instigator in this regard, and as number crunching performance improves, all stakeholders will have an opportunity to make useful and influential concurrent inputs.

6.   Critical Framework

Based on the experience of my doctoral candidates over the years, I would say that developing a convincing critical framework often seems to be a stumbling block for designers. (The PhD may seem an odd arena to evoke in this context, but I believe it bears clear similarities to the challenge of persuading an urban development authority, for instance, to engage with something beyond their imagination.) At the commencement of their doctorates articulating a conceptual framework already seems challenging enough: they know broadly what motivates them and where they want to end up, but setting down a pathway seems to be harder than one would expect. But it is towards the end of a typical candidature, the 'write up', that furnishing a credible critical framework becomes absolutely vital, for this is the vehicle that the examiners and ultimately the readers beyond the examination process can use to evaluate the proposition. Radical new urban design proposals are in equal need of a critical framework allowing non-designers to engage with the work. Here, design computation that has been sensitively explicated has a notable role to play, as it can assist in visualising the design concept as well as signal paths to fruition, but only if both are equal in sophistication and credible enactment.

7.   Opportunity and Opportunism

In thinking about our future urban environment there is obviously an opportunity for far greater engagement with radical design. When students engage with systems thinking in studio one often hears the complaint that it is not 'real architecture', in contrast to the object-based view of design. Such conservatism is laudable in any environment predicated on self replication, but today's challenges clearly require fresh and more holistic thinking. The fiscal structures of most university progammes (disciplines) place every conceivable obstacle in the way of a progressive mash-up of related disciplines, and emerging architects, in the main, will most likely work towards maintaining the status quo.

At the same time civic enterprises such as the in-house architectural departments of local councils, which have the advantage of corridor encounters with related professions and departments, have to deal with

327

the constant threat of their work being outsourced to external consultants. In the private sector the opportunities for serendipitous exchange are more limited; what takes its place is a contrived transdisciplinary conversation – a formal relationship that might well seem like one cost too many given conventional consultancy arrangements. There is a big difference in the financial implications of the two approaches – working together throughout the design process, compared to a brief being written in isolation from the designers, responded to as a series of design propositions, critiqued by committee and signed off.

With opportunity comes opportunism – accommodating and adapting to an actual situation. In this sense opportunism ought to encourage entrepreneurship, and today's emerging young designers might be well positioned to gauge fresh opportunities and alternative courses of action. How well does our education system accommodate entrepreneurial activity? This is not about teaching entrepreneurship, which is widely considered to be an instinctual and unteachable skill, it's about ensuring that entrepreneurial designers are guided in their studies to become well-informed opportunists.

8. Politics

The failure of design to achieve an effective political dimension in many countries is at least partly responsible for the failure of architectural education to deal adequately with collective civic decision-making – we are part of a self-fulfilling legacy that ensures a continuing gulf between designers and those who commission and construct our built environments. How might this be addressed effectively? Schools typically include historians to ensure that students have a strong sense of the past, but how do you ensure that students interact with history sufficiently in the studio?

Ideally studio would interface more with the various public agencies that determine what gets built and where. While some staff would oppose this, arguing that students' creative horizons would be foreshortened by the exigencies of real-world politicking (after all, they have the rest of their careers to engage with this), it is clear that opportunities for different kinds of creative outcomes are being missed, not least among them the negotiating skills required for politics. If these could be practised early enough, it would give young designers a head start to being influential and operating from the front foot.

Design Computation as an Agent for Radical Shifts in Urban Design Practice and Education

We can do a lot more with data than ever before. While the example of Plan Cerdà makes it clear that this development cannot be attributed solely to the computer, digital design computation undeniably gives data a more radical role in shaping decisions. Re-evaluating the work of pioneers such as John Frazer and his team more than a generation on from its initiation in the 1970s, it seems that not so much has changed in terms of the ideas, irrespective of the powerful advances in the computing equipment used to express them. Indeed, it is the constellation of ideas that is vital in my view, well ahead of more visually compelling results that are often insufficiently argued in terms of urbanism. As scripting has become less esoteric over the last ten years, the employment of algorithms, agents and swarm theory all create powerful links between data and physical expression.

What is interesting is the contrast between the initiator and the 'digital uptaker', and the risk that adapting a piece of code to suit one's immediate purposes might not be as profitable as decomposing the 'problem' into a set of logics and building a computational model explicitly around the task in hand. Comparing scripting and parametric design is also valuable. In scripting the code-writer has the choice of either starting with a blank piece of paper and developing a generative process from a careful consideration of the data to be explored and its application, or alternatively adapting not only an existing algorithm but also its scripted recomposition for the same purpose. Parametric design software, by contrast, almost invariably demands that its user formulate a tree of relationships, constraints and dependencies which on the one hand gives the designer as much flexibility as possible, but on the other forces them to organise the design workflow schematically with a logic that might only emerge during the design process itself.

There is an essential paradox here. We push for more data to inform the design – and sophisticated computational tools have been created to assist us – but the more data we are able to generate from a diverse range of sources and the more sophisticated the computation, the more easy it is for the designer to get tied up in knots computationally and become dependent on the services of others. Increasingly we are seeing offices employ coders to build the generative tools that designers specify but are largely unable to produce for themselves. The education of architects might need to take this more into account if we are seeking to influence the

001

Marcus White: TOD rhetoric

002

Kokkugia/Emergent Architecture: Yeosu Theamatic Pavilion 2010

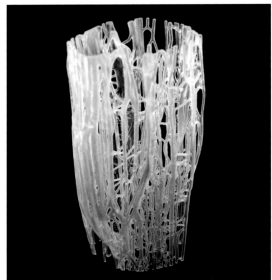

003

Kokkugia: FIBROUS TOWER 2008

design by streams of data with live deliberations along the way, rather than simply using data as a means to set the scene for a specialist to work within.

Parametric design is an unfortunate term for what is simply a more explicit framing of the relationships between design parameters and the way these parameters vary computationally within defined constraints. As soon as several parameters are considered together unfortunate inconsistencies can be discovered. Let us take the example of the facade of a tall building that faces the sun. We might have one optimisation algorithm demanding that as much light as possible enter each room, while another might try and limit solar heat gain by reducing window size. An optimum result might emerge which is a happy medium – rooms not too hot and with almost enough light – so-called satisfying Pareto-optimal mathematical formulae which deal with matching the benefits of a range of values to one situation which, at the same time, may be detrimental to a different situation of equal value as the first. Adding further dimensions such as cost or airflow further complicates the situation. Scaling up to urban size we can see that these are still early days and rapid feedback from complex interactions between large datasets remains elusive.

The other big change of the last decade has been the availability of large real-time datasets coupled with cheap sensors and enhanced miniaturised wireless connections. For the first time a live data stream can be tuned to have an impact on a design model in real time. The problem is that this takes designers into unfamiliar territory, with the consequence that many installations that interact with real-time data streams are more 'interesting' than 'useful'. This is set to change as designers, signals processors, computer scientists and interaction specialists begin to work together to model in real time what a building optimally needs to be in order to respond positively to all this data. This process further exposes the shortcomings of available technology to fulfil this potential – beyond blinds that close automatically and other relatively trivial responses.

Concluding Notes

This brief summary of the divergence between the ambition and the reality for the design and realisation of future urban environments is not intended to dampen morale or put the brakes on our resourcefulness. At the level of nature we have termite mounds, swarms and coal reefs, whose organisational force is something we shall continue to aspire to understand

and learn from. At the self-organisational level we have evidence of the dignity that lifts the inhabitants of the favelas out of the slum mentality. And as a precedent we have Cerdà's Barcelona and its continuing adaptation since it was initiated over a century and a half ago. I believe that this is a point in history when we will have to redefine collaboration to involve rather than merely consult professionals and end-users alike. We will probably have to engage quite differently with global, national and local politics in an effort to make 'design' better understood.

Sadly Barcelona might be a fairly unique example of a city that routinely plans itself well: imaginative, clear-sighted, regardless of prevailing external circumstances such as cyclical economic challenges, civil war, dictatorship and a centralist government that seems remote to most Catalans. But rather than attempt to copy adaptive ecology cities such as Barcelona physically, the point is to draw intellectual inspiration from them. Cities of the new world like Melbourne (from where I write) have had every advantage, yet have failed to live up to their own expectations and rhetoric. I have addressed the credibility gap between the envisaged and the achievable as a single issue. This gap ought to motivate us all to plot a more navigable route to achieving the profound shifts that need to take place if we are to balance our aspirations for a richer architectural outcome at the urban scale with a sustainable use of resources. In effect an enthusiasm for digital technologies versus an instinctive belief in the superiority of analogue tools, techniques and materials may be a false dichotomy in our pluralist age. Our hands are not really so tied: an artist who is a master of oil painting is not necessarily uncompetitive in an art market where they are competing with those more inclined to engage with digital processes and mechanical contrivances. When setting out ideas and strategies we all delineate what we regard as technologically achievable, and the publication of this book, with its focus on adaptive ecologies, seems a timely opportunity to examine the whole issue of design credibility in the world of bold experimentation. In Cerdà's day his revolution was all about the fluency of people movement within a planned polycentric and egalitarian urban sprawl. It is perhaps still early days for us, but even now we seem to be homing in on the opportunities offered by digital fabrication as the twenty-first panacea for a new architecture that can deal cost-effectively with burgeoning urban growth in the context of diminishing resources.

Image Credits

Page 85 (Top)
© Artists Rights Society (ARS), New York/
ADAGP, Paris/Estate of Le Corbusier

Page 85 (Bottom)
Gemeentemuseum, The Hague

Page 86 (Top)
© Massachusetts Institute of Technology

Page 86 (Bottom)
The Paul Rudolph Foundation
and the Library of Congress,
Prints & Photographs Division

Page 87 (Top)
Frank Lloyd Wright Foundation,
'FLLWF Property'

Page 87 (Bottom)
Andrea Branzi Architect

Pages 88, 90, 91
Collection FRAC Centre, Orléans
Donation Nelly Chanéac

Pages 94, 95 (Top)
Collection FRAC Centre, Orléans
Photo: Philippe Magnon

Pages 95 (Bottom Left and Right), 96–97
Collection FRAC Centre, Orléans
Donation Nelly Chanéac

Pages 98, 100–101, 102–103, 106–107
Kikutake Architects